The Uncertain Self

The Uncertain Self

Essays in Australian Literature and Criticism

Harry Heseltine

Melbourne
OXFORD UNIVERSITY PRESS
Oxford Auckland New York

OXFORD UNIVERSITY PRESS

Oxford New York Toronto
Delhi Bombay Calcutta Madras Karachi
Singapore Hong Kong Tokyo
Nairobi Dar es Salaam Cape Town
Melbourne Auckland
and associates in
Beirut Berlin Ibadan Nicosia

National Library of Australia
Cataloguing-in-Publication data:

The Uncertain Self.
    ISBN 0 19 554743 8.
    1. Australian literature — History and criticism —
    Addresses, essays, lectures. 2. Criticism —
    Australia — Addresses, essays, lectures. I.
    Heseltine, Harry, 1931–
A820'.9

Edited by Sarah Brenan
Designed by Peter Shaw
Cover design by Sandra Nobes
Typeset in Times Roman 10/11pt
by Syarikat Seng Teik Sdn. Bhd., Kuala Lumpur, Malaysia
Printed by Kyodo Shing-Loong Printing Singapore.
Published by Oxford University Press, 7 Bowen Crescent, Melbourne
OXFORD is a trademark of Oxford University Press

Contents

Acknowledgements

To the editors of the following journals I am grateful for permission to reprint some of the essays in this book:

Southerly, for 'Wrestling with the angel: Judith Wright's poetry in the 1950s', 'The metamorphoses of Henry Kendall';

Overland for 'Between living and dying: the ground of Lawson's art';

Meanjin Quarterly for 'Criticism and the individual talent' and 'Diversions and obsessions: A. D. Hope and Robert D. FitzGerald';

LiNQ, for 'The confessions of a beachcomber';

Review of National Literatures, for 'The uncertain self: notes on the development of Australian literary form'.

'The criticism of Arthur Phillips' was first printed as the Introduction to A. A. Phillips, *The Australian Tradition*, 2nd edition reissue (Longman Cheshire, Melbourne, 1980); 'Criticism and the universities' in *Criticism in the Arts* (Australian National Advisory Committee for UNESCO, Canberra, 1970); and '"A rich surplus of consciousness": a response to the poetry of Francis Webb' in *Occasional Paper No. 1* (English Department, Faculty of Military Studies, University of New South Wales, 1983). I am grateful to the publishers for permission to reprint these essays.

Finally, I must thank the Australian National Library, Canberra, the Mitchell Library, Sydney, and the Australian Broadcasting Corporation for permission to use documentary material held in their archives.

Preface

Of the fifteen pieces collected here, all but two were written within the past decade — most of them much more recently. Ten have been previously published, with some small differences, in literary journals or other places; five are now printed for the first time. For the sake of the record, I have indicated in each case the year of either first publication or composition.

The work I have chosen for this volume represents only part of ten years' output, but it is an important part, reflecting some of my strongest professional interests over that time. These include the problems of literary historiography, the question of how to represent key figures within an historical framework without distorting either the framework or the individual achievement, and the special challenges of literary autobiography. The selection of material arising out of such interests has produced, I hope, a book with the unity of at least certain recurring themes and attitudes of mind, if not that of a single, closely-argued thesis.

The two chronological exceptions I mentioned earlier are 'Criticism and the universities' and 'Criticism and the individual talent'. Since the whole book betrays a concern with literary criticism and its application to Australian culture, I thought it as well to indicate, through these pieces, some of my early attempts to formulate the views I now hold. I was especially moved to do so because, as I gather, I continue to be regarded (branded?) in some quarters as an unrepentant and unreconstructed New Critic. In some measure I suppose I am. Nevertheless, I hope that these essays may demonstrate, if nothing else, that young New Critics are capable of growth and change even as they subside into middle age.

Harry Heseltine
Duntroon
January 1986

To Sandy, Tim and Jane

The uncertain self

Notes on the development of Australian literary form

1982

> What do I know? myself alone,
> a gulf of uncreated night,
> wherein no star may e'er be shown
> save I create it in my might.
>
> Christopher Brennan
Poems 1913, No. 42[1]

> On a swing at midnight in the black park. Between poplars which are towers of light for a hidden street lamp and inky she-oaks my arc is maintained. From lighter to darker I go, from dark to light; but only, as ever, to return.
>
> Chris Wallace-Crabbe
'The Swing'[2]

The main vantage points from which Australian literary history has been viewed are familiar enough: they have permitted us to discern in its development thematic patterns, ethical patterns, colonial patterns giving way to nationalist patterns, and so on.[3] One vantage point, however, which has until now attracted very few observers is that which reveals works of literature as shaped out of the interaction between the creating self, whatever audience the artist believes he may address, and whatever materials may be to hand to form the subjects of his art. It is exactly to that interaction that I shall address myself in this essay, in the hope less of furnishing a comprehensive interpretation of the national literature than of providing some suggestive notes from which such an interpretation might be constructed.

For the historian who takes the creating self as the focus of his attention, the crucial fact about the literature of modern Australia is the period of its beginnings — the late eighteenth century. In 1788, when the First Fleet dropped anchor in Sydney Cove, Dr Johnson was barely three years dead, William Blake was already at work on the *Songs of Innocence*, England's American colonies were ten years lost, the French Revolution barely twelve months in the future; Adam Smith had published *The Wealth of Nations* a decade earlier, a decade later Wordsworth and Coleridge would publish the first edition of their *Lyrical Ballads*. An English colony was founded in the remote South Seas, that is to say, at the very moment when the value systems by which English society lived were in a state of radical change, and when literature was caught between competing conventions of style and form. That bare fact made an indelible impression on the subsequent history of virtually every aspect of Australian culture, not least the understanding that the literary artist would hold of his own imagination, his own identity. Thrust as it were into a cultural vacuum, without the support of a sanctioned tradition, his central task became that of authenticating his own uncertain self in an unfamiliar world.

The paradoxes which attended the foundation of Australian literature find their emblem in one of the first significant events in the public culture of the colony: the performance on the night of 4 June 1789 of Farquhar's play, *The Recruiting Officer*. A scant six weeks before the Bastille fell at the assault of a Paris mob, Australian theatre was born, on the occasion of the birthday of George III, with a performance by a convict cast, to an audience of military overseers, of a comedy of manners which mirrored the customs and mores of an England a hundred years gone. Convict satire apart, everything about the event seems in retrospect to have been designed to divert the imaginations of all concerned from the actualities in which they were enmeshed. Diversion, indeed, was the principal function of the Australian theatre for the next one hundred and fifty years.

Although a vigorous theatrical industry had been established by the middle of the nineteenth century, no corresponding body of native play texts appeared. It was as if a society brought into being with no sure sense of the writer's role was unable to produce that branch of serious literature which, most of all, demands a confidence strong enough to create selves quite distinct from the author's own. That there was implanted deep in Australian culture a dreadful uncertainty about the creating self is further suggested by the fact that even as late as 1964 Harry Kippax, a leading critic of our theatre, could lament the stop–go quality of what he called our 'stalled drama'. Addressing himself to signs of a quickened growth after the appearance of Ray Lawler's *Summer of the Seventeenth Doll* in 1954, Kippax nevertheless detected in some of the best plays of the 1950s and 1960s flaws which argued a persistently unhappy confusion about the play-wright's sense of his own role and identity, his relation to the society he portrayed. Two weaknesses he noticed in particular: the first, a 'failure to relate action to dramatic purpose', the second, a 'resort . . . to melodramatic contrivance to express dramatic purpose'.[4]

If Kippax was right in his diagnosis (as I believe he was), then Australian drama was failing at a quite fundamental level, and in a way that suggests a radical weakness in the national culture. In the years since 1964, however, there have been some astonishing changes in our dramatic achievement. The evidence for consistent improve-ment in both quality and quantity of dramatic writing is laid bare in the pages of the new edition of Leslie Rees's standard text, *A History of Australian Drama*.[5] Volume I, covering the years between 1788 and 1969, occupies 435 pages; Volume II, 'Australian Drama in the 1970s', runs to 270 pages. After nearly two hundred years, Australian drama seems to have caught up (in excellence and consistency of achievement as well as in output) with the other literary forms. While I shall make no further direct examination of this curious phenom-enon in our drama, the general problems that it implies will underlie all that I have to say about our poetry and prose.

During the first quarter-century after the settlement of 1788, easily the most accomplished (and seemingly dominant) literary form in the colony was descriptive prose, documentary reportage. Examples of the form are numerous enough and of an excellence which suggests that its failure to assume a permanently central role in our literary tradition can only be a matter of regret. The causes, however, of the initial pre-eminence of documentary prose and of its early decline are not far to seek. Here, on the one hand, was a new country offering new data for assimilation to the European-trained mind and eye. On the other, there were readily available the conventions of Enlightenment prose, perfectly suited to the public purposes of disseminating information to an ignorant, interested and far-removed audience. The reports of First Fleeters like Watkin Tench and David Collins, for instance, manifest a complete assurance about the purpose they were serving and the public they were addressing. Men of the middling kind, steeped in the habits of common-sense ration-ality, their aim was to convey information without fuss, if possible under aristocratic patronage. They aimed at (and achieved) a formal-ized syntax and an impersonal tone calculated to suggest a public duty honourably performed.

The first quarter-century, then, of colonial life produced a rich harvest of physical and social notation. Yet as a formal manoeuvre of the creative imagination, its possibilities were soon exhausted — and not simply because, as a generation of native-born white Australians grew up in New South Wales, the need to send back reports to a public 12 000 miles away was in some measure diminished, nor because Augustan conventions of prose were more and more felt to be stilted, outmoded, false. There was something in the Australian experience itself which soon made the artifice of Augustan reportage utterly inadequate to the needs of the truly creative imagination. When Charles Sturt sailed down Sydney Harbour for the first time in 1827, he registered a response which contained the seeds of one of the central developments of nineteenth-century Australian prose:

It was with feelings peculiar to the occasion, that I gazed for the first time on the bold cliffs at the entrance of Port Jackson, as our vessel neared them, and speculated on the probable character of the landscape they hid; and I am free to confess, that I did not anticipate anything equal to the scene which presented itself both to my sight and my judgment, as we sailed up the noble and extensive basin we had entered, towards the seat of government.[6]

'I . . . speculated on the probable character of the landscape': the enormous adjustments required of the earliest settlers in learning to live with the unfamiliar antipodean world have often been noted, the new responses demanded of the creative imagination perhaps less frequently. Among the most creative responses was clearly the urge to explore. The annals of Australian exploration are full of episodes at once heroic and extreme, sometimes fatal. In almost every instance, however, it seems that creative energy was so fully absorbed in the act of exploration itself as to make speculation on the landscape, aesthetic contemplation, beyond the reach of the explorer's imagination. Edward John Eyre may stand as a case in point. His journey across the southern face of the continent in 1840–41 plainly demanded every resource of body, nerve and spirit that he could muster. A hundred years after the event, Francis Webb could wring from it that extraordinary poem, 'Eyre All Alone'. The best registration that Eyre himself could manage of one of the most extreme moments of his ordeal is couched in a colourless prose style disguising rather than revealing the intensity of the experience he had been through:

The frightful, the appalling truth now burst upon me, that I was alone in the desert. He who had faithfully served me for many years, who had followed my fortunes in adversity and in prosperity, who had accompanied me in all my wanderings, and whose attachment to me had been his sole inducement to remain with me in this last, and to him alas, fatal journey, was now no more. For an instant, I was almost tempted to wish that it had been my own fate instead of his. The horrors of my situation glared upon me in such startling reality, as for an instant almost to paralyse the mind.[7]

In writing such as this the conventions of eighteenth-century prose reach the dead end of their expressive possibilities. From the 1840s onward, discursive prose, which had promised so bright an achievement, fragmented into a myriad more modest purposes — social commentary, literary criticism, anecdote and memoir. Thenceforward, the best energies of our prose writers would be channelled into fiction. The novelist emerged as the type of imagination most apt to contemplate the land rather than traverse or conquer it. Unwilling or unable to find the aesthetic resources for that searing personal confrontation which Eyre knew in 1841, he could yet slough off the restraints of Augustan artifice and find in narrative a means of transforming insight into art.

Alexander Harris's *The Emigrant Family* (1849) is wholly characteristic of the mid-century Australian novel. In its pages a frankly documentary and informative intention is incorporated into a narrative which permits a minimal concern for fictional characters and (quite as importantly) for the developing variant of the English language through which white Australians were beginning to take hold of their environment. Not only representative of the best qualities of 'guidebook fiction', *The Emigrant Family* also labours under a general aesthetic difficulty of fiction composed out of a new and relatively raw culture. The famous paragraphs in Henry James's life of Hawthorne are probably the best-known enunciation of the view that fiction finds in a new society a sadly thin diet when compared with the dense complexities of older civilizations. Some twenty-three years before James lamented the absence from the American scene of Ascot, the Derby and the rest, Frederick Sinnett in 1856 had deplored a similar lack in the young country below the equator:

No storied windows, richly dight, cast a dim, religious light over any Australian premises. There are no ruins for that rare old plant, the ivy green, to creep over and make his dainty meal of. No Australian author can hope to extricate his hero or heroine, however pressing the emergency may be, by means of a spring panel and a subterranean passage . . .[8]

The difficulties of creating fiction in a largely unformed society are real enough, though not perhaps as desperate as they have sometimes been represented. In Australia, the difficulty (however dimly or clearly apprehended) seems to have been answered by two fairly distinct lines of formal development in the novel. One was to enter into the pleasant pastures of romantic action, using the local data without really examining them, forcing them into patterns of narrative and character largely derived from Sir Walter Scott. Two of the best-known of Australia's colonial novels reveal the pattern quite clearly: Henry Kingsley's *The Recollections of Geoffry Hamlyn* (1859) and Rolf Boldrewood's *Robbery Under Arms* (1882–83).

Neither writer was a serious artist, as we understand art today; undisturbed by any profound self-searching, they were able to compose undemanding romantic tales out of whatever colonial experience came their way. Henry Kingsley, the younger brother of the author of *Westward Ho!*, made a comparatively brief visit to Australia but was nevertheless able to make of *Geoffry Hamlyn* 'a novel which probably influenced the writing of Australian fiction more than any other single work of fiction about Australia during the nineteenth century', as John Barnes says. The level at which that influence operated is, however, fairly indicated by Barnes's further comment that 'Hamlyn's style is characterized by an almost boyish enthusiasm for his characters and the stories he has to tell about them'.[9] The effect of *Geoffry Hamlyn* may have been to direct Australian novelists towards some readily usable structures but it was almost certainly to diminish the creative impulse, the effort to use fiction as a means of bringing the literary artist, the environment he was still learning to look at, and the society he must learn to live with, into some kind of rapport. The same kind of charge can be laid against Rolf Boldrewood. Combining readiness of invention, a superficial fluency and Victorian habits of industry, he constructed a career as a novelist in the course of which he observed Australian manners far more scrupulously and in greater detail than had Kingsley. *Robbery Under Arms*, however, enjoys its reputation among historians of Australian literature by virtue of what was for Boldrewood a most untypical narrative strategy — that of telling the tale in the first person, through the mouth of one of its principal characters. The novel represents the first significant occasion in Australian prose narrative when the Australian language became an integrated, organic element in the very form and substance of fiction.

By and large, however, Boldrewood did little to lift the nineteenth-century Australian novel above its function of providing a romantic gloss on native experience. His solution to the problem of the artist's status and identity was to remove both to the area of technical-commercial skill. That, however, was not the only path open to the Australian novel in the middle and later years of the nineteenth century. Henry Savery's *Quintus Servinton* (1830–31), antedating *The Emigrant Family* by almost twenty years, had indicated another route that it might follow. The fact that Savery's plot is largely displaced autobiography is of less consequence than that it is ferociously melodramatic. Curiously, although the novel has no right to be taken with any real seriousness, it manages to convey the sense that it is a melodrama not of concocted romance but of experiential extremity. Eyre would discover what Australia could impose on those who sought to penetrate her; Savery had already sensed, in an oddly impressive way, the means by which such knowledge might be brought within the ambit of fiction. The mode of Gothic allegory offered Australian fiction one of its most significant early successes in the form of Marcus Clarke's *For the Term of His Natural Life* (1870–72).

Clarke's professed purpose in this novel was to prevent the recurrence of the social injustices wrought by 'the System', and to that end he had undertaken some documentary research. Furthermore, he was by the 1870s building on an already existing corpus of convict literature of a predominantly documentary or protestant kind. Yet his signal achievement in *For the Term of His Natural Life* was to wring from a violent history a symbolic vision of crime and punishment, suffering and redemption. Symbolic allegory was not, however, the only solution available to other writers of Clarke's generation who might wish to make the country's convict beginnings the object of their artists' speculation. Price Warung, for instance, forged from convict material not the vivid shapes of allegory but the intensities of irony, protest and disgust. The other feature, of course, which distinguishes Warung's work from Clarke's is that of scale. Where Clarke's concern with the System was concentrated into one massive encounter, Warung's traffic with the convict past was spread over a decade's contributions to the Sydney *Bulletin*. The short story was the ideal vehicle for his bitter snapshots of warders and convicts; it also had for Warung the kind of psychological value it must have for many writers anxious about their stature as artists. For such writers, the short story provides the opportunity of saying something important to themselves without risking the full-scale revelations entailed by the novel. Warung's convict tales, in the savage treatment of their materials, in the terse irony of their tone, betray, it seems to me, an imagination possessed by its subject but unsure of its power to possess.

Orthodox histories identify the short story of the 1890s as the form in which Australian literature first achieved unequivocal excellence with a distinctive national hue. The key figure in such a reading of our literary development is Henry Lawson, whose work is regarded as both the apogee of the colonial imagination in prose and the fountainhead of mainstream Australian writing for at least half of the twentieth century. From the point of view of cultural diagnostics, however, perhaps the most significant fact about Lawson's career is the profound insecurity on which it was based. Manning Clark's recent study[10] has made the deep divisions of Lawson's life abundantly plain, and it may be that it is precisely those divisions which make Lawson the supreme representative of Australian life in both the nineteenth century and our own. Nothing suggests more acutely the motif of the uncertain self running through our colonial literature than the brief success and long tragedy of Lawson's life, the handful of great stories wherein the conflicting fragments of his sensibility coalesce into a splendid art.

Although the idea of 'mateship' has been so strongly attached to Henry Lawson, the most elaborate version of this socio-ethical code to be found in our nineteenth-century writing grew in the mind of the writer who, of all his generation, was most literally isolated — Joseph Furphy. Sixty years old when his masterpiece *Such is Life* was published in 1903, he had composed it in Shepparton, far removed from the centres of literary polity in Melbourne and Sydney. It was perhaps this very innocence of literary coteries, together with his long experience as bushman and bullocky, that gave Furphy the confidence to attempt the extraordinary comic masterpiece which is *Such is Life*, of which the intricate complexities of plot create an enormous gap between the ultimate purpose of the novel and the stuff of which it was made. By a tremendous effort of the will and imagination Furphy bridged that gap through the very artifice of his plotting, an effort which for once allowed a nineteenth-century novelist almost to escape the tyranny of an uncertain self.

Almost, but not quite. The rock against which all criticism of *Such is Life* founders is the need to distinguish between the author Joseph Furphy and the alleged author Tom Collins. There is in *Such is Life* an aesthetic ambivalence which in the end must be seen as a like ambivalence in the writer's felt situation as artist and individual. Furphy's uncertainty about his audience can be sensed in the false aplomb of the Introduction to *Such is Life*; about his created narrator in the insistent, mocking identification of Tom Collins with Hamlet. If Furphy's original simplicity of motive anywhere survives, it is in the opening sentence of the review of his own novel that he wrote (at A. G. Stephens's behest) for the Sydney *Bulletin*: 'Nowhere is literary material more copious in variety, or more piquant in character, than in legendless Australia'.[11] *Such is Life* is nothing less than an attempt to use the resources of the self as the means of celebrating a nation as yet unstoried, artless, unenhanced.

Such a claim stands good even in the face of that other great fictional compilation of nineteenth-century Australian experience — Henry Handel Richardson's *The Fortunes of Richard Mahony* (1917 –1929). Richardson's unique distinction is that, where Furphy celebrated the still-new society, she flayed it open, anatomized it to reveal the tragic bones of colonial experience — individual and social, both. The controlled modulations of style from *Australia Felix* to *Ultima Thule* have often caused the trilogy to be seen as the point through which Australian fiction turned from a nineteenth- to a twentieth-century aesthetic. Just as truly, those same phenomena of language could be regarded as the culminating improvisation on the motif of the unattached, insecure self in our nineteenth-century prose.

For the hundred years after 1788, our poets grappled with basically the same problem as that which tasked the writers of prose: how to realize the demands of the creating self in the kind of cultural vacuum to which they were condemned. The poets' answers were at once more extreme and more tentative than those of the prose writers. Relegating the documentary possibilities of literature to folk song and ballad, the poets for most of the century floundered uneasily in the hiatus between rationalism and Romanticism; unattached to any certain beliefs or reliable aesthetic conventions, they fell back more and more upon the resources of self, without understood means of artistic realization. The range of improvisations attempted by our nineteenth-century poets is resumed in the life and work of three of their number — Charles Harpur, Henry Kendall, Christopher Brennan.

Born in Australia in 1813, Harpur from the outset of his career was certain of only two things: that the new nation needed a tradition of poetry, and that it was his destiny to found it. As a teenager he confided his ambition to the lines entitled 'To the Lyre of Australia':

> Wild Lyre of Australia, in song could I vie
>   With the strength of a Burns, of a Byron the fire,
> Oh, then I would raise thee in glory on high,
>   As the guardian of beauty, of valour the sire:
> And might I but hope that one song I may waken,
>   As a voice in the gale that drives over the glade,
> Should ride, when my country her empire hath taken,
>   On the flood of her ages, I'd count me repaid.[12]

There was little else, however, of which Harpur could feel sure. What he might say or what needed to be said, how to reach his Australian audience, how even to go about writing poems — these were matters on which the circumstances of colonial Australia could offer him no serviceable guide. Born to the English language, he perforce looked to the poetic traditions it enshrined — acquired indeed an impressive acquaintance with all of them from the days of

Chaucer through to Robert Browning. But born into a penal colony of a metropolis itself caught up in doubt and change, he could find no principle for selecting among all the models he so earnestly assimilated. His writing in consequence exhibits a bewildering array of modes and manners — Augustan prospect poems, formal verse satire, a sonnet sequence, Romantic outpourings (after Wordsworth, Coleridge, Keats), Miltonic epic, Shakespearean pastiche. The very range of Harpur's formal experiments bears pathetic testimony to the difficulties of being a colonial poet. The landscape resisted his best attempts to humanize it into the likeness of a northern world he had never seen; his inner experience remained locked within the prison of inert conventions; the society of which he wrote remained apart from him, untouched by the demand for attention his verse implicitly placed upon it.

Early in his career Harpur confidently instructed his compatriots in their public duties, admonished them on general principles of conduct. Their almost total disregard of his injunctions, however, more desperate even than contumely or contempt, led in his later years to a bitterness towards his countrymen who had failed to form the enlightened audience just as necessary to a poetic tradition as the poets themselves. At the head of the 1863 manuscript of his work he placed the following note:

I cannot forbear adding to the above Memory, that it is my somewhat unpleasant impression, the future (capable) reader of the Manuscript, will be anything but gratified by the fact, that the Poems which make up the contents of it, should for a period of twenty years, have gone a begging as it were — and in vain about the land of their inspiration . . .[13]

By the end of his career (pursued almost literally to his deathbed) Harpur was reduced to composing an extraordinary verse narrative, 'The Witch of Hebron', of which the sole arbiter would be himself.

Harpur's immediate successor, Henry Kendall, in selecting out from the older poet's achievement what he found most congenial, narrowed the possibilities of nineteenth-century Australian poetry. Of a more vivid and volatile temperament than Harpur, though of less intellectual gravity and power, he thrust the tradition initiated by Harpur in the direction of Romantic specialization. No longer seeking to domesticate landscape under the guise of eighteenth-century topography, he made of the mountainous coastal region that he knew the arena of an idealized Romanticism. That Romanticism, which he discovered mainly within his own disturbed personality, never sat quite happily within the confines assigned to it. The result is, even in Kendall's best nature poetry, a certain crudeness of technique and (by implication) a coarseness of sensibility. On other occasions, when landscape does not mediate between Kendall and the inner tensions which constitute the true subject of nearly all his poetry, his work was potentially of greater power and penetration than anything that Harpur wrote. But potential was never fully converted into achievement because, again, Kendall could neither discover nor master a creative apparatus apt to the purposes of an imagination still unattached to cultural tradition or social actuality.

The most dramatic evidence of the massive internal difficulties which marred the work and nearly destroyed the man is to be found in Kendall's complete nervous breakdown at the age of 32 — what he afterwards referred to as 'the Shadow of 1872'. We cannot now be sure if that collapse was cause or consequence of Kendall's embracing the poet's vocation; we can say, however, that it is a fit emblem of the disaster which, in one form or another, overtook so many of the individuals who essayed the poet's role in nineteenth-century Australia. Kendall was more fortunate than some, in that in the middle 1870s he contrived a partial reconstruction of his personality; in a manner, however, which represented a retreat from that whole-souled commitment to art which had characterized his earlier years. After 1872 he wrote (or pretended to write) as much for money as for art's sake.

Yet in his later work Kendall did point the way towards a further advance for Australian poetry — its closer liaison with the stream of popular ballad and song which had flowed so strongly ever since 1788. There is in a piece like 'The Song of Ninian Melville' an infusion of unpretentious, salty colloquialism which promised a healthy antidote to the Swinburnian preciousness of so many of Kendall's lines before 1870. The tendency for the popular and serious streams of Australian versifying to meet and mingle was hastened in the 1890s, most famously in the work of 'Banjo' Paterson and Henry Lawson. Where Paterson brought an aristocratic insouciance to his jaunty treatment of outback tales, Lawson depended on an unabashedly sentimental display of nationalism, social protest or commonplace feeling. Both writers have become enshrined as culture heroes of the 1890s. Neither really succeeded in wedding the language of the tribe to the purposes of high art; neither significantly influenced the subsequent development of Australian poetry.

In that regard, a figure of much greater consequence is Christopher Brennan, author of *Poems 1913*, notoriously the most 'difficult' book of verse to have issued from our nineteenth-century literary culture. Brennan and his book have produced one of the largest 'industries' in Australian literary scholarship, so perhaps little more need be said here other than that his career, which came so close to being that of our first great literary master, was ultimately a failure, and that that failure was probably as much the measure of the shortcomings of a whole culture as of a single individual.

In brief, *Poems 1913* is a *livre composé* — a sequence of 105 inter-related poems composed according to a Mallarméan aesthetic, and constituting the chronicle of an individual's search for identity within the mode of myth. For a decade and more Brennan so dedicated himself to the task of self-discovery through the means of poetry as progressively and woundingly to detach himself from everything which had originally given his life its meaning — faith, family, friends. Even in the middle 1890s (seemingly his most confident years) his only answer to the question 'What do I know?' had been 'myself alone'. By 1908 that solipsistic response had taken on the quiet desperation of the close of the 'Wanderer' sequence:

> I am the wanderer of many years
> who cannot tell if ever he was king
> or if ever kingdoms were . . .
>
> and saying this to myself as a simple thing
> I feel a peace fall in the heart of the winds
> and a clear dusk settle, somewhere, far in me.[14]

The author of *Poems 1913* had come, it seems plain, to the dead end of the first great movement in our poetic history. The creative artist, uneasy in his lack of received conventions and understood materials for the making of poems, had turned inward on himself to find both material and means for his art, and in so doing had been brought finally to nought.

There can be no doubt that *Poems 1913* conveys a sense of things ending. Yet, just as *The Fortunes of Richard Mahony* was the fulcrum for Australian fiction's movement from its colonial to its modern phase, so did Brennan's lines perform the same function for Australian poetry. The continuities between our nineteenth- and our twentieth-century poets are plainly marked in the work of our first great 'modern' poets — Kenneth Slessor and Robert D. FitzGerald, born in 1901 and 1902 respectively. Of the two, Slessor seemed easily the more 'modern' to their contemporaries in the 1920s and 1930s. In spite of his acknowledged debt to Tennyson, Slessor unmistakably displayed the ironic flair, the edgy timing, the paradoxical wit which were to his generation the hallmark of modernism everywhere. From another point of view, however, his work is just as plainly an exten-sion of Brennan's. Where Brennan's imaginative wanderings brought him at last to the bleak solipsism of 'The Wanderer', Slessor moved through his century of poems towards an even more thorough-going nihilism of feeling and belief. 'Five Bells', the great elegy which stands much in the same relation to twentieth-century Australian verse as Robert Lowell's 'The Quaker Graveyard in Nantucket' does to American, is marked by a hopelessness beyond despair:

> I felt the wet push its black thumb-balls in,
> The night you died, I felt your eardrums crack,
> And the short agony, the longer dream,
> The Nothing that was neither long nor short;
> But I was bound, and could not go that way,
> But I was blind, and could not feel your hand.[15]

In lines such as these the substantive thrust of Brennanism reached its dead end. If Slessor's work significantly forecasts later trends in our verse, it may be in its heavy reliance on what Alec King called the physical imagination, 'a sense of objective things vividly present but not deeply imagined in feeling'.[16]

Against Slessor's surrender to darkness FitzGerald has stood firm throughout his career. Often suffering under such labels as 'Romantic optimist', he has steadfastly regarded human life as a quest of the spirit which, in the face of all the odds, can bring to mankind at least a measure of hope and fulfilment. In his earliest work he took over from Brennan, even more obviously than Slessor, the image of the Wanderer, but discovered in it themes and attitudes quite the reverse of those it revealed to his contemporary. Characteristically it is to the future that FitzGerald turns in the closing stanza of his major collection, *Forty Years' Poems*:

> But more than to look back
> we choose this day's concern
> with everything in the track,
> and would give most to learn
> outcomes of all we found
> and what next builds to the stars.
> I regret I shall not be around
> to stand on Mars.[17]

Such Browningesque exhilaration in the face of the universe has not, it must be said, recommended itself to many of FitzGerald's successors. Where Slessor's chief legacy to later Australian poets has perhaps been a mode of sensibility, FitzGerald has demonstrated to them the utility of certain formal structures. The poem which first brought FitzGerald widespread recognition was the sesquicentenary prize-winning piece, 'Essay on Memory' (1937). His successful management of contemplative-discursive verse not only heralded some of his own later master-works but also pointed the way to some of the most distinguished poets of later generations — James McAuley with his 'Letter to John Dryden', for instance, or Bruce Beaver's 'Letters to Live Poets'. A much later work of FitzGerald's, 'The Wind at Your Door' of 1959, is no less significant than 'Essay on Memory' in focusing some of the major formal and modal achievements of twentieth-century Australian poetry. Like 'Essay on Memory', 'The Wind at Your Door' concentrates itself finally to personal meditation, but the meditation grows out of historical narrative rather than discursive argument. And again there can be no doubt that one of the singular features of contemporary Australian poetry has been its engagement with verse narrative. McAuley's 'Captain Quiros', Douglas Stewart's 'Worsley Enchanted', John Couper's 'The Book of Bligh', Francis Webb's 'A Drum for Ben Boyd' — the list speaks for itself. Australian poets, we may say, working out their themes in the arena of their own identities, could arrive at a union of meaning and action long before our dramatists were able to achieve that *sine qua non* of dramatic art.

Slessor and FitzGerald, then, severally and in relation to each other, typify whole tracts of twentieth-century Australian poetry. Even the inevitable coupling of their names seems to betray a recurring pattern. Slessor and FitzGerald, Stewart and Wright, Hope and McAuley, Shapcott and Hall, Murray and Lehmann — there is something here other than cultural accident. The pendulum swing between Slessor and FitzGerald of substance and sensibility, theme and form, optimism and pessimism summarizes what we may describe as the whole trend of Australian poetry since it turned through *Poems 1913* into the twentieth century. That trend may be described something like this: since Brennan was defeated on the very ground of self to which his own imagination and all prior Australian poetry had directed him, our verse writers have not been willing to quit that territory but have sought to avoid its uncertainties by great polarizing swoops between opposing tendencies in form, attitudes, styles.

One of the clearest substantive manifestations of this polar oscillation is in the lines of Chris Wallace-Crabbe which stand as the second epigraph to this essay. Day and night, light and dark, reason and irrationality have been the opposing themes between which our poets have characteristically moved in their efforts to make art out of their experience of this country and their relation to their compatriots. It is possible to view the formal history of modern Australian poetry in the same way — a pendulum-like swinging between extremes of behaviour in order to control (or avoid?) the difficult centre position where so much damage had been worked in colonial times. One of the extremes of Australian verse has thus been the lyric, which (like narrative) has been cultivated in this country with greater single-mindedness than in other English-speaking societies. Many of our twentieth-century poets, indeed, have operated by translating their perceptions into the mode of song, making melodic rapture out of the light and darkness of the world, out of their joys and distress, out of their very observation of the world of things. John Shaw Nielson, Hugh McCrae, Mary Gilmore, Douglas Stewart, Judith Wright — the line is clear and unmistakable, and (with variations) is projected right down to the present time.

To subdue the uncertain self through the power of song has not, however, been the only manoeuvre attempted by our more recent poets. Substantively, we may say that the work of A. D. Hope and James McAuley makes them poets of sweet reason, of the light. Formally, their distinct achievement has been to wed sweet reason to the lyric mode — to give Australians an Apollonian as well as a Dionysian song. They are artists for whom the imagination comprehends high intelligence as well as irrational energy, for whom a tough reasonableness is an essential concomitant of any lyric grace. Their example has been followed by a line of poets as impressive in its way as that of the Romantic singers. It includes, for instance, Vincent Buckley, Chris Wallace-Crabbe, Evan Jones — and later, and in a curious way, even Rodney Hall and Thomas Shapcott, David Malouf and Geoffrey Lehmann.

The aspiration towards an Apollonian radiance is, I believe, a comparatively late phenomenon in our verse; it appeared, furthermore, as a counter to not only Romantic song but also a darker, more anarchic form of Bacchic energy. The chief theoretical text of that energy is probably Norman Lindsay's *Creative Effort* (1920), its most dogmatic exponent, William Baylebridge. But the willingness to grapple head-on with unreasoning darkness has had no more impressive issue than in the poetry of Francis Webb. Webb's *Collected Poems* of 1969 reveals an imagination that works characteristically in the expressionist mode in order to confront all the least orderly elements of its own identity.

Webb, too, has had his latter-day successors — notably Michael Dransfield and Charles Buckmaster, young men whose wild integrity brought them both to untimely death. In one respect at least, however, neither was able (though both most certainly tried) to match Webb in a vital element of his art — the use of an internalized landscape as a means of bringing the anarchic self under control. And, indeed, some of the most striking successes of our twentieth-century poets (no matter what their intellectual persuasion, their stylistic habit) have been effected when they have referred theme, form, self to the Australian land. I am thinking here less of an organized movement like the Jindyworobaks than of individual poems by FitzGerald and Slessor, Stewart and Wright, Hope, even, and McAuley. Or, if we are to search for a current instance, we need think only of Les Murray. Murray can be wilfully countrified or citified or knowingly cosmopolitan. But when he writes out of the Australian earth, few poets now at work have the power so to stop the mind and heart. His career reassures us that in this generation, as in every generation since Brennan, our poets have been able to make some few poems which exist at the point of balance between those sweeps between light and darkness which characterize our poetic history since 1900.

Not even Murray's verse, however, can surpass the feeling for the *genius loci* which animates the most astonishing starburst of our recent fiction, Xavier Herbert's *Poor Fellow My Country* (1975). This mammoth novel is perhaps the most passionately knowledgeable speculation on the Australian landscape ever to have shaped itself in the mind of a white Australian. At the same time, it is committed to action as a metaphor for the human condition with the kind of absolute conviction which, as H. G. Kippax felt, was lacking in our drama even into the 1960s. *Poor Fellow My Country*, that is to say, in one sense may be thought of as a realization of the urge to an imaginative possession of Australia which Sturt had felt in 1827. Even more than Patrick White's *Voss*, Herbert made this country his by right of vision.

If *Poor Fellow My Country* represents at last the triumph of self through its absorption into the numinous, it is at the same time the culmination of a major structural tradition of Australian fiction which has not always been put to that purpose. Ever since Henry Handel Richardson, our novelists have seemingly felt the need to work out their themes in fictions of quite remarkable length — often in trilogies or even tetralogies. Vance Palmer, Katharine Susannah Prichard, Miles Franklin, Frank Dalby Davison, Eleanor Dark, George Johnston, George Turner, Donald Stuart — the list speaks for itself. In one series after another, our novelists have endeavoured to authenticate their still-uncertain selves by submission to some dominant theme of wide extent — time, national history, socio-economic fact, cultural aspiration.

Some of these prolonged essays in national definition command respect more for their earnest application than their artistic success. Throughout the first half of the century, however, any apparent community of national purpose could not conceal deep divisions of sensibility and commitment. The most obvious polarization was in matters of style. One characteristic attempt to synthesize a national personality out of local experience was through the cultivation of eloquence — rhetorical or lyrical. Miles Franklin might be thought of as representative of the tendency. More general, however, was the opposite practice of a deliberately low-keyed utterance, a reaching out to the phenomenal world through an antipodean equivalent of Joyce's 'style of scrupulous meanness'. Vance Palmer formulated the aesthetic of a whole generation when in 1942 he endorsed Verlaine's advice to 'take eloquence and wring its neck'.[18] Perhaps, however, the finest practical vindication of that aesthetic is to be found in the short stories of the 1940s — a decade which saw a flowering of the form reminiscent in both quantity and quality of the 1890s. Gavin Casey, Brian James, Peter Cowan, Davison, Palmer himself (to name only a few) achieved in their shorter fiction an assured under-statement through which they annexed whole tracts of Australian experience as their own.

The stylistic extremes of eloquence and laconic reticence produced by the 1940s an extraordinary jostle of attitudes and stances; Jindy-worobak and Angry Penguin, left-wing nationalist and right-wing Australia Firster competed for supremacy in an atmosphere rendered electric by the fact of war. The variety of directions and postures attempted in those years suggests that an analysis into polar opposites is far too simplistic. So various indeed was the literary achievement of the 1940s that some effort at large-scale synthesis can be seen in retrospect to have been more and more needful. The need was answered with the return of Patrick White from London after demo-bilization from the RAF, and the publication of that series of novels which begins with *The Tree of Man* in 1955.

That White's mastery over his self, his situation and his art would be won hard and at some cost was signalled as early as 1948 in the phrase from Henry Miller which appears as part of the epigraph to Part II of *The Aunt's Story* (1948) — 'the great fragmentation of maturity'. After a century and a half of European experience in this country, White grasped unhesitatingly what had become the unavoid-able theme and the most potent threat to the Australian literary imagination, and converted it into a source of power. The story of Theodora Goodman offers an idea of personal maturity radically at odds with the liberal–humanist dogmas of the previous hundred years.

In the years following *The Aunt's Story* Patrick White, through characters like Voss, Himmelfarb, Hurtle Duffield, continued his radical assault on Australian pieties held too easily or too long. His prose style was no less calculated to unsettle fictional orthodoxies. His attack on 'dreary dun-coloured . . . journalism' is widely known. Less familiar, although occurring in the same essay ('The Prodigal Son'), is White's positive description of what he hoped his language might achieve: 'Writing . . . became a struggle to create completely fresh forms out of the rocks and sticks of words'.[19] An aim at once so austere and so melodramatic, united to the thematic radicalism of White's writing, has undoubtedly thrust Australian fiction towards new kinds of perception. Yet his massive contribution to our literature has not been, as I say, without personal cost, but a cost of a different kind from that paid by earlier Australian writers — Kendall, for instance, Lawson, Brennan, Slessor. White has neither suffered personal disintegration nor fallen into silence. The price he has paid to keep the imagination vigorously alive is shown rather in his work — most of all, perhaps, in that increasingly strained articulation of his vision which (as some commentators believe) marks his writing from, say, *The Vivisector* on.

Whatever the difficulties or the costs, no other writer has come anywhere near to White's capacity to assimilate his Australian experience to his vision and his art. What has been evident, especially in our fiction, in the years since his influence began to be felt has been not only a higher level of professional excellence but a more intense concern for the aesthetic of the novel. Many of the old polarities persist, now expressed in structures of greater complexity than before. The old Dionysian urge, for instance, continues, in the comic mode and located in the industrial world, in the work of Peter Mathers and David Ireland. Thea Astley and Thomas Keneally, sharing memories of a Catholic childhood, continue to explore the polarities in our treatment of love and violence, social satire and spiritual aspiration, the light and dark of all our lives. Where Dal Stivens in a novel like *A Horse of Air* (1970) acclimatizes to Australia Nabokovian subtleties of personality, Frank Hardy has learnt in *But the Dead are Many* (1975) the means of relating the themes of social and personal division in a work which relates him more powerfully and directly to the Lawson that Manning Clark revealed to us than any of the turgid social comment of his first novel, *Power Without Glory* (1950). Neither Stivens nor Hardy has so far been able to synthesize so much of life and of art as Patrick White. Yet they, along with many of our best writers since *The Tree of Man*, have accepted and used what is perhaps White's supreme gift to his fellow Australian writers: the confidence to make of the divided self the subject and support of a complex, sophisticated and penetrating art.

That the accomplishments of Australian literary prose have broadened as well as deepened during the past two decades is attested by the new excellence discovered in autobiography. While Australian autobiography is almost as old as Australian literature, most of the earlier examples of the form either exist in isolation or retain interest chiefly as sociological observation. In the 1950s, however, autobiography as a genre seems to have taken firm enough root in our culture to start producing an abundant and continuing harvest. One of the first important works from this period is Alan Marshall's *I Can Jump Puddles*, of 1955. We need not be mindful of the special appeal of this work (the triumph of a country boy over the tragedy of poliomyelitis) to accord it a secure place among our leading autobiographies. Marshall's particular distinction is to have convincingly identified the joys and sorrows of the young lad who was himself with the common experiences and emotions of a whole people. Too often in our writing such an identification has remained at the level of dogmatic assertion; in *I Can Jump Puddles* it is a matter of realized fact. Marshall's instinct served him well when he chose as title for his next autobiographical volume *This is the Grass* (1962) a phrase from Walt Whitman, the poet par excellence of the merging of the single, separate person with life *en masse*.

Other recent autobiographies — those for instance of Douglas Stewart, Katharine Susannah Prichard, Martin Boyd, Colin MacInnes — have been more personal than Marshall's, in the sense that the experiences they record are less fused with a whole way of life than those of *I Can Jump Puddles*. Nevertheless, all these autobiographers write with the assurance that Australian life has become dense enough to make an account of growing up worth telling for its own sake, as well as for its representative quality. It is as if the Australian artist no longer feels himself condemned to that thin diet of observation that James imputed to Hawthorne; Australian lives are now rich enough in themselves and in their social connections to make autobiography both possible and worth while.

None of our recent autobiographers is more persuaded of this fact than Donald Horne. He prefaces *The Education of Young Donald* with a remark which provides the rationale for more autobiographies than his own:

Technically this is an autobiography, but "autobiography" seems to suggest a sense of self-importance that is so far from what I had in mind that when people first used the word I had the feeling of someone who looks over his shoulder to see what is being talked about . . . since the central character is presented as a social animal, his adolescent revolt shaped and coloured by social circumstance, I would use the word "sociography" rather than "autobiography".[20]

Horne's bold coinage does not, however, quite fit the work of our most distinguished autobiographer, Hal Porter. His three works of autobiography, starting with *The Watcher on the Cast-Iron Balcony* in 1963, brilliantly catch nuances of national tone and attitudes, but they are by no means the deliberate exercises in socio-cultural reconstruction that *The Education of Young Donald* sets out to be. What is more usually perceived as the dominant theme within Porter's idiosyncratic manner (neither flat nor rhetorical but coruscatingly exact in its registration of feeling and sensation) is a sense of deprivation at the impermanence of human attachments. Porter himself, however, reveals what is the deepest motif of his autobiographical writing in a passage from the second volume of the series, *The Paper Chase* (1966):

The most discomposing paradox in my luggage of new information is that I prefer to live alone because I am too fond of those I love.
One wants to be alone, fundamentally, not to escape others but to escape oneself, the versions of self compelled into existence by others. It is safer for me to be mere wood than to be wood painted to look like wood.[21]

Such an assertion may well affront that code of 'mateship' which the conventional wisdom has been telling us for so long is the special Australian contribution to practical ethics. Nevertheless, and as I have tried to indicate, it can also be construed as a definitive statement of the contemporary situation of the most successful Australian literary artists. In Porter's autobiographical prose, the anxious solipsisms of the past, the aesthetic and cultural indecisions, the fundamental reliance on the physical imagination, have at last modulated into a personal utterance no longer apologetic for the form it takes or the ground on which it stands.

The rise of autobiography during the 1950s and 1960s is (outside drama) the most recent formal manoeuvre of the creative imagination identifiable to Australian literary historians. The patterns assumed by contemporary experiment must for the present remain conjectural. In closing these remarks, however, I must record one of the most widely accepted conjectures about our current writing if only for the sake of bringing a highly selective survey a little closer to the immediate present.

Writing in the *Australian Book Review* of August 1970, Thomas Shapcott asserted the appearance of a new generation of young poets, the 'generation of 1968'. Nurtured by the upheaval in values, lifestyles, beliefs which characterized the decade, these new writers tended to avoid the established channels of literary culture, rejected traditional canons of metrics and prosody, cultivated a style that mixed, in varying proportions, public exhortation, intimate self-revelation, and truncated *aperçus* into social or environmental data. From among their number, at least some poets have emerged with personal staying power and a talent which seems likely to last: Robert Adamson, Richard Tipping, John Tranter are three names selected arbitrarily from among a group whom it is still invidious to 'rank' into any kind of hierarchy. The brief careers of Michael Dransfield and Charles Buckmaster, tragically closed by early death, are all too representative of that quality of personal extremity which has characterized so much of the verse of the past decade.

The notion of a major break with the literary tradition is not, however, restricted to the younger poets. Michael Wilding makes the same sort of claim for the new prose writers in an essay appended to his anthology of *avant-garde* fiction, *The Tabloid Story Pocket Book*. As Shapcott had argued for verse, so Wilding asserts a major hiatus in the development of our prose fiction in the late 1960s. The near side of this watershed has a number of discernible features: a concerted attempt to woo a 'counter-culture' audience, a determined effort to expand the subject matter of fiction (especially into the areas of sexuality and libertarian politics), a conscious rejection of the 'Lawson–nationalist' tradition in favour of narrative freer in both form and attitude. The older traditions of Australian prose (like those of verse) are now felt to be a constraint upon the imaginations of those writers most vitally in touch with contemporary Australia.

As with poetry, so the welter of new prose has produced at least some few authors whose work seems likely to last — (again by arbitrary selection) Wilding himself, Peter Carey, Frank Moorhouse. Moorhouse in particular, working away at what he calls his 'discontinuous narratives', is notable as much for the inventiveness of his fictional forms as for his keenly observant eye. In basing his writing on documentary observation, Moorhouse is, of course, maintaining a function for prose that goes back to its very beginnings in this country. Indeed, in this respect as in many others, Moorhouse's status may be regarded as emblematic of a great deal of new Australian writing. Self-consciously international in outlook, it cannot avoid a native colouration; restlessly searching for new forms of expression, it discovers them in areas defined by the very conditions of settlement two hundred years ago; turning its back on mainstream traditions, it cannot avoid the pressure of the past. By the very act of proclaiming their polar discontinuity with their immediate predecessors, it may be that our newest writers continue one of our major literary traditions, are absorbed into the systolic rhythms of our culture.

The metamorphoses of
Henry Kendall

1981

If during the last decade of his life Henry Kendall worked in what he called 'the Shadow of 1872', it may be that those of us latter-day academics who have the temerity to concern ourselves with the poet do so in the shadow of 1979. For it was in 1979 that Barry Oakley's one-act play *Scanlan* was first performed to the kind of enthusiastic audience it has commanded ever since. In *Scanlan* Oakley created a university lecturer in English whose mediocrity is attested and personal breakdown consummated by a lecture on Kendall delivered to a seminar on twentieth-century Australian literature — a seminar organized by his arch-rival and nemesis, one Dr Grigsby. With so fearful an example before me, I might be thought of as possessing unexampled bravery or unparalleled foolhardiness in addressing myself to the subject of Henry Kendall's life and achievement.

Nevertheless, I approach my theme with some confidence because I am persuaded that some useful and important things remain to be said about Kendall. To be sure, we no longer regard him (whether for good or ill) just as the poet of 'Bell Birds'. Yet our possession of Kendall is distinctly ambiguous, because incomplete. With the gifted parodist's ability to nail the truth to the masthead of his mockery, Oakley has deftly suggested how various, how undecided, our responses to Kendall still are. This is how Scanlan rehearses some titles for his own exposition of the poet: 'Henry Kendall and the Poetry of Possibility. Or, Henry Kendall and the Forests of the Heart . . . or, Henry Kendall and the Metrics of Ambiguity . . . or the Prosody of Pain . . . or the Dactyls of Defeat . . . or, Henry Kendall: Bo Diddley or Baudelaire . . . that should just about please everyone'.[1]

Indeed, it is possible to find a counterpart in the serious commentaries on Kendall to virtually every one of Oakley's witty suggestions.

The anthology of selections compiled by Professors Hope and Kramer is, for instance, centrally concerned with issues of form and prosody and their cultural implications. It was Donovan Clarke who suggested a connection between Kendall and *symbolisme*; as it was he who documented those defeats of body and spirit which led to the poet's several committals to Gladesville Hospital. Or Adrian Mitchell's study resumes under its title of 'The Radiant Dream' most of the leading ideas about Kendall's religious idealism, his Romantic perception of the natural world and the discrepancy between his aspirations and actual experience.[2]

But in spite of our uncertain possession of Kendall we remain, in a curious way, possessed by him. For all the many failures of his art, the defeats of his living, there is yet at the core of his history a hard, bright grain of striving, success even, which no interpreter of our literary culture has ever been able to deny or ignore. My purpose in this essay is to sketch in one perspective on the poet's life and work in the hope that, by so doing, I may contribute to an understanding of that effort of the imagination which gives a colonial career continuing value to our own later twentieth-century lives. I do not, let me hasten to add, hold up my Henry Kendall as inherently superior to Alec Hope's Kendall or Leonie Kramer's Kendall or anybody else's Kendall, but simply to defend him from Dr Grigsby and, perhaps even more to the purpose, Scanlan.

The starting point, then, for my own account of Kendall's achievement lies in a recollection of his eldest son, Frederick Clarence. In a memoir composed in refutation of the views promulgated by Mrs Hamilton-Grey in *Kendall, Our God-Made Chief*, he looked back on those happy times when the poet was reunited with his wife and children in Camden Haven, on the north coast of New South Wales:

Beyond the clearing to the south was what we called the "Bush Paddock", the forest primeval of towering blackbutt, turpentine, tallowwood and stringy bark, with thick scrub undergrowth. Here it was my father loved to take my brother and myself for walks, when smoking a clay pipe, crammed with "Conqueror" or "Yankee Doodle" he would answer our childish questions with wonders of the great outer world, with mythic or historic tales, adapted to our minds. He would cut for us bush stilts or make "bull-roarers", whirling the latter around him to our huge delight.[3]

The scene is an engaging one — the world-weary poet, self-exiled from Sydney, re-creating himself among the beauties of the natural world by recounting legendary and mythic tales to his infant children. In it, it is Kendall's interest in myth narratives that most excites my curiosity, for it was by no means a late interest fostered in order to give pleasure to his young family. Quite the contrary; Alexander Sutherland asserts that such stories came to Kendall in his earliest childhood, were in fact indelibly imprinted on his imagination:

When at last the father was able to do no more than crawl out into the sunshine or crowd close in to the fire, the boy [Kendall] sat by his side, an affectionate companion, holding his hand and listening to the history of bygone ages; the myths of Greece, the exploits of Rome, the glories of England.[4]

In a letter to Sheridan Moore dated 29 June 1877, Kendall indicated that his mother too had been a source of his acquaintance with these compelling tales:

I was introduced by [my mother] to the then current translation of Homer, and took a genuine boy's delight in the book; and in Bunyan's stalwart hero, Greatheart. Every bush I came across was either an Achilles or a giant.[5]

The burden of my argument in this essay is that myths and legends, drawn from three chief sources, played a fundamental role in Kendall's imagination, provided him in effect with an indispensable means of organizing his often inchoate perceptions of the world into a sustaining identity. For Kendall, falling as it were by chance into the poet's vocation, had no firm self-image on which to build a literary career in the uncertain culture of nineteenth-century New South Wales. He certainly had not experienced that decisive moment which was granted to Harpur, his predecessor, who at the age of eleven had his life's destiny made plain to him in the sudden concatenation of storm and self and insight:

> Strange darings seize me, witnessing this strife
> Of Nature; while, as heedless of my life,
> I stand exposed. And does some destined charm
> Hold me secure from elemental harm,
> That in the mighty riot I may find
> How through all being works the light of Mind?
> Yea, through the strikingly external see
> My novel Soul's divulging energy!
> Spirit transmuting into forms of thought
> What but for its cognition were *as nought*![6]

Unblessed with any revelation of that kind, Kendall seems to have drifted into a writing career through the set of circumstance and the happy recognition of a latent talent. Only on the threshold of manhood, and through the influence of cultured patrons did he begin to believe that he might have it in him to be a poet. Those patrons, of course, included Nicol Stenhouse, Woolley and Badham of the still-young Sydney University, even (after 1863) Henry Parkes. It is a measure of Kendall's youthful uncertainty about how to play his elected role that he permitted himself more than one sneer in his private correspondence at those very pillars of respectable society who were opening the doors of colonial culture to him.

The external evidence concerning Kendall's first efforts to create for himself a literary personality is at best partial and fragmentary. The work that he published between, say, 1859 and 1865, on the other hand, makes abundantly clear how unformed was any awareness of self which might give coherence and authority to whatever particular poems he might attempt. Even the well-known initials NAP (Native Australian Poet) are little more than a gesture towards a vague nationalist ideal that Kendall made no attempt to realize in its minute, practical particulars. Some thirty-five years before the young Henry Lawson penned 'The Star of Australasia' the young Henry Kendall advocated in 'Australian War Song' a similarly bellicose mode of national definition:[7]

> Men have said that ye were sleeping —
>   Hurl — Australians — back the lie;
> Whet the swords you have in keeping,
>   Forward stand to do or die . . .
>
> Patriot fires will scorch Oppression
>   Should it dare to draw too near;
> And the tide of bold Aggression
>   *Must* be stay'd from coming here.   (*pp. 261–2*)

This, and 'Australian Volunteer Song' of the same year, did not, however, constitute the limits of Kendall's earliest efforts to use his verse to bring a national identity into being. The deeds of the explorers provided a source at once close to home and sanctioned by the attention of, among others, Charles Harpur and 'Orion' Horne. But there is no continuity of purpose, no coherent vision animating 'Australian War Song' on the one hand, and his tribute to Burke and Wills, printed in the *Empire* of 9 December 1861 under the title of 'The Fate of the Explorers', on the other.

In only one kind of verse did the tyro writer give real promise of a popular talent which might justify the title of Native Australian Poet. 'The Song of the Cattle Hunters' combines a jauntiness of expression with a felt acquaintance with its subject to suggest that

somewhere underneath the literary personality that Kendall sought
to construct for himself there lurked a folk balladist:

> While the morning light beams on the fern-matted streams,
> And the water-pools flash in its glow,
> Down the ridges we fly, with a loud ringing cry —
> Down the ridges and gullies we go!
> And the cattle we hunt they are racing in front,
> With a roar like the thunder of waves;
> As the beat and the beat of our swift horses' feet
> Start the echoes away from the caves!   *(p. 14)*

There is nothing, nevertheless, in either the biographical record or
the poems themselves to indicate that the deliberate creation of a
national poetic culture rated high among the priorities of the youthful
Kendall. In social terms, he was attracted as much to the local as to
the national. Among his very early poems for instance, is 'Lines
Suggested by the Death of L. H. Ladvenu', published in the *Empire*
on 3 August 1859. An obituary tribute to a European musician who
had visited Sydney, the piece foreshadowed what was to be one of
the constant elements in Kendall's verse: occasional poems relating
directly to events and personalities of colonial Sydney. He was
particularly given to the composition of obituaries — on prominent
figures like Stenhouse or John Dunmore Lang or (with greater
personal feeling) on fellow writers such as Marcus Clarke or Adam
Lindsay Gordon. All these works are reasonably successful exercises
in public poetry but have nothing to do with martial fervour or heroic
exploration, or outdoor occupations.

The most pervasive characteristic of the early poems is an under-
current of personal feeling so powerful as to flow into almost any
subject that Kendall essayed. Even a work like 'God Help Our Men
at Sea', ostensibly an occupation poem, is given its basic colour by
the poet's uneasy fascination with death by water, a motif which, as
Donovan Clarke has pointed out, is to be found very frequently in
Kendall's lines:

> I am watching by a pane
> Darkened with the gusty rain;
> Watching through a mist of tears,
> Sad with thoughts of other years:
> For a brother I did miss
> In a stormy time like this.   *(p. 16)*

Profoundly representative in their melancholy hue, these lines
seem to carry an autobiographical reference which is at best obscure.

At the time when 'God Help Our Men at Sea' was composed, Kendall's twin brother Basil was certainly not dead — was, indeed, probably droving in Queensland. What, however, is not obscure is Kendall's compulsive treatment in poem after poem of a fraternal relationship which is converted into a specialized treatment of the *doppelgänger* theme. The accident of a twin brother was simply one of the many elements in the poet's life which generated intensely felt and often ill-understood feelings capable of thrusting their way into the most unlikely lines of his verse.

This pattern of obsessive feelings taking control of his poems is nowhere more evident than in the nostalgia for a life that might have been that again and again takes over Kendall's writing. The sense of life as undefinable loss quite extraordinarily commands, for instance, the whole of a poem such as 'Sitting by the Fire', written in the poet's twenty-third year:

> Barren Age and withered World!
> Oh! the dying leaves,
> Like a drizzling rain,
> Falling round the roof —
> Pattering on the pane!
> Frosty Age and cold cold World!
> Ghosts of other days,
> Trooping past the faded fire,
> Flit before the gaze   (*p. 17*)

Had Heinrich Heine walked the streets of Sydney in 1862, he might well have remarked of the young Kendall, as he did in Paris of the young de Musset, 'There goes a young man with a promising past'.

Kendall's dismayed sense of worlds just beyond his apprehension most regularly attaches itself to feelings of sexual loss or failure, or to the idea of an elusive spirit of nature forever out of reach. The early poems are replete with Ethelines and Aileens, Maids of Gerringong and Bellambi — beautiful young women never attained, and now locked into an untouchable past. There are equally frequent attempts at realizing the numinous spirit of the physical world that Kendall knew best — the temperate rainforests of coastal New South Wales.

Nationalist fervour; songs of occupation; personal melancholy; the celebration of nature — Kendall's beginnings as a poet fit perfectly Stephen Leacock's image of a man leaping on his horse and galloping off in all directions at once. If there was any centripetal force at work in his imagination it was probably the very act of versifying. There is no mistaking his prosodic and metrical practices, and the 'musical' effects of his verse were widely admired by his contemporaries. Euterpe, in fact, is twice directly addressed in the canon of Kendall's poetry (the only Muse so honoured), and there are numerous musical allusions of one kind or another in his lines. That ear, furthermore, would have to be stone deaf which failed to detect the aggressive alliterations, the heavy accentual stresses, the strong end and mid-line rhymes which are the staple of Kendall's technique. These tricks combine to make music of a kind, but by and large its appeal is obvious and crude. The more important effect of the instantly recognizable technique is, it seems to me, to act as the vehicle of a certain kind of poetic sensibility — a sensibility desperately announcing its need for self-expression but quite unsure of what that self might be or how to go about expressing it with any fullness or subtlety.

So oddly incoherent but compelling a body of early work cries out for some sort of explanation, and several might be proposed: a failure to appreciate that poetry must submit to the shaping power of the imagination, uncertainty (heightened by Kendall's cultural situation) about the possible or appropriate forms of versification, simply perhaps an overdose of Edgar Allan Poe. The one, however, which seems to me to be the most convincing (because it subsumes the rest) is an undeveloped definition of the poet's deepest being, its relation to the poetic vocation, its place in the world. Having fallen into a literary career more or less by chance, equipped with enthusiasm, a fund of unexamined feelings, and a crude technique, Kendall could do little else than flail about in the hope that his random performances sooner or later might coalesce around a poetic identity of some weight, stability and authority.

Between 1862 and 1869 (between that is to say, *Poems and Songs* and *Leaves from Australian Forests*) Kendall gave some signs of moving towards such a coalescence of talent, ambition and self-understanding. He was attempting, in other words, the transformation of his fragmentary powers into an integrated imagination. His verse, particularly the idealist-nature poems, began to exhibit a new confidence; just as importantly, he was working his way towards a limited but coherent theory of the poet's role. In a letter to Mrs Selwyn dated 2 January 1864 he set down for the first time an idea which exercised a talismanic power over his conception of his own self for a decade and more:

Men and women, with the poetic temperament, are generally sorry creatures; if their sense of enjoyment is keen, their sufferings are extreme. They seem to lead a twofold life; constantly overbalanced, and surrounded by exaggerations. In my case, I have enough of that acute sensibility to work myself into a constant flutter with excitement. And therefore depression of spirits is, with me, the rule, and momentary elevation, the exception. It cannot be otherwise, it should not be otherwise.

Under the rubric of the 'twofold life' Kendall sought to harmonize many of those dichotomies and contrarieties which were the stuff of his life and art: the agony and the ecstasy of the emotions, the polarities of pleasure and pain, the hiatus between the real and the ideal, the paralysis of action and the free play of fantasy. Its adoption as a personal model of creativity encouraged him to pursue Augustan and Romantic ideals almost simultaneously. His pastiche Augustan satire, 'The Bronze Trumpet', for instance, was printed within twelve months of his most famous Romantic effusion, 'Bell Birds'. The idea of the twofold life, furthermore, reconciled his sense of the poet's superiority to a philistine crowd with his belief in his own unmerited suffering at the hands of the world. It gave, in sum, his life a *gestalt*, but at the expense of a dangerously limited understanding of motive, behaviour, capacity for personal relationships.

The latent dangers of the 'twofold life' were realized, in the kind of tragic coincidence which dogged Kendall's career, at a time when he might have expected to know the greatest happiness and joy of his young manhood. On 7 March 1868 he married Charlotte Rutter, a distant relation and the daughter of a Sydney physician. The court-ship, it might well be argued, had been built on impossibly high expectations and demands. Kendall's very first letter to Charlotte, dated from November 1867, reads in part like this:

Peace, Trust and Truth are the handmaids of pure Love. The passion sanctifies its subjects. Falsehood has no life in its atmosphere; but a white sincerity sits in its high places. Am I too serious for my dear Lottie? I hope not. It is my wish to be her anxious teacher, as well as her devoted lover. Her extreme youth needs a guide, and who is likely to be kinder than myself. I have enshrined her with all sorts of bright attributes, and she must help me to keep the structure entire. Her task is easy enough. She has only to love me, and her maidenly love will keep her in the right and direct way.[8]

Very few young women, even those born into mid-Victorian times, could be expected to live up to such steam-heated idealism. Unhappily for Kendall and his bride their relationship was even further threatened by events quite beyond their control which took place early in their married life. The deaths, within weeks of his marriage, of both Harpur and J. L. Michael removed from Kendall two very powerful and reassuring father figures.[9] At the same time he found himself labouring under severe financial difficulties, further compounded by the behaviour of his family. His irresponsible mother and sisters plunged him into debt; his brother made a hasty departure for Queensland, fleeing crimes (forging and uttering) virtually identical with those of which Kendall believed his father guilty. There is evidence from his correspondence that by the middle of 1868 he had borrowed heavily from Henry Parkes (a debt never fully repaid). Early in 1869 J. le Gay Brereton senior tried to help by making his cottage at Gladesville available for Kendall's use. By that time, however, nothing could avert the impending disaster. With the threat of bankruptcy and dismissal from government service hanging over his head, Kendall left Sydney in what amounted to a flight. By June 1869 he, his wife, and infant daughter Araluen were established in Melbourne. With the collapse of his material security, the attempt to construct a self on the model of the twofold life also failed.

For several years before he fled, however, Kendall had experimented with at least one kind of verse potentially capable of breaking through his self-restricted vision to a deeper and more fructifying awareness of his own being: the re-working of myths and legends. The sources of such poems, as we might expect from his son's and his own recollections, were three-fold: Aboriginal, religious and classical. During an infancy passed in the Illawarra district Kendall had made contact with Aboriginal people still living within their tribal culture. Along with 'Bell Birds', one of his best-known poems is 'The Last of His Tribe', first printed in the *Sydney Morning Herald* on 3 September 1864. The piece is often read as a gesture of sympathetic identification with a race already approaching extinction, an early act of contrition on the part of the white conquerors of Australia's native people. Read in association with the other pieces that Kendall devoted to non-white races, however, 'The Last of His Tribe' takes on a further, complementary meaning. Of such poems there are four, all published in 1860–61. One, 'Urara', has an Australian Aboriginal setting; the others derive, apparently, from Kendall's experience in the South Pacific. Two, 'The Ballad of Tanna' and 'A Legend of Tanna', are closely-related versions of the same tale. The title of the other, 'The Cannacha's Death Song over his Chieftain', suggests the element common to the whole group. Whether the overt subject is Aboriginal or Melanesian, Kendall in every case bases the emotional appeal of his lines on the death of a powerful authority figure defeated in battle by men of his own race. The dream of all these poems is the dream of obliteration — of self, or of some personality perceived as wielding profound influence over the teller of the tale. While it is only in the poems derived from the legends of non-European races that Kendall entertains the notion of the most radical transformation of all, self-annihilation, nevertheless all the products of his mythopoeic imagination address themselves to metamorphoses through which an insecure identity may assume a completely different substance and outline.

When he turned to the religious mythology of Europe for his subjects, Kendall used not the *Pilgrim's Progress* that his mother had taught him to admire but a source even more fundamental and surely quite as familiar to one who boasted missionary forbears: the Old Testament. What is perhaps his earliest scriptural piece, 'Achan', derives (somewhat distantly) from the story of Jephtha's daughter, told in the Book of Judges. In his own version of the sacrifice of the girl to her father's integrity, Kendall ascribes a deeply passionate love of the maiden to the messenger Achan, the speaker of the poem. The climactic stanza becomes the expression of a desperate erotic frustration:

> 'She glides, like a myrrh-scented breeze, through the willows,
> O Ada, behold it is Achan that speaketh!
> I know thou art near me, but never can see thee,
> Because of the horrible drouth in mine eyelids.'   (*p. 60*)

The intensity of the expressed emotion, combined with Kendall's characteristic refusal to develop his material beyond its barest episodic base, suggests that the value of the dramatization lay largely in the symbolic displacement of feelings of central importance to the poet himself onto the narrative material.

Similar displacements can, I believe, be observed in all Kendall's dealings with Old Testament themes. During 1864, for instance, he published several pieces which use their ostensibly scriptural subjects to dramatize his concern for the American Civil War, then at its height. Even in these, however, it seems clear that Kendall was using both narrative source and political motif as means of exhibiting elements of his own identity. 'Elijah', published in the *Sydney Morning Herald* of 27 June 1864, not only hints at similarities between the Old Testament prophet and President Lincoln but also uses the internecine nature of the American conflict to dramatize the *doppelgänger* theme, the fraternal tension so deeply embedded in his own psychological make-up.

Only two months later, on 30 August 1864, Kendall once again addressed himself to the American Civil War by way of biblical allusion. In this instance, the devotion of Rizpah, the concubine of Saul mentioned in the second Book of Samuel, is contrasted with the sexual looseness and promiscuity which Kendall, oddly enough, singles out as one of the remarkable features of the faraway struggle:

> And the harlots — the shameless, the nameless
>   Who stand in the market place, winning
> Our souls with their cunning devices,
>   And the flush — and the signs of their sinning —
>
> Oh! hearken sweet daughter of Zion,
>   To the noise from the sides of the ships, now;
> And look to the mariner's forehead,
>   And the scorn like a worm on his lips now . . .
>
> "How long", we have howled from the wall-tops,
>   "Shall we wait for the Christ to deliver
> Our lives, from the Passion that strangles
>   For ever, and ever, and ever?"   (*p. 302*)

As late as April 1867, some two years after silence fell at Appomatox, Kendall returned to the character of Rizpah. Finding yet again its ostensible theme in 'the Strife That shook America for five long years', the second poem with this title becomes in fact an idealization of long-suffering, faithful womankind. The oscillation between fascinated disgust at the erotic allure of women and an idealization of their beauty of conduct is utterly characteristic of Kendall. All that is remarkable is that he found even in poems devoted, seemingly, to current affairs, the means of projecting the jostling, confused elements of his own self. For even in these Old Testament pieces, the techniques of dramatization brought him no closer to understanding and synthesizing the muddled components of his personality. He had found only the means of projecting some of the causes of his unease, not of bringing them into a harmonious unity.

Not surprisingly, as the 1860s drew towards a close, Kendall's traffic with the Bible seemed to be proposing a more drastic approach to the needed construction of his own identity. 'King Saul at Gilboa', published in the *Empire* on New Year's Day 1869, has been properly praised by Alec Hope for its skill in achieving the aims implied in its sub-title, 'A Battle Piece'.[10] Quite as interesting, it seems to me, is the fact that it repeats, in a different context, the psychological motif of pieces like 'The Last of His Tribe' and 'A Legend of Tanna' — the immolation, that is to say, of a heroically defeated leader. Through his description of the death of Saul, Kendall, at one of the traumatic periods of his career, was finding consolation in the fantasy of annihilation as a means of escaping the stresses of his own life. In one of his rare excursions into the New Testament, composed at much the same time as 'King Saul at Gilboa', he contemplated an equally radical, if more hopeful, metamorphosis of self. 'To Damascus', in its account of the conversion of Paul, plainly offered Kendall the wish-fulfilment dream of a similarly triumphant transformation of his own self and situation. Significantly, however, the poem ends with the hope of transformation rather than its actual achievement.

> For now we may judge of the Truth through a glass;
> And the road over which they must evermore pass,
> Who would think for the many, and fight for the mass,
>   Is the road to Damascus.   (*p. 83*)

In the end, it seems, Kendall came to recognize the motive force behind his repeated use, throughout the 1860s, of biblical material. Above the second of Kendall's poems to bear the title 'Elijah', Bishop Reed in his edition prints an extract from a letter written by the poet to Adam Lindsay Gordon, which says (in part) the following: 'the beauty of your verse and its relation to my late loss [of his daughter Araluen], caused me to carry it away in my head where it became fused with the ideas that led to *Elijah*'. Given such a critical awareness of the deep personal needs his biblical poems were meeting, it is hardly surprising that the conclusion of this second 'Elijah' is not only the clearest but the fullest scriptural representation of the poet's sense of his own situation:

> one
> Made godlike with that scholarship supreme
> Which comes from suffering; one, with eyes to see
> The very core of things; with hands to grasp
> High opportunities, and use them for
> His glorious mission; one, whose face inspired
> Would wear a terror for the lying soul,
> But seem a glory in the sight of those
> Who make the light and sweetness of the world,
> And are the high priests of the Beautiful.   (*pp. 369–70*)

It may be that personal and cultural inhibitions prevented Kendall from using his biblical sources as fully as he might have done to probe the nature and possibilities of his own being. No such impediments, however, attached to classical lore, and his treatment of Greek mythology in the period between 1862 and 1869 is, if anything, of greater consequence than his reworking of scriptural narrative. Twice in 1866, for instance, Kendall turned to classical themes, in 'Merope' and 'The Voyage of Telegonus'. The first of these deals with one of the daughters of Atlas and Pleione who, in marrying the mortal Sisyphus, forfeited, as the *Sydney Morning Herald* explained in a footnote to the first printing on 9 November 1866, her dowry of light. Kendall's version, conflating several myths, stresses, on the one hand, the close bond between mother and daughter and, on the other, the desperate unhappiness of Sisyphus in his separation from his bride. Sisyphus's closing speech in particular is another variant of that sexual longing which so often appears in the verse of the young Kendall, on this occasion modified into what could pass as the chaste calm of a classic style:

> "Therefore," he saith, "I am sick for thee, Merope,
>   faint for the tender
> Touch of thy mouth, and the eyes like the lights of an
>   altar to me;
> But lo, thou art far, and thy face is a still and a
>   sorrowful splendour!
> And the storm is abroad with the rain on the perilous
>   straits of the sea."   (*p. 138*)

'The Voyage of Telegonus' even more patently strains towards a style capable of subduing its material to a classical moderation. The opening lines conclusively demonstrate the poem's stylistic dependence on Tennyson's 'Ulysses':

> Ill fares it with the man whose lips are set
> To bitter themes and words that spite the gods:
> For, seeing how the son of Saturn sways
> With eyes and ears for all, this one shall halt
> As on hard hurtful hills; his days shall know
> The plaintive front of Sorrow; level looks
> With cries ill-favoured shall be dealt to him;
> And *this* shall be that he may think of peace
> As one might think of alienated lips
> Of sweetness touched for once in kind warm dreams.   (*p. 93*)

The whole subject of 'The Voyage of Telegonus', of course, also derives from the epic career of Ulysses, recounting the unwitting slaying of the great hero by Telegonus, his son by Circe. In dealing with parricide Kendall touched on one of the recurring subjects of most mythologies. 'The Voyage of Telegonus' transmits an emotional power rare in his canon because, as I shall suggest, it opened up a path towards one of his own deepest conflicts.

In one other important poem Kendall combined a Tennysonian manner with Homeric material: 'Ogyges', first printed in the *Colonial Monthly Magazine* for April 1869. As Kendall admitted in a footnote, his specific models were Tennyson's 'Tithonus' and R. H.

Horne's 'Orion'. His theme, following particularly Tennyson's hint, is that of spiritual paralysis, impotence. While this poem, in my view, does not probe as deeply as 'Telegonus' into the fundamental causes of Kendall's behaviour, it is clearly a projection of his own situation at the time of its first appearance. By April 1869 the pressure of family and financial crises had brought the poet to exactly that state of inaction mirrored in his poem, a state from which he hoped desperately to be relieved by some miraculous transformation.

Little wonder that in a series of three myth poems printed between November 1868 and August 1869 he addressed himself to legends in which art combines with physical metamorphosis as a protection against sexual threat. 'Syrinx', thus, recounts the transformation of one of Ladon's daughters into the reed that bears her name in order to escape the assault of Pan. The syrinx, of course, remains to this day an alternative name for Pan's pipes. 'Daphne', equally, is based on the metamorphosis of a sexually-threatened nymph into a natural form which acquires the permanency of art. Daphne, another daughter of Ladon, was beloved by both Apollo and the mortal Leucippus. Leucippus was slain by Daphne, who in turn, and at her own entreaty, was changed into a bay tree to avoid the pursuit of Apollo. The bay tree, again, became sacred to the god. In 'Galatea', finally, Kendall retold the legend of the nereid who loved the mortal Acis and was loved by the Cyclops Polyphemus, a situation which was resolved when Acis was crushed under a rock hurled by Polyphemus and Galatea was transformed into a river which bore the name of her mortal love.

In two of these poems Kendall achieved an art as successful and impressive as anything in his *oeuvre*. Only 'Daphne' is marred by a climax which falls into that bathos which was a recurrent failing in his verse:

> Pallas, friend of prayerful maid,
> Lifted dazzling Daphne lightly, bore her down the breathless glade,
> Did the thing that Zeus commanded: so it came to pass that he
> Who had chased a white-armed Virgin, caught at her, and clasped
> a tree. (*p. 70*)

Happily, the actual moment of metamorphosis is rendered with far greater success in both 'Syrinx' and 'Galatea'. Here are the relevant lines from 'Syrinx':

> While Arcas of the glittering plumes
> Took Ladon's daughter lightly,
> And set her in the gracious glooms
> That mix with moon-mist nightly.

> And touched her lips with wild-flower wine;
> And changed her body slowly,
> Till in soft reeds of song and shine
> Her life was hidden wholly.   (*p. 119*)

In all three poems, Kendall stresses in the events which precede the transformation the brutal lust of the pursuing male, while he plays down the aesthetic significance of the natural object — syrinx, daphne — into which the female is transformed. Without pressing too precise a significance on Kendall's year-long concern with transformation legends, it does seem fair to argue in it a simultaneous and ambivalent sense of sexual guilt and a deeply personal need to idealize womankind.

It is equally true of these reworkings of Greek legends that, like the poems drawn from Aboriginal and biblical sources, in the end they succeed only in projecting the problems they symbolize rather than confronting or resolving them. The whole history of Kendall's mythopoeic art in the 1860s, in effect, bespeaks an effort to find in legend the means to make himself anew, to escape his own limiting past and present; an effort finally unsuccessful because the legends he chose for his versifying could not carry him deeply enough into the heart of his own mystery. They left untouched some basic conditions of his being which, until admitted, would block every endeavour to create an identity appropriate to his times and talent.

In only one of his myth poems, 'The Voyage of Telegonus' did Kendall come close to the insights he needed to free himself from the claustrophobic conditions of his creative life in the 1860s. 'The Voyage of Telegonus' deals with parricide. Now we need not rely on the scanty biographical evidence to suggest that Kendall's feelings about his own father's life and death were the very nub and core around which his creative life turned. Alexander Sutherland, drawing on a letter from Charlotte Kendall, provided the account of Basil Kendall's death on which all later commentators have depended:

. . . the night was far advanced when [the twins Henry and Basil] returned with the physician. There upon the bed lay the thin and chilly face of the dead father, and by his side a huddled heap, the equally unconscious mother.[11]

For Kendall the memory of his father's squalid end was compounded not only by the image of the drunken mother but also, so Donovan Clarke has suggested, by the guilty belief that his father had committed the crimes of forgery and uttering. In addition to the slight documentary record, however, are the poems themselves. As Bishop Reed has pointed out, there are at least five pieces (written or re-written between 1860 and 1869) in which Kendall refers to the death of his father.

The first appeared in the *Empire* for 24 August 1860 under the title of 'A Death Scene in the Bush'. It is an account in some 173 rhymed verses of the death and burial of a bush shepherd. No background is given to his life, and the only other character of any consequence is his faithful wife. On 2 November 1861, again in the *Empire*, Kendall published another piece, 'In the Depths of a Forest', in which the same basic situation is made quite explicitly to refer to the death of his own father. The three quatrains assert remembered affection for Kendall senior, but again provide no information about the kind and quality of his life. When Kendall does fill out the basic situation with (presumably invented) biographical data, they invariably indicate an existence of some emotional and physical squalor, invest the writing with uneasy feelings of shame and guilt. Hence, 'Orara — A Tale', which first appeared in the *Sydney Mail* for 15 April 1865, provides the shepherd with a convict past. Hounded unjustly by his wife's kin, he has known better days before his death in the wilderness during a howling storm. After his burial his widow returns to England, to learn some years later of the death of the brother who had persecuted her husband. Kendall reprinted this narrative, with several omissions and under the title of 'A Death in the Bush', in the *Illustrated Australian Annual* for 1869. In the same volume he published 'Orara — A Fragment' — yet another direct reminiscence of his father, and an acknowledgement of the melancholia which invariably attended such an act of recall.

The series of poems plainly does not constitute a full or infallible diagnostic record. Yet it undoubtedly points to a disturbed and compulsive obsession with the death of a father who aroused in the son obscure and shameful feelings which he tried for ten years to exorcise. In the end, however, Kendall could not achieve that full possession of his feelings which would have delivered him from their stultifying grasp. Unable to uncover the deepest springs of his being, thwarted in his efforts to construct a self appropriate to the poet's vocation, Kendall at last suffered that complete breakdown of personality he was later to call 'the Shadow of 1872'. Once the flight to Melbourne had failed of its promise and hack-writing had proved utterly inadequate to his family's needs, he returned to Sydney a broken man, estranged from his wife and mourning the death of his daughter, Araluen. Degraded by drink and drugs, charged with the same crimes — forging and uttering — that had been ascribed to both father and brother, the murderer in fantasy of his own child, he discovered in himself an image of all the old familial betrayals which had blocked the full development of his art. Collapsing at last into total disintegration, he was admitted to Gladesville Lunatic Asylum on 5 June 1871. His dark night of the soul lasted for something like two years, culminating in a readmittance to Gladesville in April 1873.[12] Only after his release in July of the same year did Kendall feel ready to attempt the reconstruction of his being out of what had been left him by the purgatorial fires. His final attempt was ready to begin.

His first steps towards rehabilitation involved renunciation and resignation. For a time he kept apart from his wife and family (they were not reunited until 1876). The solitariness of his personal life was matched by a deliberate severance from his literary past. Scarcely willing to think of himself as a writer, avoiding the companionship of other writers, he began to characterize his earlier existence (and adversely) as 'Bohemian'. A letter to P. J. Holdsworth of 4 September 1874 contains a summary dismissal of his previous career: 'I haven't a scrap left of my Bohemian writings'. As late as 20 March 1879 he was even more vehement to Thomas Butler, the editor of the *Freeman's Journal*: 'I would rather turn bullock driver than go back to the ragged old Bohemian life'.[13] Perhaps, however, the most vigorous expression of this attitude of mind came in a letter of 16 January 1880 to N. W. Swan, the author of *Luke Mivers' Harvest*: 'in that wild bleak Bohemia south of the Murray I went through *Gethsemany* and I am only a grey shadow of the young man who began to write with so much enthusiasm in 1861'.[14]

Not even Kendall could entirely repudiate his past, and his earliest positive moves towards creating himself anew derived from the love of nature he had known from his youth. Poems such as 'Mooni' and 'Narrara Creek' eloquently demonstrate the continuing power of natural phenomena to bring the poet ease and refreshment of spirit. Such established techniques, however, constitute only a small part of Kendall's efforts to discover a new identity. He began to cultivate, for instance, a newly sardonic attitude towards himself and the world. The high old Romantic motives for writing poetry were now cast aside, along with cultural pretensions of all kinds. Economic considerations now dominated his approach to writing. 'Coin in these days is everything', he wrote to Holdsworth on 16 November 1874. 'My *Freeman* squibs are not written by one with a passion for scribbling', he confessed to Sheridan Moore on 6 March 1878, 'but rather by a poor devil who needs *coin*'. Undoubtedly Kendall did need money, and his immediate aim in writing after 1874 was financial. Yet the consequences of this changed outlook were curiously beneficial to his art. Released from the overpowering need to see himself as a 'poet', he could all the more readily turn to journalistic prose, suffering no queasiness about the betrayal of literary values.

Many of his prose articles display a pleasing vivacity and wit. Many, too, were written over one or other of the *noms de plume* that Kendall adopted during the years of his rehabilitation. While one of the reasons for adopting these pseudonyms must have been financial, those that he chose suggest further aspects of his reconstructed personality. 'Tiresias', presumably borrowed from Tennyson, indicates a writer who, having opted out of the common struggles of humanity, composes with the weary calm of one who has nothing further to lose. 'The Mopoke', too, is emblematic of a solitary and unshakable melancholy. 'Jokoki' (sometimes shortened to 'Joker'), on the other hand, promises a new element in his literary identity. An Aboriginal expression of delight, it hints at a popular vigour unknown in Kendall's work up to 1869. Out of his renunciation of things past and pretensions best forgotten, Kendall discovered in himself a salty, democratic streak hitherto barely given expression.

This new popular vigour is acknowledged in the very letter (of 19 June 1874) to Holdsworth which speaks of the 'sorrowful gift of the poet's two-fold life':

Still don't stick yourself upon 'intellectual stilts'; and look persistently over the heads of the poor devils associated with you; because a thistle, although scarcely an inviting plant, has still its uses. But I have no doubt you are involuntarily, most likely, too careful a student of humanity to overlook even its poorest side.

This attitude was soon sufficently assimilated into Kendall's sense of himself as to control some of his most impressive new writing, in prose as well as verse. An ear newly attuned to bush phraseology, for instance, resulted in an article on that topic in the *Town and Country Journal* of June 1879. He began to produce, too, a looser, more colloquial mode of poetry than anything he had written before, a poetry in which comedy and verbal irony are the controlling elements. One of the first poems to find an idiom more or less adequate to its impulse is 'Bill the Bullock Driver', printed in the *Town and Country Journal* of 1 April 1876:

> The leaders of millions — the lords of the lands
>   Who sway the wide world with their will,
> And shake the great globe with the strength of their hands,
>   Flash past us — unnoticed by Bill . . .
>
> As straight and as sound as a slab without crack,
>   Our Bill is a king in his way:

> Though he camps by the side of a shingle track,
> And sleeps on the bed of his dray . . .
>
> Poor bullocky Bill! In the circles select
> Of the scholars he hasn't a place;
> But he walks like a *man* with his forehead erect,
> And he looks at God's day in the face.   (*pp. 165–7*)

Kendall's newly found democratic insouciance gained further expression in pieces like 'A Hyde Park Larrikin', 'Billy Vicars', 'Kingsborough', and 'Jim the Splitter'. Probably, however, the most famous example of his anti-Romantic energy is 'The Song of Ninian Melville', so vigorous in its satire on a contemporary politician that it had to be hastily deleted from *Songs from the Mountains*, Kendall's last collection of verse, which appeared in 1880. The conduct of this poem offers, indeed, an instructive contrast with 'The Bronze Trumpet'. Forsaking the stilted formality and artifice of the earlier work, 'The Song of Ninian Melville' depends on the exploitation of a pungent popular idiom to achieve its satirical effects.

By turning his back on accepted notions of what was 'poetic', that is to say, Kendall discovered a new voice for his writing, a new sense of himself as a writer. A transformation of self so complete as to obliterate all his former attitudes and values was, however, beyond his powers. Through the middle and late 1870s there recur themes and feelings in his verse left over, as it were, from his earlier life. They are equally distributed between poems which participate in his new toughness of outlook and those which repeat the old self-defeating Romanticism. Through 1881, the last year of his life, Kendall was working on 'The Austral Months' — a series of allegorical nature descriptions so often akin to his manner of the 1860s that he could quite appropriately allocate a piece from that time to the month of 'September'. Its mixed success, its manner compounded of old and new, provide a fair gauge of how far and in what direction Kendall had travelled at the end of his career in search of a restructured imagination. His death, on 1 August 1882, brought to a close a programme of self-transformation vigorously pursued but still tragically incomplete.

In this brief survey of Kendall's career I have stressed the theme of metamorphosis for several reasons. In the first place, it provides, I believe, a nexus between his life and his writing more satisfactory than any other — within its compass every element of his career takes its place in a comprehensible design. It allows us, furthermore, fully to appreciate the heroism of his career, and in that heroism resides the continuing importance that Kendall can claim in our culture. The need to construct a self, we may say, was the primal need of all our nineteenth-century poets, the final inability to do so the unavoidable condition of their colonial situation. In his persistent refusal, however, to admit defeat in what should have been a self-defeating enterprise, Kendall made possible a literary tradition that many of our later masters have successfully exploited. Without Kendall's efforts to make and re-make his personality, for instance, Brennan could probably not have written 'The Wanderer' nor Slessor have manoeuvred his way from the brilliant surfaces of his early poetry to its ultimate silence; without them, there would have been no place for Eve Langley's astonishing transpositions of sex and identity or the symbolic strategies of Randolph Stow's *Tourmaline*; without them, there would have been no matrix to nourish Alec Hope's dream of man's spiritual evolution or Patrick White's concept of the mature spirit gambolling among infinite choices of behaviour; without them, Bruce Beaver could not so readily have explored the exigencies of being in *Letters to Live Poets* or David Malouf have imagined into existence the author of *Metamorphoses*.

These, to be sure, are large claims, and would require the detailed justifications of a major literary history to support them. I remain convinced, however, that such a history could be written and that it well might take as its central type and emblem the Henry Kendall whose major quest, albeit unsuccessful, was the mythologizing of an uncertain self into a sustaining identity.

Between living and dying

The ground of Lawson's art

1982

The strident controversy that attended the publication of *In Search of Henry Lawson* in 1978 in some measure obscured what must surely be the most obvious implication of Manning Clark's title: that his subject still awaits a full and true discovery. The conflicting views of Clark and Colin Roderick, indeed, merely schematized a prevailing pattern in Lawson commentary. Virtually every new account of our most enigmatic author has achieved its own conviction only at the expense of blotting out some of the central features of its predecessors. It is not my aim here to support either Clark or Roderick in their opposing claims concerning Lawson as a profoundly representative figure of our culture. What I do assert is that neither (at least in *In Search of Henry Lawson* and Dr Roderick's response to that work) provides adequate reasons why, through and in his writings, Lawson can be claimed to be profoundly representative of anything. It is not enough repeatedly to claim that Lawson 'knew what life was all about'; nor, on the other hand, to insist simply that 'his work mirrors the yearning of man to refine the human condition'.[1] If the public property we call Henry Lawson is to be worth anyone's ownership, there must be demonstrated in his writing particular proofs of an actively searching, successfully expressed creative imagination.

In other words, as often as competing arguments about Lawson's cultural significance are raised, it becomes the responsibility of literary criticism to submit his work, once again, to its own procedures — the only procedures by which, in the long run, we can test whether he merits the high national importance imputed to him by Manning Clark, or Colin Roderick, or anyone else. To address myself to that task is precisely my aim in this essay. Not that I shall offer anything so pretentious as 'My Henry Lawson' or 'Henry Lawson: A Revaluation'. My modest purpose is to examine a comparatively small and well-defined part of Lawson's prose writing with the intention of demonstrating in it one instance of that creative dynamism which, multiplied a hundredfold, is the mark of the major literary artist.

My starting point then, is the year 1892, a 'year [as Manning Clark would phrase it] of miracles' (p. 52) in Lawson's life. Clark sees 1893–94, too, as 'halcyon years' (p. 57). And there would be few to dissent from his belief that it was during the three- to four-year period from 1892 to 1895 that Lawson reached the high-water mark of his career. Some of the major stories of that time will constitute my subject; the ground of Lawson's art, my theme. In adopting that phrase I do not wish primarily to indicate the importance of place in Lawson's prose narratives. Enough has been made, for instance, of the bush as a source of passion, meaning, value in his tales. The meaning of 'ground' that I have chiefly in mind is its musical one: 'the plain-song or melody on which a descant is raised'. Now all great writers have such 'melodies' playing to their inner ear; their books become the descants raised upon them. If we can detect even one such motif stated and restated in Lawson's stories, we will have at least one possible starting point for arguing his mastery as a writer, and consequently his importance as a figure in our culture.

One particular interplay between ground and descant, one source of creative dynamism, has struck me more forcibly than before in the re-reading of Lawson's work demanded of me by the Clark–Roderick conflict of opinions. I can identify it most clearly in that story which, as Clark would have it, initiates the golden period of Lawson's artistic life. 'A Day on a Selection' was published in 1892. Only four pages long, this bitter, plotless snapshot of up-country living has generated some remarkably diverse responses. Here, for instance, is Manning Clark's comment:

In this work a wondrous thing began to happen. On the surface it was a description by a man who had begun to feel bitter about life . . . On the surface the life of the selector seemed hopeless . . . At the end of the story an attempt is made to portray the majesty and absurdity of life in the bush . . . He had managed to confer a might, a power and a glory on what had previously been dismissed by the cringers to overseas culture as the affairs of the sliprail, the cow-yard and the chook-house.   (*pp. 51–2*)

This, by way of contrast, is Denton Prout's assessment of the same story, in *Henry Lawson: the Grey Dreamer*:

The whole sketch . . . is filled with scorn for the fantasy-ridden idealists who live in a world of slipshod incompetence and haven't the willpower, "guts", or initiative to improve their lot by physical action . . . It is a picture of the "bad" side of the "intellectual ferment" of the nineties.[2]

Such divergencies of opinion I find neither surprising nor distressing. For there is that in Lawson's own words which permits, enforces even, a range of response limited only by the number of his readers. To me, the unavoidable feature of 'A Day on a Selection' is its style of scrupulous meanness, a style which, in reducing human life to mere event and observable action, evacuates from the whole performance the possibility of guiding its readers to any single moral or emotional judgement. In 'A Day on a Selection' Lawson, no less than Joyce in *Dubliners*, remains within or behind or beyond his handiwork, allowing the primal facts to speak as they will. It is perhaps the first thoroughly (and compellingly) depersonalized work of fiction in Australian literary history. The means of achieving this remarkable *tour de force* (and it is nothing less) are obvious enough — the consistent use of the passive voice ('A boy is seen to run' . . . 'The thick milk is poured into a slop bucket'), the recurrent elision of narrative connections, the dependence on a tone of voice wholly apart from the action or any moral significance that might conceivably attach to it. The full result of Lawson's method is a representation of the enigma of sheer existence, of that order of human experience captured by T. S. Eliot in 'The Hollow Men':

> Shape without form, shade without colour,
> Paralysed force, gesture without motion.

My allusion to Eliot is neither arbitrary nor, as I believe, unwarranted. For in 'A Day on a Selection' Lawson committed himself, at the beginning of his major phase, to the depiction of that state of spiritual nullity, that kind of life-in-death, in which the author of 'The Waste Land' was so expert. Even before 1892, indeed, there had been preliminary soundings of what during the middle years of the decade was to become the very ground of his most important fiction. As early as 1890, in the Albany *Observer*, he had surveyed the inhabitants of the continent's western third and dismissed them in a single phrase: '*the people of West Australia have no existence*'.[3] As social observation, the remark must be allowed a measure of exaggeration; as the expression of one man's state of mind and heart, it registers the personal vision for which Lawson, in succeeding years, had to invent plots and characters, that it might enjoy a local habitation and a name.

The exact phrase, 'they have no existence', does not occur (to the best of my knowledge) in any of the major stories of 1892–95. They exhibit, however, their own recurring verbal motif, summing up the hollowness that Lawson felt in himself and sensed in so much that he looked out on: 'it doesn't matter'. The phrase occurs, almost parenthetically, in 'A Day on a Selection':

Sometimes the boy's hand gets tired and he lets some of the milk run over, and gets into trouble; but it doesn't matter much, for the straining-cloth has several sizeable holes in the middle.   (*p. 44*)

It forms the theme of the old shepherd's obituary spoken over his friend's remains in 'The Bush Undertaker': 'Brummy . . . it's all over now; nothin' matters now — nothin' didn't ever matter, nor — nor don't' (p. 56). Its most striking appearance is in the climax of 'The Union Buries Its Dead':

[The grave digger] tried to steer the first few shovelfuls gently down against the end of the grave with the back of the shovel turned outwards, but the hard, dry Darling River clods rebounded and knocked all the same. It didn't matter much — nothing does.   (*p. 83*)

The whole of 'The Union Buries Its Dead', as we now see, is probably less in praise of union solidarity than in recognition of that state of spiritual paralysis which its author could project so tellingly upon his characters because (we must believe) he knew it so well himself. Every significant element in the story testifies to this view — action, setting, comedy, social observation, most of all, perhaps, its rejection of the sentimental comfort of literary convention ('I have left out the wattle — because it wasn't there' — p. 83). Even the detail which so taxed Colin Roderick — the shadow cast by a fence at noon — can be explained (if not finally defended) in terms of this reading of the tale.[4] Richer and more fully dramatized than 'A Day on a Selection', 'The Union Buries Its Dead' yet takes up exactly the same theme: 'shade without colour,/Paralysed force, gesture without motion'.

'The Union Buries Its Dead' appeared in the *Bulletin* on 16 April 1893[5] — during the year, that is to say, which followed the publication of 'A Day on a Selection'. These two stories portray with a thoroughness never surpassed in Lawson's canon his sense that it is man's lot to be held somewhere between living and dying. To the very extent, however, that they succeeded in sounding the ground-tone of his fiction, they represented a barrier to its further development. It is not to my purpose to enquire into the psychological genesis of the tune which played so insistently to Lawson's inner ear, merely to examine its energizing effects on his creative patterns. Even within the limits of such an enquiry, however, it is possible to suggest that few human beings could bear to remain stalled in that perception of nullity which characterizes 'The Union Buries Its Dead' — particularly one as alert as Lawson was to human potentiality. In such a situation Lawson almost inevitably sought for a release from the imaginative impasse he had revealed to himself in his art. The mode and substance of that release are to be detected in a new descant he began to raise upon the ground of his narratives, a descant first unmistakably heard in 'The Bush Undertaker', published in the *Antipodean* of Christmas 1892.

Colin Roderick finds the primary significance of 'The Bush Undertaker' in its traffic with the Australian bush:

[Lawson] wanted to retain the notion of Nature's indifference to human activity, to leave the impression of the bush brooding over the grim episode . . .[6]

This view or something like it represents the common wisdom about the story, and has accordingly directed a good deal of attention towards the well-known final paragraph — especially the critical acumen (or otherwise) exhibited by Lawson and his editors in the various alterations and omissions of the early printings:

And the sun sank again on the grand Australian bush — the nurse and tutor of eccentric minds, the home of the weird, and much that is different from things in other lands.   (*p. 57*)

Whatever uncertainty Lawson may have felt about the ending of 'The Bush Undertaker' is of less consequence, it seems to me, for his representation of the Australian bush than for his status as a creative artist in the culture in which perforce he operated. I shall return to this issue later; for the time being, however, I wish to comment on a strand of meaning in the story much less obvious than the impact of the bush — what might be called its inside narrative. I do so not for the sake of contesting prevailing interpretations but in order to lay bare what I have described as the descant that Lawson came to weave about the theme of spiritual nullity.

The main action of 'The Bush Undertaker' takes place on Christmas Day.[7] The heavy-handedness of the irony should not, however, blind us to its importance. For the tale is last, if not first, a tale of death and rebirth. The opening sequence, wherein a solitary shepherd goes in search of some old bones in what is probably an

Aboriginal grave, does more than establish the pathological eccentricity of an individual condemned to a solitary life in a remote corner of the bush. It establishes the motif of the (here quite literal) resurrection of the dead: the nature of the bones may remain problematical, but they are most certainly exhumed. The narrative then develops along a line of ironic counterpoint: after the shepherd has uncovered the long-dead occupant of the grave, he discovers an unburied body, that of his old friend Brummy, awaiting ritual committal to the earth. It may be imputing too great a subtlety to Lawson to discover a pun in his description of the skeleton as 'thunderin' jumpt-up bones' (p. 54), yet observation of the possible play on words confirms the prevailing meaning and emphasis of the entire tale.

The fugal opposition between the shepherd's Christmas dinner of 'boggabri and salt meat', on the one hand, and the meal the goanna makes of Brummy's remains, on the other, cannot be gainsaid. Nor is it possible to overlook the resolution of opposing themes — of death and rebirth — in the closing scene. As the shepherd commits the remains of his old mate to the ground, his hope is that Brummy will find 'a great an' gerlorious rassaraction' (p. 56). For all the grotesque comedy of its realized action, 'The Bush Undertaker' finds its deepest motivation in the juxtaposition of an absolutely hopeless, sterile existence with the possibility of redemptive change.

I make this claim for 'The Bush Undertaker' with all the greater confidence because exactly the same dynamic structure can be shown to inform many of Lawson's other stories of the same period. It is foreshadowed, for instance, even in the city tales which precede the great bush studies of 1892–95. The irony, thus, of dating Arvie Aspinall's death (in 'Arvie Aspinall's Alarm Clock') during the Easter holidays may be as heavily pathetic as the Christmas setting of 'The Bush Undertaker' is deliberately grotesque; it points quite as clearly to Lawson's dream of renewal. Nor should it go unnoticed that in 'Jones's Alley' Mrs Aspinall lived in dread of her husband's 'daily resurrection' (p. 35), and that rescue from imminent eviction at the end of the story takes on the appearance of a funeral:

When the funeral reached the street, the lonely "trap" was, somehow, two blocks away in the opposite direction, moving very slow, and very upright, and very straight, like an automaton.   (*p. 42*)

After these tentative experiments Lawson was ready to confront, in story after story, death-in-life with the hope of release by dying into a new identity. A recurring feature of this interplay between the

ground of his art and the new motif he wove around it is set out with
singular clarity at the beginning of 'The Mystery of Dave Regan':

"And then there was Dave Regan," said the traveller.
"Dave used to die oftener than any other bushman I knew. He was always
being reported dead and turnin' up again."   (*p. 326*)

Time and again the pattern is repeated. The bush worker disappears
up-country, seemingly dead, only to return, unannounced, to his
former surroundings. Time and again the faint hope that he may be
renewed, especially through the influence of romantic love, is
disappointed. The expression of the pattern may be comic (as in 'The
Mystery of Dave Regan'), pathetic, grotesque, but its activating
elements remain the same. Mitchell, for instance, is made to undergo
a representative experience in one of the briefest pieces Lawson ever
wrote, 'A Love Story'. 'He went up-country and was reported dead'
(p. 141), says Mitchell to his mate, patently projecting his own case
onto an imaginary third person. But there is no comic sequel to this
disappearance:

"He was reported to have been drowned while trying to swim his horses
across a billabong. His girl broke her heart — and mended it again; then he
turned up alive, and drier than ever, and married her, and broke her heart
for certain. And — she died."   (*p. 141*)

The only release he can know is the bitter, familiar comment 'Ah,
well — never mind . . . The billy's boiling, Joe' (p. 141). Mitchell is
required to suffer a remarkably similar experience in 'On the Edge
of a Plain', while the situation to which Lawson condemns him in
'Some Day' is even harsher. He speaks his tale of lost love from the
outback itself, the outback from which he knows he will never return.
Descended into purgatory, he knows that there can be no
resurrection.
    If the farthest reaches of the bush could hold an itinerant pastoral
worker like Mitchell captive for months or years, Lawson knew of
other ways in which the Australian earth could literally swallow those
who inhabit its surface. The conditions of shallow-shaft gold mining,
with which he was so early familiar, provided him (as it did later
Henry Handel Richardson) with potent images. The motif of the
miner dying underground was quite as vivid to him as that of the
pastoral worker wandering the land in hope of resurrection. Indeed,
exactly that motif is at the heart of the very first of Lawson's prose
narratives, 'His Father's Mate'. In that piece the father's desire to
work underground is the direct cause of his son Isley's death, through

a fall to the base of the mine shaft. As an afterpiece to the main action, the long-lost elder son returns home to find his father dead of a broken heart.

The ironic symmetry of 'His Father's Mate' clearly prefigures the design of 'The Bush Undertaker', while its substance is repeated in a number of important stories, notably 'When the Sun Went Down'. This tale tells of a quarrel between two brothers, both helping to sink the same shaft. The quarrel is resolved (before the sun goes down) when the elder brother Tom saves Jack from a cave-in, only to die of heart failure at the very moment the rescue is effected. As one brother is resurrected into life, the other goes down into the darkness of death. 'The Golden Graveyard', by way of contrast, uses the mining material to create a comic variation of Lawson's central theme. In their search for a rich reef of gold, Dave Regan and his mates drive straight underneath a cemetery, literally uncovering the coffins of the dead as they strike towards their hoped-for wealth. In a farcical climax, one of the diggers momentarily thinks he has met the devil when he comes face to face with a Negro driving in to the gold from another direction. It is life, however, which finally triumphs — life in the form of drunken Mrs Middleton, as she saves her husband's grave from threatened despoliation by the diggers.

Comic, pathetic, or tragic, the hope (never more than half-believed in) that there may be some release from the state of death-in-life by a redemptive rebirth is the animating force behind nearly every significant story that Lawson wrote in the middle years of the 1890s. In many, as in 'Brummy Usen', it determines both the substance and the mode of the telling. Brummy, thus, experiences the rare difficulty of being declared unofficially dead by his bush companions and subsequently being unable to convince them of his continued existence. He becomes that loneliest type in all Lawson's range of characters — the solitary traveller, the 'hatter'. The terrible detachment of his life from the rest of humanity is revealed in the conclusion of the story, when the narrator unwittingly reveals that, in recounting Brummy's history, he has been recounting his own.

Perhaps, however, the most extreme instance in Lawson's fiction of the 'hatter' as a man condemned to live, in Eliot's phrase, 'in death's other kingdom', is the story entitled 'Rats', first published in the *Bulletin* of 3 June 1893. Its experiential extremity is further complicated by an ambiguity of meaning quite as marked as that which attaches to 'A Day on a Selection'. The ambiguity in the case of 'Rats', however, derives less from any scrupulous meanness of style than from rival interpretations produced by its alternative endings. The editorial crux is the propriety or otherwise of printing a single sentence as a coda to the main narrative:

And late that evening a little withered old man with no corks round his hat and with a humorous twinkle instead of a wild glare in his eyes called at a wayside shanty, had several drinks, and entertained the chaps with a yarn about the way in which he had "had" three "blanky fellers" for some tucker and "half a caser" by pretending to be "barmy".[8]

That sentence did not appear in the original *Bulletin* printing; it was added for *Short Stories in Prose and Verse* (1894), and completely altered the meaning and tone of the tale. The later version uses the final sentence to produce a sort of 'trick' ending to which the entire episode must be regarded as leading. Without the coda, however, 'Rats' becomes accessible to a much more ambiguous and, I believe, satisfying interpretation. The opening scene, thus, in which Sunlight, Macquarie, and Milky first see the hatter apparently struggling with a human opponent in the middle of a dusty track, becomes crucial in establishing the ground-tone of Lawson's meaning. The three shearers are sufficiently interested by the prospect of witnessing a fight to abandon their 'smoke-oh' and move, without undue haste, towards the encounter. Their interest becomes urgent, however, when they decide that one of the participants is a woman:

"It's a funny-lookin' feller, the other feller," panted Milky. "He don't seem to have no head. Look! he's down — they're both down! They must ha' clinched on the ground. No! they're up an' at it again . . . Why, good Lord! I think the other's a woman!"   (*p. 57*)

It is only when a sexual element is introduced into the scene that 'they dropped swags, water-bags and all, and raced forward' (p. 57). While it is certainly possible to account for this haste as a gesture of outback chivalry, it is quite as fair to regard it as the behaviour of sexually frustrated men excited by the prospect of near contact with a woman. Neither interpretation is invalidated by the fact that when the shearers come near the hatter they discover that he is in fact wrestling with his swag.

Even when the truth of the matter has been established, however, the behaviour of the three shearers continues to offer psychological interest. Seemingly untouched by Rats's neurotically disabled condition, they encourage him in his pathetic parody of the ritual contest of the boxing ring. Sunlight and his mates take a sadistic pleasure in the old man's antics that Lawson is at no pains whatsoever to conceal. If, however, the overt actions of the shearers vibrate with implicit aggression, the behaviour of Rats himself in the latter part of the story is even more ambivalent in its psychological implications. 'Well, old Rats, what's the trouble?' asks Sunlight, and his question encapsulates what is perhaps the deepest motif of the tale. Rats's manifest behaviour cannot be accounted for by any generalized appeal to the alienating effects of the prolonged solitude in the Australian bush. It is reported with an exactness of detail which demands a detailed response.

Once the symbolic boxing match has been concluded, Rats, borrowing a piece of meat for bait, goes through the motions of fishing in the dust. There is no need to rely on accepted literary convention to account for this behaviour as displaced male sexuality. There is ample evidence elsewhere in Lawson's own fiction to justify such a reading of 'Rats'. Rivers in his stories are regularly (if not universally) associated with romantic love between men and women; one tale in particular, moreover, provides striking evidence in support of a sexual understanding of Rats's pathetic angling in a sterile bush track. In 'The Hero of Redclay', Mitchell tells the narrator of the sad history of 'Lachlan', who has condemned himself to a living death outback in order to preserve the honour of the girl he loved. Mitchell himself had been peripherally involved in that history, to the extent that he had observed some of the meetings between 'Lachlan' and his girl while he himself was fishing. Mitchell's report of one such incident leaves no doubt that his fishing excursion was a quite direct attempt to 'catch' a woman of his own:

"About a week before that I was down in the bed of the Redclay Creek fishing for 'tailers'. I'd been getting on all right with the housemaid at the Royal . . . She mentioned one day, yarning, that she liked a stroll by the creek sometimes in the cool of the evening. I thought she'd be off that day, so I said I'd go for fish after I'd knocked off. I thought I might get a bite. Anyway, I didn't catch Lizzie — tell you about that some other time." (p. 297)

Rats's fumbling with meat and string, that is to say, may be seen as the symbolic gesture of a man spiritually paralysed through prolonged deprivation of the company of women. So understood, the whole story must properly end at the comment which insists on the ambivalent existence of a man completely without hope of restoration:

When they turned their heads again, Rats was still fishing: but when they looked back for the last time before entering the timber, he was having another row with his swag; and Sunlight reckoned that the trouble arose out of some lies which the swag had been telling about the bigger fish it caught. (p. 58)

So radical a reading of 'Rats' must provoke questions about Lawson's intentions in writing the story, about the validity of a commentary so completely based on a doubtful text. My own position on the matter is simple enough. Whatever Lawson's conscious 'intentions', his imagination was demonstrably capable of entertaining at least two possible interpretations of the same events. My inclination in such a situation is to prefer the richer reading. In any case, if there is any discrepancy between the pattern that Lawson finally decided on and that urged on him by the deeper promptings of his imagination, the question of primary interest concerns the nature of that discrepancy and the reasons for its appearance. An inspection of the whole range of Lawson's stories written in the middle 1890s, furthermore, reveals that indecision about the final status of a text is by no means unique to 'Rats'. On the contrary, variant printings of the stories seem to be the rule rather than the exception.[9] To be sure, many of the textual emendations can be accounted for, as Colin Roderick has pointed out,[10] by the interference of editors less perceptive than Lawson himself. Even those which can be shown to have authorial sanction are often the result of Lawson's desire to heighten, say, the dramatic impact of a particular tale, or the naturalness of its idiom. Nevertheless, the very fact that Lawson had to suffer (and accept) frequent editorial interference indicates something of the uncertain status of the Australian writer of his generation. His own need, furthermore, to tinker with his texts (sometimes with profound consequences) suggests that such uncertainty was not entirely a matter of external pressure; it existed within the man himself, as a radical element of his creative apparatus. Manning Clark is, thus, right to draw attention to the codas so often appended to Lawson's stories. In perceiving them, however, as a 'signature tune, a Lawson comment . . . on life in general' (p. 52), he was missing much of their significance in the larger patterns of Lawson's art. For nowhere more than in these end pieces and in Lawson's seemingly unavoidable need to tinker with them is there more acute evidence of his uncertainty about his own self, the very basis of his being. The textual history of these final paragraphs suggests as potently as any other data marshalled by Clark the actuality of that divided and ambivalent self which the whole sweep of *In Search of Henry Lawson* aims to demonstrate.

Curiously, however, what might be construed as fundamental weaknesses in his life and personality proved to be the strength and buttress of his art. The great stories of his flowering time are precisely those in which he refuses to let ambivalence, uncertainty, distress be resolved by the comforts of doctrine, any absolutes of belief or action. His primal sense, that is to say, of human existence held between living and dying stubbornly opposes the seductive symbols of death and rebirth to which it is so regularly submitted. However great the temptation to convert the motif of resurrection into a faith, an explanatory myth, he steadfastly refused to succumb, at least in the middle 1890s, to any certitude which would falsify his sense of the enigmatic, the ambivalent, in man's life. The Christmas and Easter symbols of 'The Bush Undertaker' and 'Arvie Aspinall's Alarm Clock' are, in spite of their diagnostic value, patently machinery (or at most uneasy devices for injecting sympathetic irony into the writing). Unlike T. S. Eliot, Lawson would never have occasion to write an 'Ash Wednesday'; the integrity of his great tales of the middle 1890s resides in his determination to hold the balance between the spiritual wasteland he perceived in his own and other lives and the tantalizing but illusory promise of rebirth he could not help but entertain.

I should make it plain that I claim no status for the patterns I am imputing to Lawson's fiction other than what in theatrical terms would be called the sub-text to a script. In other words, I do not wish to challenge the validity of orthodox readings of such tales as 'Rats', 'The Bush Undertaker', 'A Day on a Selection', and 'The Union Buries its Dead', which locate their meanings in the interchange between men and the Australian bush. All that I wish to suggest is that the manifest meanings of these stories can be made to bear the burden of cultural representativeness and value so often demanded of them in part because the 'melodies' I have attempted to describe can be heard, by the well-tuned ear, playing at their very core. It is also, and finally, true that, just as from the late 1890s on Lawson's life began its long disintegration, so too did his art begin to lose the authority it derived from the tense balance it had once held between the ground-tone of existential dis-ease and the several variations on the theme of resurrection. From the end of the decade on, indeed, Lawson's career had at least this in common with Christopher Brennan's: both men acted on the metaphoric prophecies of self-destruction that they had dared to create in the flowering time of their imagination. Just as the latter part of Brennan's career is, in a sense, contained and predicted in 'The Forest of Night', so too is Lawson's life, from, say, his journey to England on, characterized by episodes in which he sought to destroy the old Adam of his former self and rise into a new and changed identity. One thinks, for instance, of the burning of his manuscripts upon his arrival in England — a symbolic *auto-da-fé*; of the abortive leap from the cliff at Fairy Bower; of the multifarious *personae* tried and discarded in the letters of his later years.

Such episodes in his life find their parallel in the conduct of his later fiction. The nexus between his awareness of spiritual paralysis and his dreams of release is all too often shattered, leaving him stranded between polarized extremes. By way of example I might cite 'That Pretty Girl in the Army', composed in 1901 and first published in the following year in *Children in the Bush*. In that tale Lawson reverts to material he had gathered on his trip to Bourke in 1892. Where, in the stories written immediately after that outback expedition, the motif of romantic love had been expressed with a tactful restraint, in 'That Pretty Girl in the Army' his treatment of women undergoes a complete polarization. On the one hand there is the sentimentalization of the 'pretty girl' of the title; on the other, an attitude towards female sexuality which produces perhaps the only coarse jest that Lawson allowed into his fiction:

The Army prayed, and then a thin "ratty" little woman bobbed up in the ring; she'd gone mad on religion as women do on woman's rights and hundreds of other things. She was so skinny in the face, her jaws so prominent, and her mouth so wide, that when she opened it to speak it was like a ventriloquist's dummy and you could almost see the cracks open down under her ears.
     "They say I'm cracked!" she screamed in a shrill, cracked voice. "But I'm not cracked — I'm only cracked on the Lord Jesus Christ! That's all I'm cracked on — ." And just then the Amen man of the Army — the Army groaner we called him, who was always putting both feet in it — just then he blundered forward, rolled up his eyes, threw his hands up and down as if he were bouncing two balls, and said, with deep feeling:
"Thank the Lord she's got a crack in the right place!"   (*p. 491*)

No story, however, more fully measures the extent to which the deepest controls of Lawson's imagination collapsed along with the externals of his life than 'The Man Who Was Drowned', not printed in Lawson's lifetime and probably composed about 1908. Its opening paragraph gives the clearest indication of the value it had for Lawson:

This is the story of a man who went away and died — or was supposed to be dead. Supposed to be drowned. He was a writer. I might have made him a "great" artist, actor, singer, musician, or poet, or anything else out of the common and great — or in the common, rather, and "great", as "great" things go now; but he was a writer. He was a writer who had been widely known and had written for many years. And he found that the more he wrote, and the more widely known he became, the less money he got for it. Perhaps it was because of the drink — and perhaps private worries had been the cause of the drink. No time nor space to enter into the mystery of drink here.   (*pp. 672–3*)

To dispel any doubt that Lawson is, in fact, writing of himself, he identifies his protagonist in the second paragraph by one of his considerable range of pseudonyms: 'Maybe his name was John

Lawrence' (p. 673). 'The Man Who Was Drowned', in other words, must be read as a prolonged and uncontrolled fantasy in which Lawson, bitter and aggrieved at himself and the world, gives way uncritically to the dream of dying into a new life.

There were of course temporary reversals of the trend — the Joe Wilson stories spring instantly to mind. By and large, however, after 1895 Lawson found it increasingly difficult to bring his fantasies under the command of his creative imagination. That fragile balance between the personal ground-tone of his fiction and the vision of Australian life that he constructed upon it more and more slipped away from his control. Only rarely could he repeat the triumphs of the major phase; hardly ever could he find some new vision of his own uncertain self to give his life and art new impetus. Near the beginnings of his sad decline, however, one story stands out, and for a single scene. In 'The Blinding of One-Eyed Bogan' Lawson strikes off an unforgettable image. His protagonist is briefly revealed, blinded in the act of saving a policeman sent to effect his arrest, naked and alone by the side of the life-giving waters of the River Darling:

. . . I've often thought since what a different man Bogan seemed without his clothes and with the broken bridge of his nose and his eyes covered by the handkerchiefs. He was clean shaven, and his mouth and chin are his best features, and he's clean limbed and well hung. I often thought afterwards that there was something of a blind god about him as he stood there naked by the fire on the day he saved Campbell's life . . .   (*p. 323*)

A fleeting glimpse of man as Adonis–Lear, and no more. Unable to find release from his wasteland, increasingly paralysed by its sterility, Lawson was condemned in his later years to the composition of fragments to shore against the ruins of his life.

The confessions of a beachcomber

1980

The title page of E. J. Banfield's *The Confessions of a Beachcomber* bears this quotation from Thoreau:

If a man does not keep pace with his companions, perhaps it is because he hears a different drummer. Let him step to the music which he hears.[1]

We have it on the authority of the naturalist Charles Barrett[2] that this was Banfield's favourite quotation from the American writer. Indeed, the range and number of his quotations from Thoreau's books suggest that the lord of Dunk Isle had a deeply familiar admiration for the hermit of Concord. Two chapters of Banfield's second book, *My Tropic Isle* (1911),[3] for instance, carry epigraphs from Thoreau. Chapter IV, 'Silences', is headed by the quotation, 'Who has not hearkened to Her [Nature's] infinite din?'. Chapter V, devoted to 'Fruits and Scents', establishes its theme through Thoreau's phrase, 'The pot herbs of the gods'. There are more than specific echoes of Thoreau in Banfield's prose. The whole of the *Confessions* is structured on much the same lines as *Walden*: in each book, opening chapters which give some account of the background to and motives for the writer's retreat from society, are followed by descriptions, varying from the lyrical to the virtually statistical, of the surroundings where he makes his new life.

Such explicit borrowings and analogies of structure seem to invite a comparison between Banfield and Thoreau, between Dunk Island and Walden Pond (between Townsville and Concord even?) as a profitable way into something like an exact understanding of the Australian writer's achievement. If I resist that invitation at least in part, it is both because the comparison is subject to some immediate limitations and because other sources are in the long run more illuminating than Thoreau. A cursory glance at the affinities between the two men, however, is worth while, if only to establish the length of time each spent withdrawn from society, their manner of comporting themselves, and their degree of isolation from humankind. Out of an inspection of their obvious affinities will grow an appreciation of their deeper dissimilarities.

There is, for instance, a distinctly exemplary purpose behind Thoreau's removal to Walden Pond which is absent from both Banfield's decision to go to Dunk Island and his motives in writing about it. Thoreau appended this quotation (from the second chapter of his book) to the title page of the early editions of *Walden*:

I do not propose to write an ode to dejection, but to brag as lustily as chanticleer in the morning, standing on his roost, if only to wake my neighbours up.

The cheery didacticism of Thoreau's last phrase cannot be mistaken. And the point of his lesson to his readers, is, of course, summed up in the most famous ethical imperative of nineteenth-century American letters: 'Simplify, simplify!'. Banfield lags far behind such vigorously educative intentions when he discusses the aim of the book in the Foreword to *The Confessions*: 'My chief desire is to set down in plain language the sobrieties of everyday occurrences — the unpretentious homilies of an unpretentious man'.[4] I am not absolutely persuaded that Banfield's stated aims square with what follows, but there is in my mind little doubt that his writing is far less informed than Thoreau's by any deliberately exemplary goal. His original purpose in going to Dunk Island was, if we are to believe his repeated assertions, a matter of quite literal self-preservation. So debilitated was Banfield by the rigours of Townsville journalism that his weight was reduced to a pitiful 8 stone 4 lbs (*My Tropic Isle*, p. 54) and he believed himself within twelve months of the end of his life.

Within months of his official arrival on 28 September 1897, however, he had gained weight, recovered his health, and had every prospect of enjoying a long and vigorous life. He chose to enjoy it, nevertheless, not back in the fleshpots of Townsville but on the island which had preserved him — dying there, indeed, in 1923, some twenty-five years after taking up residence, in his seventy-first year. Thoreau, by way of contrast, occupied his house at Walden Pond on Independence Day 1845, and, having proved his point, left it some two years later. During those two years he seems to have lived a genuinely frugal, independent, but by no means isolated life. Dunk Island is, to be sure, a good deal further from Townsville than the mile and a half which separated Walden Pond from Concord. Nevertheless, throughout his quarter-century stay in his offshore retreat,

Banfield does not appear to have lacked for company. Indeed, he took the precaution of taking with him his wife, several Aboriginal friends and (a fact which is revealed in my edition of *The Confessions* only by a photograph) a faithful Irish servant called Essie. With the frequent passage of coastal steamers, and fairly regular visits to Townsville, he can scarcely be thought of as the compleat anchorite. Charles Barrett was right when he wrote of Banfield, his wife and Essie, that 'Their way of living was a compromise perhaps; not too simple and not too far from the comfort that middle-class folk demand' (p. 171).

Barrett was also right, however, to insist (along with A. H. Chisholm) that the life Banfield led on Dunk Island was far from that of a lotus eater. Here is Barrett's testimony on the matter:

I must tell you that Banfield's energy kept me on the move. Readers of his books may imagine him as a leisurely man, happiest when lazing on the beach or sauntering among palms and his fruit-trees. As I knew The Beach-comber, he was active and alert, even sometimes energetic in talking. (*p. 170*)

Chisholm also points to a hard-working, physically active existence when he reminds us that 'in the nature of his semi-isolated case The Beachcomber was faced with a wide range of workaday tasks — did he not confess to being a slave to his own wheelbarrow?' (*Confessions*, p. xiii).

In other words, it seems to me that, starting with the very choice of *nom de plume*, Banfield was constructing in *The Confessions* a literary personality a good deal further removed from the historical individual called Edward John Banfield than the speaker of *Walden* was from Henry David Thoreau. My chief interest in the rest of this essay will be to delineate the created personality of *The Confessions*, to discover the attitudes and assumptions that went into its making. I can most usefully begin to do so by altering my point of reference from the American writer to the literary figure inevitably suggested by Banfield's title — Jean-Jacques Rousseau. I do not know whether Banfield ever read the *Confessions* of Rousseau. Nevertheless, the identity of titles implies a common cultural tradition — of which Rousseau was an initiator and Banfield a late antipodean inheritor. I refer of course to Romanticism, a phenomenon at the height of its power in Europe in 1788, when British settlement began in Australia. Transmitted vigorously, if with some variation from its northern source, through the nineteenth-century, Australian Romanticism finds at least three characteristic modes of expression in *The Con-*

fessions of a Beachcomber, all directly descended from the doctrines developed by Rousseau or his European and English contemporaries. They relate to the self, society and nature.

Rousseau's *Confessions* opens with a celebrated hymn of praise to the actuality, force and value of the individual self:

> *Je forme une entreprise qui n'eût jamais d'exemple, et dont l'execution n'aura point d'imitateur. Je veux montrer à mes semblables un homme dans toute la verité de la nature; et cet homme, ce sera moi.*
> *Moi seul. Je sens mon coeur et je connais les hommes. Je me suis fait comme aucun de ceux qui existent. Si je ne vaux pas mieux, au moins je suis autre.*
> [*I am formulating a plan which has no precedent and which will, in its execution, have no imitators. I want to demonstrate to my peers a man in all the truth of his nature; and that man will be myself.*
> *Myself alone. I am aware of my own innermost self, and I am acquainted with other men. I am not made like anyone else in existence. If I am not worth more, at least I am different.*]

Banfield patently knew neither the unaffected egotism which animated these lines nor the raging talent which supported it. Within his own modest compass, indeed, he apparently felt so little confidence in the reality of his own self that he used his books to create one which the world might find of some interest. If that creation started with the choice of *nom de plume*, it continued through a whole range of imaginative extemporizations, appeals to some of the most respected cultural models of his generation. Most notable among them, of course, was that of his elected isolation — the adoption (at least for literary purposes) of the role of anchorite. Now, while English and European Romantic literature can offer some few examples of the hermit as hero, it seems by and large to have been a role which very few Romantic writers in the northern world were inclined literally to embrace. The literal enactment of the myth of the isolated self is a mode of romantic behaviour which seems to have acquired a special prestige among creative artists in Australia. It is certainly true that from the end of the nineteenth century on, the decision to withdraw more or less from human society for greater or lesser periods of time has been if not endemic among Australian artists, at least widespread. Only two years after Banfield beat his retreat to Dunk Island, John le Gay Brereton walked out of Sydney on that excursion which found literary expression in *Landlopers* (1899). Further south, E. J. Brady made Mallacoota Inlet his headquarters and his home in the early years of this century; was visited there in 1910 by Henry Lawson on one of the several occasions during Lawson's declining years when his friends persuaded him, however temporarily, that a bucolic retreat might be a cure for his ills of body and mind.

Queensland in particular seems to have been conducive to behaviour of this kind. One thinks of McLaren's solitary years from 1911 to 1919 on his coconut plantation on Cape York Peninsula; of Vance and Nettie Palmer at Caloundra between 1925 and 1929; more recently of Ian Fairweather on Fraser Island; Xavier Herbert's attachment to the Daintree River and later Redlynch; Thea Astley's setting up residence on the banks of the Barron River, remote even from the village of Kuranda. In his representation of the fate of the Australian artist through the career of Hurtle Duffield, White displayed a profound instinct for the truth when he sent his protagonist to a solitary shack on the edge of a gorge north of Sydney to undergo one of his great moments of self-discovery.

If, in this regard, Banfield may appear to be the fountainhead of a local tradition, there can be little doubt that his own decision to stay on Dunk Island, once it had worked its initial therapy, was intimately connected with attitudes he had inherited (along with so many other Australians of his generation) from the English Romantic poets. These included the belief that Nature was a more amenable environment for the discovery and definition of the self than human society, because less corrupt. *The Confessions of a Beachcomber* is full of assertions about, on the one hand, the corrupt and corrupting influence of civilization; on the other, the restorative power of the natural world. In the section of his book which describes the 'official landing' Banfield attributes his decision to live on Dunk Island to a desire to escape 'the mauling paws of humanity' (p. 5). He maintains the image of a bestially destructive humanity a few pages later when he speaks of 'the rude hoofs of civilisation' (p. 9). Elsewhere he makes his dislike of 'the formal courtesies of the crowd' (p. 11) and 'The cares of . . . town life' (p. 41) equally plain. In his own way, Banfield felt with Rousseau that all the evidence of civilization pointed to the fact that social man, although born free, is everywhere in chains.

The complementary attitudes, the positive endorsements of nature, are derived just as clearly from the Romantic tradition, particularly that of the English Romantic poets. Banfield's language when describing natural phenomena characteristically draws upon the fund of images and metaphors bequeathed to the nineteenth century by Wordsworth. Banfield, for instance, tends to view Nature as feminine, nourishing and protective, its beauty clothed in the physical features of the created world. On arriving at Dunk Island, as he writes at the opening of Chapter II of *The Confessions*, he was 'eager to know how nature, not under the microscope, behaved; what were her maiden fancies, what the art with which she allures' (p. 34). The personification of Nature as a figure of female beauty is implicitly carried through in many descriptive paragraphs, of which these are representative examples:

lovely in its mantle of varied foliage, what better sphere for the exercise of benign autocracy could be desired?   (p. 5)

Most of the range is heavily draped with jungle.   (p. 10)

the bingum arrays itself in a robe of royal red.   (p. 11)

Coral gardens — gardens of the sea nymphs, wherein fancy feigns cool, shy, chaste faces and pliant forms half-revealed among gently swaying robes. (p. 40)

Faithful to the Romantic tradition, Banfield, furthermore, regularly adopted an attitude of worship towards this soft, feminine spirit of Nature. From the very first morning spent on the island, his response to his surroundings takes on the tones of adoration:

Feebleness and dismay vanished with the first plunge into the still sleepy sea, and alertness and vigour returned, as the incense of the first morning's sacrifice went straight as a column to the sky.   (p. 7)

The quasi-religious needs of his being were especially fulfilled on Dunk Island by the abundance of bird life, which he came to know in intimate and loving detail without ever losing the sense of birds' traditional significance as symbols of spiritual aspiration.

Banfield's emotional response to the natural world was by no means limited to rather genteel expressions of Romantic awe and rapture. At least as much of his emotional involvement in Nature is Keatsian as Wordsworthian. One does not need to track down the Keatsian quotations embedded in the text to realize that especially in his love of scents and fragrance Banfield is close in spirit to the poet of 'St Agnes Eve' and the great Odes. Charles Barrett has reported, and Banfield's own books confirm, the intensity of his delight in the sweet odours of his island; while his unalloyed pleasure in handling, plucking, above all eating tropical fruit like papaw and mango bears comparison with Keats's ecstatic enjoyment of an apricot: 'it went down with all the delicious embonpoint of a beatified strawberry'.

The Keatsian pleasure in pleasure could, on occasion, merge into the Keatsian pleasure in languorous idleness — a mode of behaviour sanctioned of course by a later nineteenth-century poem, Tennyson's 'The Lotos-Eaters', to which the inevitable allusion finds its way into *The Confessions*. More interestingly, perhaps, Banfield's intense sensory awareness of nature led him to contest that view of the

Australian world which had been promoted by Marcus Clarke's Introduction to Adam Lindsay Gordon's poetry. Throwing back Clarke's words in his face, Banfield defends at least the tropic north from the celebrated slurs on our flora and fauna:

the scent of the wattles, the eucalypts, the boronias, the hoyas, the gardenias, the lotus, etc., are among the sweetest and cleanest, most powerful and most varied in the world; . . . many of the birds of Australia have songs full of melody . . . . (*p. 47*)

To adhere to Romantic notions about society and nature involved for nineteenth-century Australians other difficulties than reconciling European natural mythology with antipodean fact: the doctrine, for instance, of the noble savage, the inherent superiority of the untutored tribesman over the man of sophisticated European experience, made for real and immediate difficulties for a colonial people who had semi-systematically destroyed the indigenous race. Banfield, on the evidence of his *Confessions*, participated in the general cultural dilemma — more intensely perhaps than many, since he, his wife and Essie enjoyed the company of several Aboriginal men and women at least during the early years of their life on Dunk Island. He seems to have been personally acquainted, furthermore, with a number of other North Queensland Aboriginals and to have made a genuine effort to familiarize himself with the culture, artefacts and history of the local tribes. For all his goodwill, however, Banfield was no more able than most white Australians of his time to free himself of the sense of the inherent superiority that those of British descent felt over whatever dark-skinned races they brought under their sway. The mixed quality of his sympathies and understanding is made clear in the very opening section of his book:

Why invoke these long-silent spectres, white as well as black, when all active boorishness is of the past? Civilisation has almost fulfilled its inexorable law; only four out of a considerable population remain, and they remember naught of the bad old times when the humanizing processes, or rather the results of them, began to be felt. They must have been a fine race — fine for Australian aboriginals at least — judging by the stamp of two of those who survive; and perhaps that is why they resented interference, and consequently soon began to give way before the irresistible pressure of the whites. Possibly, had they been more docile and placid, the remnants would have been more numerous though less flattering representatives of the race. (*p. 4*)

The whole of the second part of *The Confessions of a Beachcomber* is given over to what in a moment of unconscious self-revelation

Banfield describes as 'Stone Age Folks'. For whatever reason, the writing of Part Two is perceptibly duller than in the first 150 pages. Its prevailing attitudes are summed up in two separate comments. In the chapter titled 'Black Art' Banfield praises the drawing of the Aboriginals in these terms:

Here is the sheer beginning, the spontaneous germ of art . . . For these pictures are . . . the earliest and only efforts of an illiterate race, a race in intellectual infancy, towards the ideal — a forlorn but none the less sincere attempt to reach the "light that quickens dreams to deeds." (*p. 175*)

The unexamined and, it must be said, somewhat unattractive patronage displayed here is even more obvious in a remark almost at the end of the book:

I am convinced that this race, despised and neglected of men, can be as devoted to one another as truly as we who are so superior to them in many attributes. (*p. 209*)

Perhaps the only saving feature of the remark is the passing allusion ('despised and neglected of men') to Isaiah 53:3 which, probably unintentionally, associates the Aboriginals with Christ, and in so doing opens up a whole new perspective not only on Banfield's anthropological observations but on the quality of the entire book.

There are not many direct quotations from the Bible in *The Confessions of a Beachcomber*, but a great many from that poet from whom generations of Englishmen — and Australians — learnt the Protestant version of Christian mythology. I refer of course to John Milton. That Banfield shared the general passion of nineteenth-century Australian poets for Milton is attested by the wealth of direct and indirect citation not only in *The Confessions* but also in *My Tropic Isle*, which is headed by two Miltonic epigraphs:

What dost thou in this World? The Wilderness
For thee is fittest place.

Taught to live
The easiest way, nor with perplexing thoughts
To interrupt sweet life.

The Confessions of a Beachcomber contains quotations from a range of Milton's poems. Two from *Lycidas* are important more for their tone of elegant allusion than for their thematic or illustrative force. In the chapter entitled 'The Serpent Beguiled' Banfield provides a serio-comic account of the defeat of a marauding snake by the placing of a china egg in a nest. The anecdote reaches its climax in a direct quotation from line 75 of Milton's great elegy:

The snake submits to the temptation of the egg coyly resting on a bunch of grass, and having made it its own, cannot let go. Then comes the abhorred fate in the shape of a gleeful man with a long-handled shovel.   (*p. 123*)

Some few pages later, writing now 'In Praise of the Papaw', Banfield again has recourse to *Lycidas* to furnish him with the slightly mocking tone he needs for his paean to his favourite fruit:

Ripened in ample light, with abundance of water, and in high temperature, the fruit must not be torn from the tree "with forced fingers rude" lest the abbreviated stalk pulls out a jagged plug, leaving a hole for the untimely air to enter.   (*p. 129*)

The richest source, however, for Banfield's Miltonic quotations is *Paradise Lost*, a poem which had obvious value for a writer celebrating the pristine delights of a garden he had created in his tiny tropic paradise. There is one particular passage in which Banfield represents Dunk Island as yet another variant on that obsessive nineteenth-century Australian dream of a rediscovered Paradise, wherein he and Mrs Banfield presumably were cast in the role of our First Parents:

The scheme for the establishment of our island home comprehended several minor industries. This isle of dreams, of quietude and happiness; this fretless scene; this plot of the Garden of Eden, was not to be left entirely in its primitive state.   (*p. 26*)

Just as this barely suppressed equation of Dunk Island with a freshly created Paradise pervades the *Confessions*, so it is equally plain that Banfield saw himself and his wife filling the roles of Adam and Eve in a manner much more Miltonic than Rousseauistic. He aspired, that is to say, to be not a noble savage, but, like the inhabitants of Milton's garden, both cultivator and cultivated. If his days were given over to the practical tasks of maintaining life and health, his favourite evening occupation was reading, or conversation with Mrs Banfield or any transient guest.

Even the freedom he enjoyed in dress as compared with his London contemporaries, Banfield could refer to in serio-comic manner as the distinction between innocent and fallen Adam: the conventionally dressed man is every moment 'reminded that he has imposed upon himself an extra to the universal penalties of Adam'

(p. 113). Even in the haven of his offshore island, however, Banfield was forced to realize that he shared some of the conditions of a mortal world. All about him, in spite of the idyllic conditions of his life, there were evidences of Adam's fall. It is, in the first place, a trick of tone for Banfield to decline to call a snake a snake but to refer to it consistently as a serpent. But the trick of diction, derived, I am sure, from *Paradise Lost*, is more deeply symptomatic of Banfield's nagging recognition that even on Dunk Island he could not escape the contingencies of a post-lapsarian creation. His awareness of his participation in the common fate of man and nature often focuses in his observation of specific phenomena. The final observation of his account of the *bêche-de-mer* is characteristic. The creature's defence mechanisms include protective camouflage, giving it the appearance of a snake:

under what charter of rights [asks Banfield] does it slink among the coral and weed affrighting God-fearing man under the cloak of his first subtle enemy?   (*p. 112*)

On at least one occasion, early in his book, Banfield extends his sense of a fallen creation to a perception of the beachcomber's role in it — compares himself, in fact, with some comic shock, with Satan wallowing in the fiery lake: 'even the hardened beachcomber walks thereon [the coral] with uneasy steps, reminding him of another outcast who used that oft-quoted staff as a support over the "burning marl"' (p. 20).

I do not offer these Miltonic echoes and allusions in the *Confessions* as evidence of any thorough-going system of ideas or structural plan; rather as suggestive of a cast of mind which found ease and comfort, which recognized itself, in the familiar concepts and characters of the great poetic myth which had shaped for generations the attitudes and assumptions of that class of Englishmen from which Banfield sprang. Only one genuinely important element in his book would, I suggest, have found its way into the book as a result of the conjunction of a mind fed on Milton with senses feasting on the rich diet of Dunk Island and its surrounding waters. From time to time, even as Banfield relished the implicit analogy between his own situation and that of Adam in Paradise, the marvellous actualities of creation that he observed all around him forced him into questioning the received myths and assumptions about them. Looking on the garden of the world as it was laid out before him, that is to say, he repeatedly observed natural phenomena which undermined his whole framework of beliefs. The experience of living in Eden made Banfield doubt the wisdom and purposes of its creator. Behind the beauties of creation he had chilling glimpses of nature red in tooth and claw; and through those glimpses came to know doubt.

His conventional belief in a beneficent God was, most frequently, brought to the test when, as in the case of the *bêche-de-mer*, he inspected the beauties of the marine life which were all about him. The coral gardens that he knew and loved could offer frightening, unexpected suggestions of a creation in which all was not perhaps for the best, in which evil existed even if it was to Banfield inexplicable. The stone fish, repulsive and lethal in a world of loveliness, could not fail to arouse his anxious speculations:

has it not a gift which would have brought it to the stake a few score years ago, as a sinful, presumptuous and sacrilegious witch — that of living for an hour or two out of its natural element? . . . if the poisonous qualities are in line with its hideousness, one can but ponder why and wherefore such a creature has existence in 'this best of all possible worlds'.   (*p. 91*)

These observations of what in *My Tropic Isle* he calls the 'primordial life' of the 'tepid slime' produce comments almost Darwinian in their contemplation of a nature whose primary principle is the law of survival. The sustained commentary on 'The Garden of Coral' in Chapter IV of the *Confessions* is typical:

A coral reef is gorged with a population of varied elements viciously disposed towards each other. It is one of nature's most cruel battlefields, for it is the brood of the sea that 'plots mutual slaughter, hungering to live'. Molluscs are murderers and the most shameless of cannibals . . .

All is strife — war to the death. If eternal vigilance is the price of liberty among men, what quality shall avert destruction where insatiable cannibalism is the rule? . . .

With all its fantastic beauty a coral reef is cruel.   (*pp. 80–5*)

To the best of my knowledge, Banfield nowhere quotes Darwin directly in the *Confessions*, and it would be a mistake to represent him as accepting the idea of evolution or capable, even sporadically, of Darwin's generalizing powers. Banfield was, nevertheless, capable of recording natural data with real accuracy and thoroughness. Indeed, it is in this quality of mind that he is more immediately related to the development of late nineteenth-century natural science than through any convincing or consistent espousal of Darwinian theory. Banfield was the inheritor of the tradition of natural observation which produced men such as John Burroughs in America and Henri Fabre in France.

Fabre, indeed, is the very type of the nineteenth-century naturalist/field observer after whom Banfield seems to have quite deliberately patterned himself. Born in 1823, Fabre devoted his long life (he died in 1895) primarily to the study of the life history, habits and interests of insects. He developed a range of interests — wasps, coleoptera, orthoptera — and a method — direct field observation — that Banfield enthusiastically adopted. Apart from his central passion for birds, some of the Beachcomber's most impressive observations are of the insect world — butterflies, wasps, spiders — and they are recorded with meticulous accuracy and fullness. That there was a genuine scientific concern as well as romantic delight behind Banfield's scrutiny of nature is suggested by the tenacity with which he sought opinions from qualified scientists, often far removed from Dunk Island. He refers, thus, to sending specimens to Brisbane and Sydney; to corresponding with scientists in England. What Banfield himself would surely have regarded as the highest reward of his scientific life came when a species of mammalian rat he discovered was named *Uromys banfieldi*.

At least one quotation in *My Tropic Isle* indicates that Banfield had some acquaintance with the writings of John Burroughs. Burroughs would have particularly appealed to Banfield. Born in Delaware County, New York, in 1837, he was like Fabre a field naturalist and observer. But, rather more amateur, he allowed his feeling for his subject to show more immediately through his prose. His especial passion was for birds and he was widely recognized in his native land as having inherited the mantle of Thoreau. Indeed, like Thoreau (and like Banfield) he would from time to time retreat from human society to some haven in the woods where he could compose himself into a proper spirit for communing with nature. Burroughs's 'Slabsides' in the Hudson River valley of New York State is in exactly the same tradition as Thoreau's hut at Walden Pond and Banfield's simple dwelling on Dunk Island.

On the face of it, there is some contradiction (if not indeed confusion) between Banfield's chosen role as scientific observer of the natural wonders of the tropics and the attitudes towards nature which he appropriated with equal enthusiasm from the Miltonic and the Romantic traditions. That the contradiction runs deeper than the surface is suggested by the fact that, at the polar extremes of his responses to nature, there exist in *The Confessions of a Beachcomber* two quite opposite (even opposing, and independent) styles. On the one hand there is self-exciting Romantic awe at the mysterious beauties of a quasi-divine Nature manifesting itself in the flashing beauty of a butterfly's wing or some wonder of the coral gardens or forest:

The dark compactness of the jungle, the steadfast but disorderly array of the forest, the blotches of verdant grass, the fringe of yellow-flowered hibiscus and the sapful native cabbage, give way in turn to the greys and yellows of the sand in alternate bands. The slowly-heaving sea trailing the narrowest flounce of lace on the beach, the dainty form of Purtaboi and the varying tones of great Australia beyond combine to complete the scene, and to confirm the thought that here is the ideal spot, the freest spot, the spot where dreams may harden into realities, where unvexed peace may smile. (*p. 12*)

In the same book, it should perhaps come as a surprise to find the quivering sensibility so severely tamped down as to produce great tracts of a prose almost deliberately stultifying and dull, of which this is a fair sample:

Examining the specimens procured, it was found that they resembled lampreys in shape, olive green in colour, with pale lemon-coloured streaks and marks. Each of the gill cases terminated in a two-edged spur, transparent as glass, and keen as only nature knows how to make her weapons of defence.   (*p. 93*)

It is nevertheless possible to read such disparate passages with equanimity, without a disabling sense of disappointment that the imagination behind them both was interested not at all in fusing them and the whole range of perceptions, assumptions, attitudes that make up *The Confessions of a Beachcomber* into a unified whole. For the character who emerges from the book is essentially a *congeries* of received feelings and opinions providing little scope for intellectual or imaginative synthesis. His simple purpose is not even self-display so much as self-revelation. If there is any psychological motive at all in Banfield's pages beyond the uncritical unfolding of a fictive identity, it is the need to authenticate that identity, the elected lifestyle, to both its creator and its audience.

The primary means of such authentication is through the most frequent set of allusions in *The Confessions* — allusions, of course, to the unavoidable cultural hero of nineteenth-century writers in the English tradition, William Shakespeare. What I am persuaded is the most endemic of the Shakespearean allusions in Banfield's writing is his tendency to refer to his home as 'the isle' rather than 'the island'. Outside his books Banfield seems to have preferred the native name 'Coonanglebah'. But once he advances beyond the 'official landing', not only does he prefer the English 'Dunk' but is also likely to insist on its status as an isle rather than island. The ultimate source of this usage, I suspect, is twofold. The first is perhaps the most famous single speech in the whole of Shakespeare outside Hamlet's 'to be or not to be' soliloquy. Certainly no nineteenth-century middle-class English reader would fail to recognize or be stirred by Gaunt's dying apostrophe, in *Richard II*, to 'this sceptred isle, this earth of majesty, this seat of Mars, this other Eden, demi paradise'.

In suggesting that, in one of the basic tropes of his book, Banfield was (consciously or unconsciously) appealing to a whole class of English bardolaters, I am also of course indicating that the hermit Banfield was writing with at least one eye on an audience. The paradox of an Australian recluse justifying himself to an overseas public is intensified by other elements in *The Confessions of a Beachcomber*, particularly those gratuitous appeals to the sentimental patriotism by which imperial Britain maintained its hold on its far-flung citizens. I quote only the most notable of several noteworthy instances:

The odour of the island may be specific, and therefore to be prized, yet it gladdens also because it awakens happy and all too fleeting reminiscences. English fields and hedges cannot be forgotten when one of our trees diffuses the scent of meadow-sweet, and one of the orchids that of hawthorn. (*p. 15*)

Whatever Banfield's motive in thus attempting to authenticate his tropical experiences to potential readers in England, he seems to have felt an equal need to authenticate them to himself. There is about *The Confessions* the air of a man who needs to proclaim to himself as much as to anyone else the enchantment of an existence asserted to be endlessly desirable. And herein, I suspect, lies the other source of Banfield's need habitually to refer to his 'isle'. If the tacit reference to John of Gaunt soothed his readers, the implicit allusion, through the same terms, to *The Tempest*, authenticated his life to himself. Repeating to himself lines like '"Cooling of the air with sighs, In an odd angle of the Isle"' (p. 123), he could fancy himself a Prospero of his own enchanted island, weaving his spells into the books it made available to him. He could thus believe himself to be both a humble man speaking humble truths and (as he often put it) 'lord of his Domain'.

Lest these speculations appear too fanciful, I must now turn back to the unquestionable fact of Banfield's habit of Shakespearean quotation. In addition to *Richard II* and *The Tempest*, *The Confessions of a Beachcomber* offers citations from or allusions to at least these plays: *Richard III, Othello, Henry V, As You Like It*, and *Antony and Cleopatra*. We know from A. H. Chisholm that a love of Shakespeare was instilled into Banfield in his boyhood. But in 'placing' it in his adult writing, we are doing more than extending that range of nineteenth-century cultural pieties that the quotations from Milton, Wordsworth, Keats reveal. We are moving closer than we have so far to the essence of the idiosyncratic personality made manifest in the pages of *The Confessions of a Beachcomber*. For Banfield's extraordinarily prolific habit of allusion and quotation suggests more than conventional gestures of obeisance to the pieties of late Victorian England, or the frequent practice of late nineteenth-century journalism. It is part of the very fabric of his imagined self. Beyond the quotations from Shakespeare, Milton and the Romantics, the most cursory examination of *The Confessions* and *My Tropic Isle* yields citations from Dickens, Addison, Carlyle, Wagner, Kingsley, Goldsmith. Out of these endless appeals to artistic idols he constructed his own unique literary personality. The final paradox of his paradoxically public solitude was that the kind of self that nature's simple priest imagined into being was essentially bookish and cultivated. If the unceasing evocation of names from the literary past suggests any exact analogue it is, oddly enough, from a century to which, outside Shakespeare, Banfield alludes hardly at all — the seventeenth.

In making this suggestion I have in mind more than Banfield's deliberate archaisms, his quirky humour. His reports from his tropic island, like Burton's *Anatomy of Melancholy* or Sir Thomas Browne's investigation of vulgar errors, grow in a matrix of the most miscellaneous information. All the inconsistencies, contradictions, conventionalities of the revealed mind of the Beachcomber are in the end reconciled in a sensibility which resembles, perhaps more than anything else, that of one of those antiquarian projectors who give the English seventeenth century its particular flavour. 'These chronicles are toned from first to last', Banfield asserts in *The Confessions*, 'by perceptions which came to the Beachcomber' (p. 40). He amplifies the assertion in a sentence which echoes the late Renaissance sonorities of a Browne or a Thomas Traherne:

perceptions which lead, maybe, to a subdued and sober estimate of the purpose and bearing of the pilgrimage of life. Doubts become exalted and glorified, hopes all rapture, when long serene days are spent alone in the contemplation of the splendours of sky and sea, and the enchantment of tropic shores.   (*p. 40*)

With the same capacity for naive wonder that underlies Sir Thomas Browne's most ornate periods, Banfield was able to incorporate virtually everything that came under his survey into a personally satisfying scheme of things. He was, as he phrases it in *My Tropic Isle*, a 'man of many avocations' (p. 45). His ready acceptance of the conventional and traditional wisdoms of his age enabled him to give these avocations full play in an invented personality of oddly unrepeatable charm, in a book still unique in our literary history. It is not, I think, a great book. Indeed, the supreme creative act of his life was located in the very removal to Dunk Island rather than in any of the books he composed there. Of his own powers as a writer he had a very exact appreciation when he wrote as the epigraph to Chapter II of *The Confessions*, 'For the Beachcomber, when not a mere ruffian, is the poor relation of the artist'. A ruffian he most certainly was not: yet he was not so much the poor relation of the artist as an artist of limited powers and in a minor mode. There is a kind of daring as well as modesty in his own gloss on his book: 'So, these my vocations drift into the gentle and devious stream of inconsequence' (p. 32).

'Wherefore I think'

Notes on the poetry of Kenneth Slessor

1977

I

Kenneth Slessor left what must be one of the most compact *oeuvres* of any major Australian poet, and criticism has by now had some forty years to gain mastery over it. If, then, I add to the catalogue of commentary, it is only because I am exercised by a curious feature of Slessor's own well-known gloss of his work, 'Writing Poetry: the Why and the How', which was first printed in *Southerly* in 1948.[1] The essay is characterized by a studious concentration on the detailed techniques of versification. It comes, then, as something of a shock to discover the agonized tones of the last sentence: 'writing poetry is still, I think, a pleasure out of hell'.

The seeming hiatus between the disinterested analysis of the essay and its profoundly emotional conclusion will occupy me in this paper, and I shall approach my topic obliquely by recording an anecdote set down by R. P. Blackmur in the last essay in his collection, *The Lion and the Honeycomb*.[2] Once a patient in a hospital ward, Blackmur found himself literally placed between opposite poles of human experience. On one side of him lay a terminal patient whose life had been reduced to pure behaviour ('the medium in which our lives take place'). He was capable only of a 'guttural, explosive cry of the single word twice or thrice repeated: Hallelujah, hallelujah, hallelujah!'. Then one day the bed on Blackmur's other side was occupied by a man whose life had been saved by a tracheotomy. Hearing the ejaculation 'Hallelujah!' for the first time, the tracheotomy patient 'sat up a little higher on his elbows, looked all round in sheer delight, and sang a long syllabic Alleluia — All-e-lu-i-a-a-a-a!'. This is Blackmur's comment on his extraordinary experience:

Here was behaviour drawn out of inspiration in pure praise: not what this man had left but what he had suddenly come on. To be between the two [the Hallelujah and the Alleluia] was to be between the *Moha* and the *Numen.* (*pp. 304–5*)

The title of Blackmur's essay is 'Between the Numen and the Moha', and he is at some pains to define his key terms other than anecdotally:

The *Numen* or *numinosus* is that power within us, greater than and other than ourselves, that moves us, sometimes carrying us away, in the end moving us forward unless we drop out, always overwhelming us . . . it is related to the rhythm which gives meaning to action . . . the *Numen* enters, though it is not in itself, behaviour. It is the reality that presses into behaviour but never reaches whole incarnation there. (*pp. 293*)

Here, by contrast, is the *moha*:

Moha . . . the uncontrollable behaviour which tends to absorb and defile both the chill and the fire of the spirit . . . is a term for the basic irremediable, irreplaceable, characteristic, and contemptuous stupidity of man confronted with choice or purpose: the stupidity because of which he goes wrong, without which he could not survive . . . *Moha* also refers to the stubborn tenacity of will — of blind, necessary action — by which man puts up with what is intolerable in his life . . .
It is what our behaviour, unenlightened and unimpeded, would leave us at. It is what we are like when we deprive ourselves of the three things reason requires of beauty: *consonantia, integritas, claritas:* harmony, wholeness, radiance. (*pp. 293–4*)

Art, so Blackmur maintains, occurs where *numen* and *moha* meet. Now, while Slessor's poetry may not occupy exactly that position, it is certainly responsive to a criticism which uses Blackmur's two key terms, especially in regard to that odd disjunction between technique and feeling betrayed in 'Writing Poetry: the How and the Why'. To suggest how such a criticism might proceed is the aim of the rest of this essay.

II

Let me turn first of all to the operations of the *moha* in Slessor's verse. A number of those poems in which it can be felt most potently are precisely those which have been singled out for their technical virtuosity. Take, for instance, the case of 'Fixed Ideas':

> Ranks of electroplated cubes, dwindling to glitters,
> Like the other pasture, the trigonometry of marble,
> Death's candy-bed. Stone caked on stone,
> Dry pyramids and racks of iron balls.
> Life is observed, a precipitate of pellets,
> Or grammarians freeze it into spar,
> Their rhomboids, as for instance, the finest crystal
> Fixing a snowfall under glass. Gods are laid out
> In alabaster, with horny cartilage
> And zinc ribs; or systems of ecstasy
> Baked into bricks. There is a gallery of sculpture,
> Bleached bones of heroes, Gorgon masks of bushrangers;
> But the quarries are of more use than this,
> Filled with the rolling of huge granite dice,
> Ideas and judgments: vivisection, the Baptist Church,
> Good men and bad men, polygamy, birth-control . . .[3]

Slessor's own comment on these lines runs like this: 'I attempt to show the solidity of the fixed opinions by square, heavy, rigid lines with images of solidity, squareness and rigidity' ('Writing Poetry', p. 168). What must be added to so severely impersonal a gloss is that the same lines transmit before all else a sense of the irremediable, the irreplaceable. In the first part of 'Fixed Ideas' the poet's stubborn will confronts and learns to put up with what is intolerable in life. The poem allows only the sparest relation between objects and anecdote, gesture, morality — anything which might give meaning to human behaviour, 'the medium in which our lives take place'. 'Life is observed', remarks the poet, and observation rather than participation remains the chief source of whatever passion is in the lines. If its lines anywhere imply a movement towards morality, it is only in the final imperative — 'Undo, loosen your bubbles!'.

A similar withholding from any action or emotion which might give meaning to behaviour is to be observed in 'Sensuality':

> Feeling hunger and cold, feeling
> Food, feeling fire, feeling
> Pity and pain, tasting
> Time in a kiss, tasting
> Anger and tears, touching
> Eyelids with lips, touching
> Plague, touching flesh, knowing
> Blood in the mouth, knowing
> Laughter like flame, holding
> Pickaxe and pen, holding
> Death in the hand, hearing
> Boilers and bells, hearing
> Birds, hearing hail, smelling

Cedar and sweat, smelling
Petrol and sea, feeling
Hunger and cold, feeling
Food, feeling fire . . .

Feeling.   (*p. 90*)

The verse impels admiration for its technical dexterity, its heartless ingenuity even. What, however, I take to be the necessary comment on its effect is that, despite its title, the poem is one of the least sensual I have ever read. It recognizes what Blackmur calls 'blind, necessary action', and little more. Most certainly, it registers behaviour quite unenlightened or unimpeded by *consonantia, integritas, claritas* — harmony, wholeness, radiance. 'Sensuality' is (by intention, I take it) a mechanism, nowhere conveying the sense of an individual will controlling or controlled by the sensations it catalogues.

That Slessor was, nevertheless, capable of imagining a sensual mechanism operating as an instrument of human consciousness is tellingly demonstrated by 'The Night-Ride':

Gas flaring on the yellow platform, voices running up and down;
Milk-tins in cold dented silver; half-awake I stare,
Pull up the blind, blink out — all sounds are drugged;
The slow blowing of passengers asleep;
Engines yawning; water in heavy drips;
Black, sinister travellers, lumbering up the station,
One moment in the window, hooked over bags;
Hurrying, unknown faces — boxes with strange labels —
All groping clumsily to mysterious ends,
Out of the gaslight, dragged by private Fates.
Their echoes die. The dark train shakes and plunges;
Bells cry out; the night-ride starts again.
Soon I shall look out into nothing but blackness,
Pale, windy fields. The old roar and knock of the rails
Melts in dull fury. Pull down the blind. Sleep. Sleep.
Nothing but grey, rushing rivers of bush outside.
Gaslight and milk-cans. Of Rapptown I recall nothing else.   (*p. 31*)

In many ways I take this to be one of Slessor's most remarkable achievements — a veritable *coup de poésie*. Yet how desolate its final assertion: 'Gaslight and milk-cans. Of Rapptown I recall nothing else'. Again we are brought face to face with 'uncontrollable behaviour which tends to absorb and defile both the chill and the fire of the spirit'. At least, however, this can be said: Slessor's espousal of the *moha* aspect of existence is as total and uncompromising as might be registered in poetry — those around him reduced, as he puts it in 'Last Trams', to 'Stars of a film without a plot,/Snippings of idiot celluloid' (p. 96).

III

So much for the presence of the *moha* in Slessor's poetry. What, then, of the *numen*? Let me proffer, as my first exhibit, 'Cock-Crow':

> The cock's far cry
> From lonely yards
> Burdens the night
> With boastful birds
> That mop their wings
> To make response —
> A mess of songs
> And broken sense.
>
> So, when I slept,
> I heard your call
> (If lips long dead
> Could answer still)
> And snapped-off thoughts
> Broke into clamour,
> Like the night's throats
> Heard by a dreamer.   (*p. 92*)

The narrow lines of verse threading their way down the page constitute a feat of virtuosity quite as impressive as any in Slessor's *moha* poems, yet the virtuosity is here put to quite different purposes. The splendid skill in versifying here becomes Slessor's shouted 'Alleluia', a triumphant celebration of 'that power within us . . . that moves us, sometimes carries us away'. Perhaps, however, the most important lines for the view of Slessor's achievement that I am trying to sketch in are the last two: 'Like the night's throats/Heard by a dreamer'. The numinous is characteristically created in Slessor's poetry by dream-work or something akin to it. It arises from fictive visions of delight. Their relation to objective reality is unimportant; the delight lies in the imagining — as, for instance, in 'Rubens' Innocents':

> If all those tumbling babes of heaven,
>   Plump cherubim with blown cheeks,
> Could vault in these warm skies, or leaven
>   Our starry silent mountain-peaks —
> O painter of chub-faced, shining-thighed

Fat Ganymedes of God — what noise
Would churn between the clouds and stride
Far downward from those rose-mouthed boys!   (*p. 7*)

This fleshy-pink paradise is no more offered as serious theology than
its opposite, 'Rubens' Hell', or, say, 'Earth-Visitors'. All three
discover the numinous in the very pleasure of invention.

Slessor may not be the only poet for whom the numinous arises
in the delighted play of the imagination, the exploitation of interior
fantasy. There is, nevertheless, one quite special feature of the
operations of the *numen* in his art: the pleasure of re-creating one's
self as somebody else. The *locus classicus* for this effect is 'Metempsychosis'. The poem starts out in a plethora of irremediable fact —
'a tin trunk and a five-pound note . . . a peajacket the colour of a
shark's behind' (p. 78), and so on. Yet this potentially squalid
material is glamourized by the poet's patent pleasure in his imagin-
ings: 'To fry potatoes (God save us!) if you feel inclined,/Or to kiss
the landlady's daughter, and no one mind'. As the poem proceeds,
the local exoticism of William Street gives way to the literal exoticism
of fascinating, faraway places: 'Behold! — a mermaid piping through
a coach horn'. Yet the real stress of theme and technique falls on the
last line of all: 'Suddenly to become John Benbow'. Transported out
of mind and place, out of his own self into another's, this is Slessor's
shout of 'Alleluia' thrown into the face of the 'Hallelujahs' of Rapptown and the rest.

IV

It is not, I think, too paradoxical to see both *numen* and *moha* borne
through Slessor's verse on the strength of its splendid technique —
apt for both the impersonal registration of irremediable fact and for
gathering itself into those rhythms that give meaning to action. Yet
Blackmur, from whom I borrow the terms of my argument, insists
that literature consists not in the mere presence of *numen* or *moha*
but in their confrontation. It becomes important, thus, to enquire if
any such confrontations are to be found within the canon of Slessor's
work.

They are, and, I believe, of several distinct kinds. In pieces like
'Polarities', for instance, and 'William Street', *numen* and *moha* face
each other in outright opposition. The subject of 'Polarities' is a
woman, of 'William Street' a Sydney thoroughfare — both subjects
seem capable of presenting contrary aspects to Slessor's imagination.
Indeed, perhaps the most interesting feature of both poems is that

the point of confrontation is the poet himself. 'Sometimes I like her swimming in a mirror on the wall;/Sometimes I don't like her at all' (p. 107); 'You find this ugly, I find it lovely' (p. 99) — in each case the focus is squarely on the first person singular pronoun. It would, however, be a mistake to think of Slessor as the subject of his own poetry; he is less its subject than its essential medium. In spite of works like 'Metempsychosis' or 'Polarities' or 'William Street', Slessor's is not a self-expressive art; the self is rather the ground on which *numen* and *moha* meet.

Indeed, the many poems that use the first person singular — 'To Myself', 'Trade Circular', 'Elegy in a Botanic Gardens', 'Wild Grapes' and 'Serenade' to list only a few — do so with a peculiarly self-deprecating air. 'My rather tedious hero', 'Personally, I have other things to do', 'But I was beating off the stars, gazing, not rhyming' — such self-descriptions abound. When he put himself at the centre of his poetry, Slessor seemed to discover that that was the last place he wanted to be. Given such an uneasy self-awareness, he might have been expected to adopt that very common manoeuvre of his poetic generation — the assumption of a *persona*. There are, in fact, several poems in which that is precisely what he appears to be doing: 'Glubb-dubrib', or 'The Vesper-Song of the Reverend Samuel Marsden', and most particularly, 'Gulliver'. 'Lashed with a hundred ropes of nerve and bone/I lie, poor helpless Gulliver' (p. 73).

Readers schooled in the theory of the *persona* must find it an almost irresistible temptation to construe such lines as an example of its practice. Yet there is, I believe, another and more accurate way of interpreting the value of such utterances in Slessor's poetry. The clue can be found in 'Crustacean Rejoinder':

> Take your great light away, your music end;
> I'm off to feed myself as quick as I can.
> You're perfectly impossible to comprehend,
> I'm such a busy man.
>
> Good God, haven't you got a circumference?
> There's not a moment I can call my own —
> My clocks, my keys, my wheels and instruments
> And that fierce Ethiop, the telephone.
>
> No doubt, it's very charming out in the sun,
> But there are other things you know. In any case,
> I've got no time, no time. There's much to be done.
> Thank God for this, my faithful carapace!   (*p. 87*)

Taking my hint from the last line, I would suggest that the idea of the *persona* is far less useful in dealing with Slessor's art than what might be described as the carapace theory of poetry. He did not, that is to say, use particular poems as a means of oblique self-display; rather, he exploited certain tricks of syntax, focus, perspective to hint at the presence of a self which covertly permeated his entire *oeuvre*. Such a tactic was essential to his verse because, if his technique was the medium in which *numen* and *moha* might coexist, his self was the ground on which they had to meet.

V

It is, thus, the self lurking beneath the polished surface of his verse which defines the essential mode of Slessor's poetry. By way of conclusion, I shall offer some brief suggestions as to how a sense of the modality of Slessor's verse, the meeting ground of *numen* and *moha*, may permit us to see some of his central works anew — 'Out of Time', for instance, 'Captain Dobbin', 'Five Visions of Captain Cook', 'Five Bells', and 'Beach Burial'.

We have learnt, thus, to see in 'Out of Time' an instance of Slessor's great theme of transience; we are fully aware of the propriety of admiring his management of the sonnet form, the dextrously circular effect of the whole sequence. 'I saw Time flowing' (p. 88) is Slessor's opening statement, and we have grown accustomed to directing our own attention through the transitive verb to 'Time', its object, until we are led to the final development of the theme: 'And Time flows past them like a hundred yachts'. If, however, we keep our attention focused on the first person pronoun, we may become more aware of the fact that Slessor is using the sequence to make poetry out of the very condition of being held between *moha* and *numen* — the brute indifference of passing time and the splendid transcendence of the experienced moment ('I and the moment laugh'). The point of 'Out of Time' is surely to acknowledge the impossibility of either escaping time or staying in the Moment. '"Fool, would you leave this country?" cried my heart,/But I was taken by the suck of sea'. To be alive is to battle against both change and stasis, to be alert to the punning significance of Slessor's title: not only are we changed by time and attempt to escape from it, we are born out of it as well.

Where 'Out of Time' makes poetry out of the poet's own entanglement in the dilemma that he registers, in 'Captain Dobbin' Slessor seems to be quite obliterated by the character who is the poem's centrepiece. Captain Dobbin may be one of Slessor's most memorable creations, yet the point that I would wish to note is that he is created only semi-dramatically. For some reason, Slessor held back from full dramatic monologue. That reason, I suggest, has to do with the characteristic modality of his verse, the characteristic use to which he put his own personality in his writing. In the last of the lines quoted below Slessor can be seen to show his hand, infiltrating his way into a poem from which a more rigorously dramatic writer would have been absolutely excluded:

> But the sea is really closer to him than this,
> Closer to him than a dead, lovely woman,
> For he keeps bits of it, like old letters,
> Salt tied up in bundles
> Or pressed flat,
> What you might call a lock of the sea's hair.   (*p. 42*)

That kind of sly insinuation is the most of himself that Slessor permits to appear in 'Captain Dobbin'. Yet it is enough to move the Captain fractionally away from that *moha* of cluttered objects in which he is embedded towards the poet's own numinous perceptions. The Captain, of course, never achieves the poet's angle of vision, but that is the exact point of the whole work — to register a state of awareness, a quality of being, in which behaviour, trapped in the past, never confronts aspiration and hence is never translated into action.

In 'Five Visions of Captain Cook', on the other hand, the confrontation is close, vital and productive. Both *moha* and *numen* are given their due weight and, again by virtue of the covert presence of the poet himself, meshed together. In brief, the first vision reveals the numinous quality of Captain Cook, which in the second is challenged by the exotic facts of the antipodean world. The third section introduces, through both the subject of the chronometers and the quasi-doggerel tone of the writing, a more acute awareness of the *moha* aspect of existence. The response of the numinous Cook to the brute fact of time, as recorded in the fourth vision, brings a lessening of his charismatic force: 'Sometimes the god would fold his wings' (p. 59). The consequences of the confrontation are finally expressed in the fate of Captain Home. The last paragraph of 'Five Visions' unfolds the emptiness of a man caught between memories of opposing principles:

> Cook died. The body of Alexander Home
> Flowed round the world and back again, with eyes
> Marooned already, and came to English coasts,
> The vague ancestral darknesses of home,
> Seeing them faintly through a glass of gold,
> Dim fog-shapes, ghosted like the ribs of trees
> Against his blazing waters and blue air.

But soon they faded, and there was nothing left,
Only the sugar-cane and the wild granaries
Of sand, and palm-trees and the flying blood
Of cardinal-birds; and putting out one hand
Tremulously in the direction of the beach,
He felt a chair in Scotland. And sat down.   (*p. 62*)

Of 'Five Bells', so thoroughly analysed in so many of its aspects, I shall assert only that it stands at the centre of that range of Slessor's poetry of which 'Captain Dobbin' and 'Five Visions' embody the extremes. In Slessor's elegy for his friend Jo Lynch, the equivalents of the physical clutter of Dobbin's life and of the transcendence of Cook — *moha* and *numen* — meet more closely perhaps than in any other of the poet's works. As memory, the need to interpret the after-images of death, drives its lines towards action and morality, 'Five Bells' reveals itself more and more to be a poem about Kenneth Slessor rather than Jo Lynch.

It is possible, indeed, to think of 'Five Bells', among all Slessor's poems, as the one in which he most fully sheds the carapace of technique to reveal the subtle self behind. That revelation discovers the numinous not in anything like Cook's godlike power or in Rubensesque fantasies of heaven but in the poet's very capacity to know the pain of consciousness:

If I could find an answer, could only find
Your meaning, or could say why you were here
Who now are gone, what purpose gave you breath
Or seized it back, might I not hear your voice?   (*p. 106*)

'Beach Burial', the signature, as it were, that Slessor placed at the end of his career, is on the face of it his most daunting acknowledgement of the power of the *moha* to wipe all significance from human action, behaviour. At its close, all hope seems, like the dead seamen, to have enlisted on another front. If, however, Slessor found any kind of optimism untenable as an overt theme for this most poignant of elegies, he did not entirely remove hope from the poem. It is there — and in a way, triumphantly — in the technique itself, the conduct of the beautifully managed lines. 'Beach Burial' is a tribute to the dead, but a tribute jerked out of the poet's overpowering awareness of the continued dazzle of living. 'Beach Burial' is of a piece with the rest of Slessor's work not through its nihilism but in the intensity of the poet's response to the fact of his own existence.

In the end, indeed, we must come to see that writing poems was Slessor's way of authenticating not merely his own existence but his existence as a sentient, conscious human being, forever the meeting

ground of *numen* and *moha*. It was such a sense of Slessor's achievement which prompted the title placed at the head of these notes, and
drawn from 'Post-Roads', the second poem in the 'Atlas' sequence:

> Ogilby
> Did not forget, could not escape such ecstacies,
> Even in the monasteries of mensuration,
> Could not forget the roads that he had gone
> In fog and shining air. Each line was joy,
> Each computation a beatitude,
> A diagram of Ogilby's ear and eye
> With soundings for the nose. Wherefore I think,
>
> Wherefore I think some English gentleman,
> Some learned doctor of the steak-houses,
> Ending late dinner, having strolled outside
> To quell the frivolous hawthorn, may behold
> There in the moonshine, rolling up an hill,
> Steered by no fleshly hand, with spokes of light,
> The *Wheel — John Ogilby's Wheel —* the WHEEL hiss by,
> Measuring mileposts of eternity.   *(p. 50)*

For the sake of a pun Slessor himself would have approved, we may
say that he put the whores before Descartes, and took as motto, not
cogito ergo sum, but *sum, ergo cogito*; better still, *sum, ergo carmina
scribo*.

Wrestling with the angel
Judith Wright's poetry in the 1950s
1977

By the beginning of the 1950s Judith Wright's career had reached a
point in its development which is not only peculiarly interesting in
itself but of general significance for the whole pattern of Australian
poetry during that decade. She was a veteran of the 1940s. Her first
volume, *The Moving Image*, had appeared in 1946, exhibiting all the
passionate intensity of the wartime years out of which it came. The
appearance in 1949 of *Woman to Man* confirmed the presence of a
writer of unique personal power. By the 1950s, that is to say, Judith
Wright's problem was neither to launch a career nor even to cope
with comparatively late success; it was quite simply to maintain the
impetus of a dazzling start. Writing poetry in the 1950s became
perforce for Judith Wright an exercise in strategic survival.

The period following a literary début — especially if that début is
a brilliant one — can be among the most difficult of a writer's whole
career, often characterized by a diminishment in either the quantity
or quality of his work. Judith Wright's output suffered no quanti-
tative decline as the 1940s gave way to the 1950s. *The Gateway* (1953)
and *The Two Fires* (1955) brought together a body of new poems
quite as substantial as that collected in *The Moving Image* and
Woman to Man. Some of her admirers have, however, felt that these
middle volumes of her career do represent a qualitative decline from
her early achievement, a moment of hesitancy and faltering in the
development of her art. The kinds of failure which have been attributed to Judith Wright's verse of the 1950s may, I think, be
summarized like this: a certain tendency to bolster assertion with
rhetoric, a loss of confidence in both the movement of the verse and
the composing self, a loosened grasp on her humanistic optimism

without even the compensation of a convincing despair. Where individual poems are held to have succeeded, they are seen as repetitions of her earlier manners and themes. 'All Things Conspire', for instance, may be construed as a variation on the passionate intimacies of *Woman to Man*; 'At Cooloolah' as a continuation of her preoccupation with the nation's indigenous people; 'Eroded Hills' as a reworking of that New England regionalism present ever since *The Moving Image*; and so on. Many of the poems of *The Gateway* and *The Two Fires* which have gained wide popular acceptance, that is to say, are precisely those in which the poet might seem to have nothing new to say, and to be saying it with an already achieved technique.

That Judith Wright herself does not think entirely ill of her work during the 1950s is indicated, if crudely, by the amount of work from that period which she has included in the several collections of her writing for which she has been responsible. Neither do I subscribe to any view of her career which would relegate ten years' striving to failure or directionless floundering. On the contrary, while I recognize that Judith Wright may not have brought off so often during the 1950s the kind of stunningly complete and self-confident poem which was almost her trademark in the 1940s, I would nevertheless argue that the work collected in *The Gateway* and *The Two Fires* represents a deeply purposeful effort to keep her art alive and vital, because responsive to new problems, fresh experiences, changed circumstances. To suggest, however briefly and inadequately, the new perspectives towards which Judith Wright was working in her verse of the 1950s is the chief burden of this essay.

I shall make only a few points, and shall seek to make them by directing attention towards several poems from *The Gateway* and *The Two Fires* which have perhaps attracted less attention than they merit simply because, at the time of their appearance, they were less readily predictable from the patterns laid down in *The Moving Image* and *Woman to Man* than other pieces published in the 1950s. Let me begin my abbreviated exercise in adjusting critical perspectives by some comment on one of Judith Wright's most famous anthology pieces — 'Bullocky', first collected in *The Moving Image*;

> Beside his heavy-shouldered team,
> thirsty with drought and chilled with rain,
> he weathered all the striding years
> till they ran widdershins in his brain:
>
> Till the long solitary tracks
> etched deeper with each lurching load

were populous before his eyes
and fiends and angels used his road.

All the long straining journey grew
a mad apocalyptic dream,
and he old Moses, and the slaves
his suffering and stubborn team.

Then in his evening camp beneath
the half-light pillars of the trees
he filled the steepled cone of night
with shouted prayers and prophecies.

While past the campfire's crimson ring
the star-struck darkness cupped him round,
and centuries of cattle-bells
rang with their sweet uneasy sound.

Grass is across the wagon-tracks,
and plough strikes bone beneath the grass,
and vineyards cover all the slopes
where the dead teams were used to pass.

O vine, grow close upon that bone
and hold it with your rooted hand.
The prophet Moses feeds the grape,
and fruitful is the Promised Land.[1]

The central subject of the poem — an archetypal figure in Australian outback poetry — attracts to the whole work an overpowering sense of the folkloric quality in Judith Wright's imagination (given classical expression in, for instance, 'South of My Days' Circle'). The further impact of 'Bullocky' depends on the irony, at once overt, potent and reassuring, of the last stanza:

O vine, grow close upon that bone
and hold it with your rooted hand.
The prophet Moses feeds the grape,
and fruitful is the Promised Land.

There is a readiness of appeal in this conclusion which comes close to historical charm. The fulfilment of the bullocky's fantasies after his death and in so unexpectedly literal a manner is the comforting perception on which the whole poem turns.

To say so much of 'Bullocky' is less to submit it to fair criticism than to account for the popular prestige it enjoys in modern Australia. That prestige, has, I believe, obscured several other equally basic facts about the poem if its value in Judith Wright's own development is properly to be understood. 'Bullocky' quite simply assumes an acquaintance with one of the central stories of the Old Testament — an acquaintance with, but not a belief in. The ironic resolution of the poem is entirely secular, demanding an acceptance of neither Moses's divine inspiration nor the efficacy of the Mosaic Law. Nevertheless the fund of cultural assumption on which 'Bullocky' draws, and Judith Wright's relation to that fund, provide, as it seems to me, a major clue to understanding the progress of her art during the 1950s, and indeed up to the present time.

There is thus a small number of poems in both *The Gateway* and *The Two Fires* which require a minimal familiarity with the Scriptures and which, at the same time, can bring all of Judith Wright's other poetic endeavours of the 1950s into focus. The most important, interestingly enough, allude to the Old rather than the New Testament. In *Woman to Man* Judith Wright had included one piece pointedly titled 'Eli, Eli', but it is vague in its execution and symbolism. In the Old Testament poem which she placed almost at the end of *The Gateway* she discovered material and a method much more useful for clarifying her own purposes. The poem is 'The Traveller and the Angel', and its first stanza runs like this:

> When I came to the strength of my youth
> I set out on my journey;
> and on the far side of the ford
> the angel waited.   (*p. 115*)

The reference is plainly to the episode from Genesis 32 wherein Jacob, on his way to meet his brother Esau, wrestles with an angel in the dark. As told in the King James Bible, the encounter involves both diminishment and triumph. The angel causes the sinew in Jacob's thigh to shrink, but his name 'shall be called no more Jacob, but Israel; for as a prince hast thou power with God, and with men, and hast prevailed'.

Judith Wright makes of the incident a metaphor for both the obscure workings of the creative imagination and whatever doubts and uncertainties she was experiencing in her own life. The image of an anguished struggle with an unidentified assailant in the dark perfectly suits her twin purposes:

> Marvellously and matched like lovers
> we fought there by the ford,
> till, every truth elicited,
> I, unsurpassably weary,

> felt with that weariness
> darkness increase on my sight,
> and felt the angel failing
> in his glorious strength.   (*p. 115*)

The closing stanzas of Judith Wright's poem, however, almost completely reverse the tone and temper of the Genesis story. Triumph in diminishment is replaced by a fearful inconclusiveness and uncertainty:

> But his voice on the air
> pierced the depths of my heart.
> "I was your strength; our battle
> leaves you doubly strong.
>
> "Now the way is open
> and you must rise and find it —
> the way to the next ford
> where waits the second angel."
>
> But weak with loss and fear
> I lie still by the ford.
> Now that the angel is gone
> I am a man, and weary.
>
> Return, angel, return.
> I fear the journey.   (*p. 116*)

The title of *The Gateway* may derive from William Blake, but 'The Traveller and the Angel' makes it abundantly clear that at the beginning of the 1950s Judith Wright saw herself in much the same terms as did the Christopher Brennan who wrote the 'Wanderer' poems: she was standing on the threshold of a journey, unsure how long it might take or where it might lead her.

She found her answers, partly at least, in the poem which holds the same place and importance in *The Two Fires* as does 'The Traveller and the Angel' in *The Gateway*: 'The Harp and the King'. Again she takes up a familiar episode from the Old Testament (one first attempted in Australian poetry by Charles Harpur), but embroiders more fully and freely on her original than she had even in her account of Jacob's dark struggle with his opposing self. Her source for 'The Harp and the King' is 1 Samuel 17, which tells of Saul's spiritual desolation in Gilead. Specifically she goes to verse 23: 'And it came to pass, when the evil spirit from God was upon Saul, that David took an harp and played with his hand: So Saul was refreshed, and was well, and the evil spirit departed from him'.

In her poem Judith Wright attempts to construct something of which the Authorized Version tells us nothing — the substance of David's song, what it was in his words which rescued Saul from his dark night of the soul. 'The Harp and the King' provides in effect a dialectical argument between experiential despair and the imagination which asserts, in spite of all, some intrinsic value in the human experience of the world. Alternatively (or simultaneously) the poem may be read as an encounter between the artist whom creativity has temporarily deserted and the distant promptings of his art.

In either case 'The Harp and the King' is to be read as a major attempt by Judith Wright to free herself from the inertia and paralysis which threatened at the end of 'The Traveller and the Angel'. This further variation on the theme of spiritual struggle is thus of enormous consequence for interpreting the whole subsequent pattern of her career. In this respect, the basic content of the poem is too important to be overlooked, regardless of the aesthetic shaping to which it is subjected. The burden of the harp's song, in response to Saul's command, 'Say something, Comfort me', is the praise of time — time, however, no longer pictured as the moving image of eternity but in metaphors of harsh despair provided by the phenomenon of an Australian drought:

> I sing the praise of time, the harp replied:
> the time of aching drought when the black plain
> cannot believe in roots or leaves or rain.
> Then lips crack open in the stone-hard peaks;
> and rock begins to suffer and to pray
> when all that lives has died
> and withered in the wind and blown away;
> and earth has no more strength to bleed.   (*p. 157*)

For all its stringency, however, it is precisely in our life in time that the harp finds its last argument for the value of human existence. The poem reaches its climax in the harp's statement in the final stanza:

> This is the praise of time, the harp cried out —
> that we betray all truths that we possess.
> Time strips the soul and leaves it comfortless
> and sends it thirsty through a bone-white drought.
> Time's subtler treacheries teach us to betray.
> What else could drive us on our way?
> Wounded we cross the desert's emptiness,
> and must be false to what would make us whole.
> For only change and distance shape for us
> some new tremendous symbol for the soul.   (*p. 158*)

The discovery of strength through betrayal, is I believe, the foundation on which Judith Wright has built her whole later career, the insight which has given her dominant theme of the duality of experience its distinctive stamp. It is the perception which has allowed her to write, in later days, a successful New Testamant poem like 'Judas in Modern Dress' where she had earlier failed in 'Eli, Eli'. It is the private concern which has united her with one of the prevailing preoccupations of Australian poetry — the Eden theme.

In addition to its substantive importance, 'The Harp and the King' also offers technical clues to the development of Judith Wright's poetry during and after the 1950s. In this respect it is the artist's movement towards dramatization which commands attention. Where, in 'The Traveller and the Angel', the dramatic mode had been subordinated to the sense of personal involvement, in 'The Harp and the King' it becomes a primary feature of the writing, opening the way to such later pieces as 'Eve to Her Daughters', 'Naked Girl and Mirror', or 'The Beanstalk, Meditated Later'. Further, in so thrusting her technique away from the lyric towards the dramatic, Judith Wright must have begun to sanction to herself that move from privacy to publicity which has characterized her later career — the entry, for instance, into the politics of ecology and conservation.

It has been my aim to suggest then that while to some observers Judith Wright's career may have seemed to falter during the 1950s, at best to repeat earlier successes, there are at least some few poems from the period (perhaps 'atypical') which were clearly of immense service to her. Through them she was able to discover and follow the later path of her development, not only as an artist but as an individual. Through them she was even prepared to discover the dispensability of poetry. She is quite clear on this point in the penultimate poem of her *Collected Poems* (1971), 'The Unnecessary Angel'. The title is, I take it, both an oblique comment on Wallace Stevens's celebrated essay on the imagination, 'The Necessary Angel', and a backward glance at her own struggles with the angel of the imagination — struggles which hold the key to her poetry of the 1950s. In 'The Unnecessary Angel', her final prescription for the makers of verse runs like this:

> Let the song be bare
> that was richly dressed.
> Sing with one reserve:
> Silence might be best.   (*p. 296*)

If by 1971 the spirit of poetry had for Judith Wright become the unnecessary angel, it remains for her, and in the face of logic, the unavoidable angel. And herein lies, for her and for us, the true significance of her work in the 1950s. Knowing the kind and quality of her earlier successes, able at will to repeat them, she yet made the harder choice of seeking, through private struggle, to wring from poetry a new vision of the world. In this enterprise, one kind of poem which proved of enormous and perhaps unexpected value was that derived from Old Testament narrative. In cultivating such verse, however spasmodically, Judith Wright can, in retrospect, be seen not only to have found a fundamentally important way of clarifying her own sense of things but also to have made a most valuable contribution to the public life of Australian poetry at that time. She demonstrated, in the first place, that the generation of wartime poets need not mark time in the war which produced them. She hinted at the possibilities of narrative verse to be more fully exploited by other poets of the decade. She demonstrated that there were more successful ways of wedding European mythologies to Australian experience than any others previously attempted. Above all, she demonstrated by her own example that the continuity of Australian poetry did not consist merely in finding transitions from the 1940s to the 1950s, from the 1950s to the 1960s, but in learning to draw on the whole inheritance of verse from Charles Harpur on.

But if Judith Wright's versifying in the 1950s retains a shared value for all of us, it is only because it was in the first place of importance to herself. I have tried to suggest that importance through the figure of a continuing struggle with the angel of the imagination. Perhaps it could be better described as the (finally successful) attempt to take from the centre of her poetry an image of time and replace it with an image of the world. Judith Wright has herself best described the transformation that the years have wrought in her verse in the last stanza of 'Shadow'.

> World's image grows, and chaos
> is mastered and lies still
> in the resolving sentence
> that's spoken once for all.
> Now I accept you, shadow,
> I change you; we are one.
> I must enclose a darkness
> since I contain the Sun.   (*p. 298*)

Diversions and obsessions
A. D. Hope and Robert D. FitzGerald
1979

The most palpable demand that A. D. Hope's *A Book of Answers*[1], makes on us is for the enjoyment of a literary *divertissement*. The 'Answers' of the title consist of twenty-six replies, witty and usually in an assumed voice, to poems (of which the texts are also printed) which have held some personal interest for Hope. Each set of poem and response is preceded by a brief prose commentary.

The pleasures of *pastiche* and parody, it may be thought, require little in the way of critical elucidation. And, indeed, there should be no excuse for collapsing Hope's elegant *soufflé* beneath the weight of needless commentary. Nevertheless, *A Book of Answers* does invite, if not a gloss, at least some few remarks on its implications and intentions.

For all its tone of light-hearted fun, thus, the collection points to several aspects of Hope's poetic personality quite as clearly as do his 'serious' works. Among the most deeply impressive of these is his self-confidence — complete and knowledgeable without any taint of arrogance. *A Book of Answers* is, in effect, an oblique debate with some of the masters of the English and European poetic traditions — Shakespeare, Donne, Milton, Pope, Baudelaire and Mallarmé, to name only a few. That the debate is sustained on such equal terms is testimony to, among other things, Hope's remarkable skills in the craft of verse. These examples of literary satire are further testimony to his command over a remarkable range of traditional metres and verse forms. A deliberate injection of comic colloquialism, however, demonstrates that they are more than five-finger exercises, are indeed deeply weighed if lightly balanced expressions of personal belief.

Some of the items of belief are, to be sure, stated most directly in the prose commentaries — notably, some succinct judgments on this writer or that: 'Shakespeare's *Sonnets* are a kind of licensed bedlam for scholars and critics in the crazy season' (p. 3); '[Tennyson] *is* a peerless poet, after all' (p. 39); 'One Hopkins is enough' (p. 46). This is the kind of thing that many of us have often thought but ne'er so forthrightly expressed. But what I take to be the most important point about Hope's forthrightness is that it springs from neither a poet's jealousy of other professionals nor the kind of scholarly ignorance sometimes attributed to critics. In the long run, the satiric thrusts of *A Book of Answers* are marked far more by charity than by spleen; that the book is grounded in a proper sense of how to use literary scholarship is demonstrated in, for instance, section VII ('Pope and Bounce') and section XIX ('Yeats and Graves'). *A Book of Answers* springs, that is to say, from a self-confidence which can produce a *jeu d'esprit* without being merely trifling.

The volume, furthermore, offers opinions and values much closer to the centre of Hope's imagination than his private ratings of assorted versifiers. His explicit identification of the seventeenth as 'my favourite . . . century' (p. 113) draws together whole tracts of his career. His admiration for the splendid rhetoric of Byron's 'Roll on, thou deep and dark blue Ocean — roll!' unabashedly bespeaks an aesthetic at odds with modern orthodoxy. Perhaps the most heart-felt statement of artistic belief, however, occurs in section XX, 'Dante, Virgil and T. S. Eliot'. The poem, entitled 'Home Truths from Abroad' and composed in *terza rima*, delineates two opposing views about the language of poetry. In reply to the attitude expressed by T. S. Eliot in the lines from 'East Coker' beginning 'So here I am, in the middle way', Dante is given a counter-argument, endorsed (I take it) by Hope himself:

> Real poets never 'try
> to use words', as you put it; your first blunder
>
> Was treating them like slaves or tools. The high
> Art that we serve begins with love and patience
> To learn to let the words use us . . .
>
> Poets do not 'raid the inarticulate':
>
> They waken sleeping images, untether
> The captive truths and lead them towards the light,
> Break time's hard frost and foster growing weather.   (*pp. 91–2*)

'Home Truths from Abroad', appearing in section XX of the twenty-six sections of *A Book of Answers*, lies well towards the latter end of the collection. And, whether by accident or design, the tone of the work becomes steadily more serious, so that the last five pieces (addressed to contemporary Australians) advance beyond either parody or *pastiche*. They include the well-known poem 'The Muse', written in response to James McAuley's work bearing the same title. The other four, less familiar, are quite as important in filling out the details of Hope's poetic territory. The lines addressed to Judith Wright, for instance, acknowledge the vein of prophetic fervour so strong in Hope's writing; those which reply to Gwen Harwood recognize the theme of a Paradise within, which has played so large a part in his later career:

> Eden is all around us, where to choose
> If only we keep time and learn to play.   (*p. 110*)

'Nec Tamen Consumebatur' (composed for Rosemary Dobson) defends the immortalizing power of art, while the final piece, a serio-comic account of Hope's entry into Heaven in the company of David Campbell, provides the occasion for asserting the supreme import-ance of harmony:

> 'Just stretch the rules a little — So, on your way!
> Get along, both of you; and don't forget:
> There'll be no lunching in Heaven from today;
> Pick up your harps from Peter, and learn to play;
> We'll expect some heavenly music from you yet.'   (*p. 116*)

Parody, it might be held, is essentially an élitist joke, designed to give those readers who already enjoy the superiority of acquaintance with the parodied originals an even sharper sense of their own accomplishments. Parody, in effect, derives from and encourages the worst kind of cultural snobbery. Such a charge might in some instances be justified: not, I believe, here. That Hope's satiric imitations are motivated by quite other (and wholly laudable) inten-tions is indicated in the dedication: to Frederick Murray Todd, late Professor of English in the University of Tasmania, and long-standing friend of the poet. Todd shared Hope's skill and pleasure in writing humorous verse. Yet the dedication of this volume does more than offer tribute to a fellow-practitioner of the marginal arts of the scholar–poet. Its point lies in the recognition that it is only in the informed acceptance of a tradition, the willing submission to an aesthetic discipline, that any art can flourish, be maintained. The authentic delight of these productions of a poet on a busman's holiday resides in their tactful critique of the tradition to which they are attached. Hope, however, makes it clear in his Preface that we may expect from him no more of their kind. Yet even that fact should not, perhaps, occasion us any regret. As the poet himself puts it,

'There should be a limit to secondary productions of this sort. As an occasional diversion it is justified, but it can easily grow into a habit and the habit into a tedious obsession. One should know when to stop' (p. xi).

Obsessional Robert D. FitzGerald's, *Product*[2] most certainly is; tedious, it is not. On the contrary, it might properly be described as creatively obsessional; it continues to worry, that is to say, at matters which will not leave the poet alone. None of the thirty-four poems collected within its covers significantly enlarges what we have come to think of as FitzGerald's characteristic range. Indeed, they demonstrate that in the 1960s and 1970s (when they were written) he was, by and large, content to work within the substantive limits set by the middle years of his career.

There are, thus, meditations on time and history, re-creations of episodes from the Australian past, lyrics of aphoristic clarity and pithy succinctness. The record of these latter decades, as set down in *Product*, confirms our sense that now, as always, living remains for FitzGerald a matter of striving, strenuous ethical self-examination, the assertion of hope in the face of all the physical and metaphysical odds. If, indeed, this volume incorporates any new subject within his scope it is the sharp outrage, the deeply personal protest dragged out of him by the Vietnam years. A small group of poems (by no means the least considerable of those included in *Product*) was written in direct response to those testing times: they include 'Deep within Man', for instance, 'Lawbreakers' and 'The Denuded World'. Characteristically, even these fight free of an uncritical acceptance of a closely espoused cause. 'Lawbreakers', extolling the exemplary careers of Robert Emmet and John Hampden, may lead to this conclusion:

> Never, I think, have the oppressed
> thrown off harsh harness, or has wrong
> been righted, till, against the strong,
> the few have put the law to test,
>
> broken it, suffered for their deeds,
> and, obstinate, have overcome
> *status quo ante*, which, to some,
> is the most sacred of the creeds.   (*p. 39*)

Yet the octave of 'Deep within Man' admits to an attitude that very few of his fellow-protesters would have confessed to:

> This does not touch me: that a splatter of lead
> punctures the jungle torpor in some broil

north of my life; but that on alien soil
men of our own intrepid young have bled
now greatly does; as do those innocent dead —
good farming folk — who, bent above their toil,
have suffered anguish rained as flaring oil
from what were once kind heavens overhead.   (*p. 36*)

Even the stubborn, gritty honesty of that opening concession, however, had been part of FitzGerald's imaginative equipment for many years before the 1960s. In sensibility as in substance, there is little that is startlingly new in *Product*. Indeed, in virtually every respect the book imposes itself as the continuing record of a poetic personality firmly entrenched in its major preoccupations. The forms and versification are no less familiar than the themes and moral attitudes. The narrative piece, 'One Such Morning', perhaps enjoys a lighter tone than earlier work of a comparable kind; in most essentials, however, the technical achievement is a case of the mixture as before.

My insistence on the projection into later years of the concerns of his early manhood and maturity is in no way intended to denigrate FitzGerald's achievement; quite the reverse. It is an insistence on the creatively obsessional behaviour of a major artist. Such repetitiveness, however, is to be distinguished from most obsessional behaviour, which (at least to those who observe it) is merely tedious. In FitzGerald's case, the distinction resides in a quality he identified as long ago as in 'Fifth Day'. 'Attitude matters: bearing', he wrote in that poem, and it is the sense of an actively maintained attitude which more than anything else gives his work — right down to *Product* — its artistic worth, its human consequence. The FitzGerald who emerges from sixty years' poems is an upright man, in every important sense of the term — in its high, old ethical connotation as well as in its suggestion of an individual who, knowing that his feet are planted in the clay, yet aspires to whatever understanding his rational intelligence may afford.

The uprightness of the poet FitzGerald could, I believe, be demonstrated by the usual techniques of close analysis. I pass over such a procedure for the sake of venturing a final assertion about the writer who presents himself in *Product* with so rare a combination of unassuming power and unflagging tenacity. His obsessional need to examine his life as it unrolls before him, I have suggested, is what drives FitzGerald to major aspiration. His relation to the craft of verse is what makes possible his major achievement. We might think that the clue to that relation is laid bare in the piece entitled 'Just Once':

I'll say, just once, I like a tune well sung,
not cranky music. As for abstract art,
the painters not their product should be hung —
dupes with the fakes; for both have built in part
this age of shoddy. And, one final curse:
Hell take freak poetries; I like good verse.   (*p. 44*)

Here, as rarely, FitzGerald's forthrightness is deceptive. The importance of 'Just Once' lies not in its apparent endorsement of old-fashioned aesthetic orthodoxies but in the unstated needs which sanction, for FitzGerald, that endorsement. As aesthetic theory 'Just Once' is at least open to disagreement; as personal statement, it reveals FitzGerald's understanding that the obsessional thrust of his innermost concerns requires the strictest ordering to transmute them into art. The chief goal of his own technique seems to me more adequately suggested in the opening lines of 'Tribute':

Now, for no reason but the trick
mind plays on memory, I have brought
straight from my youth a shape of thought.   (*p. 2*)

'A shape of thought' — that is the goal and, at its best, the effect of all FitzGerald's technical effort. Fidelity to a strict versification is the best means he has discovered to bring thought alive, to turn the materials of mind, memory, and the world into what in 'Height' he calls 'Fact/for use' (p. 19). And if it will not provide facts for use, poetry is of no importance to him. It has been said that FitzGerald's individual poems can manifest a studied avoidance of charm amounting almost to an aesthetic defect; if that is so, it has been the price that he has been prepared to pay in the effort to make of his poems candid declarations of complex concerns to which charm is utterly irrelevant.

The *panache* of Hope's *Answers* and the strength of purpose which announces itself in *Product* are, oddly, both made possible by allegiance not to a common aesthetic but to a common acceptance of poetry as a disciplined craft which can be learned, studied, mastered. We need concur in neither Hope's classic conservatism nor FitzGerald's rejection of what he calls 'freak poetry' to recognize and admire in the work of both poets that element which has sustained two such notable careers — an idea of culture and tradition larger than and beyond the self. That, or something like it, is what keeps these artists still in so fresh a relation to their art as to permit one of them to relax into the diversions of parody, the other to thrust obsessions now half a century old into lines of continuing vigour and integrity.

'A rich surplus of consciousness'

A response to the poetry of Francis Webb

1983

When I first wrote on Webb's poetry, some sixteen years ago,[1] I was seized by that marvellous happiness we all feel on first encountering a rare creative talent; additionally, I experienced something like what I imagine to be the special exhilaration of a cryptographer who succeeds in cracking a peculiarly difficult code. For, in coming close to Webb's art, I had immediately felt the challenge of its intensely personal symbolic system, had judged that this was the issue in his verse which, before all others, it was the responsibility of literary criticism to confront.

In returning now to that same poetry, I find the joy of discovery transmuted into a pleasure of somewhat different colour, texture, tone; the sense of being akin to, say, Michael Ventris laying bare the secrets of Linear B eludes me altogether. For whether I was successful or not in deciphering the messages which radiate through Webb's verse, that task, once attempted, is behind me, in the past. My attention now is much more urgently drawn to a different kind of problem, a problem more usually associated with the prevailing tasks of literary criticism: the need to establish a more exact appreciation of the quality of Webb's art, some assessment of its value to us, its worth.

In thus shifting the grounds of my interest in Webb's creative achievement, I shall not abandon the method I adopted in that earlier enterprise: basically I shall pursue a qualitative linguistic analysis of Webb's text in the hope of discovering the patterns, the modes, the levels of expression which make his poems what they are, locate them in what Webb himself called in his late poem 'Pneumo-Encephalograph', the 'cabin of art'[2] rather than the psychiatric ward. If I venture beyond these limits, it will be only to attempt some comparisons with poets whose work bears directly on our understanding of Webb's. The method, I freely confess, is inexact, unscientific; but so is literature. In attempting his own kind of diagnosis the literary critic must be prepared to take at least some of the same risks as the writer whose work he is diagnosing. I use the term 'diagnosis' here quite deliberately, as a means of suggesting, right from the outset, what I perceive to be the common ground between literary criticism and psychiatry — and the differences. In the first place, both critic and clinician seek to collate, describe and classify symptomatic behaviour in order to identify and understand particular states of being. Where they part company, of course, is that the critic is exclusively concerned with linguistic behaviour, while the psychiatrist takes within his ken a much broader range of symptomatic gestures. The psychiatrist differs from the critic, further, in that he is likely to take a sustained interest in any 'case' only if there are strong indications of pathology, the cure of which it will be a primary aim to effect. The critic, on the other hand, is less likely to assume that the abnormalities with which he deals are in any way disabling, he certainly has no professional drive to 'cure' his subjects, and finally, he is perhaps more likely to live in the hope that his diagnostic techniques will reveal some response to the human condition hitherto unknown, unidentified, unvalued.

In attempting my own critical diagnosis of the poet Francis Webb I shall make no appeal to the clinical history now available to us; not because I deny its importance but because of my belief that a response to his writings as creative literature promises the best contribution that academic criticism can make to understanding the coexistence in a single individual of unique artistic achievement and significant mental disorder. Only one other preliminary remark is necessary. My survey of Webb's accomplishment will be based on the *Collected Poems*, published by Angus & Robertson in 1969. This decision, while largely a matter of convenience, is partly based on the view that it is on that volume that his artistic reputation must stand or fall. Within the *Collected Poems*, furthermore, I shall direct my attention largely (though not entirely) to the poems first printed in *Birthday* in 1953 and those of the subsequent collections — *Socrates* (1961) and *The Ghost of the Cock* (1964). This is less a matter of convenience; it depends on the belief that there is a direct correlation between Webb's retreat from the quasi-dramatic form of 'Ben Boyd' and 'Leichhardt in Theatre' and his use of elements of his own personality in the making of his poems.

In *Collected Poems*, then, there begins on p. 216 a sequence bearing the general title 'Clouds'. The first line of the first poem, 'Inland', has provided me with my title: 'The rich surplus of consciousness rots at the wharves'. Through a meaning I wish to impose (not, I believe, arbitrarily) on its opening phrase, 'a rich surplus of consciousness', I shall aim to explore the kind, quality and value, especially of Webb's later poetry.

At least three important issues are implicit in my title: the cornucopian abundance of the materials that Webb poured into his poems (their "richness"), the poems' capacity to assimilate those materials (their "surplus"), the level of awareness at which the poems were composed and make their appeal (their "consciousness"). The first of these matters barely needs arguing beyond asserting that the materials of Webb's poems are predominantly images — of a particular kind to be described later. Quotation from almost any poem will suffice to make the point. 'The Telescopes', from the early volume *Leichhardt in Theatre* (1952), is as good as any:

> Wind trembles, intense with Fall; the headlights of a car
> Break steeply on the campus — sudden false dawn, or snow
> In a flurry of rippling the voiceless interview
> Of summer and nearing winter. But shooting far
> To the shining hemisphere of Bloor and Yonge,
> They vanish. Slashed with blue hieroglyphs, a wall
> Buckles and shifts, slithering off like a scroll
> Eluding thumbs of light. Each tautly strung
> Nerve of the night relaxes, the melted road
> Skyward hardens and deepens where the dome
> Of Convocation breasts an exhausted cloud:
> A simple curve of peace and shadow of home.   (*p. 54*)

It would be a truly astonishing poem which could cram a greater profusion of images than we have here into the same number of lines. Indeed, it is the rapid succession of stimuli, the abrupt shift from one object of concern to the next, which commands most general attention in Webb's verse, establishes the effect, at once bedazzling and benumbing, of a mind whizzing at random between nodes of interest. The barest outline of the image sequence in 'The Telescopes' — wind–autumn–headlights–campus–snow–stars–hieroglyphs–thumbs–nerve–breast–cloud–home — establishes beyond the need of further analysis the tumbling richness of lexical content to be found on virtually every page of the *Collected Poems*. Two further examples will clinch the case, the first from 'Good Friday, Norfolk', the second from 'Gustav Mahler':

> Conscience of the late tractor that straddled cloud,
> Was hammer on nailhead, jogs into dozing rumour
> Along the sacred stolid flanks of land.

Peter de Draiton, hasten from your shroud
To the church of St Margaret, your beloved bird.
But voices. Eight static centuries pry as wind
Into His darkness; staccato forgiven hammer
Broods in the third hour; and the omnibus
With portly moon-faced grief
Blunders up and down certain hills to know His Cross.   (*p. 210*)

Brummagem buttons and fingernails of the freak
Warder thunderstorm in old jail of time,
The scowling bass, the tingling sky's rhetoric
As the ribald yellow scrawl
On a grubby public wall;
And innocence weaving a song of the earth . . . (*p. 195*)

In both passages image gives way to image with the same unpredictable speed as in 'The Telescopes'. In only the first two lines of 'Good Friday, Norfolk', thus, perception must leap from 'conscience' to 'tractor' to 'cloud' to 'hammer' to 'sleep' and 'rumour'; similar acrobatic feats of adjustment are required by the opening stanza of 'Gustav Mahler'.

The richness of the creative stir is undeniable, but the difficult question remains: do the manifold images arrange themselves into designs possessing a coherence greater than the apparent sum of their parts? On the answer to this question turns our whole sense of Webb's status as a poet. For if we cannot answer it in the affirmative, if, that is to say, we can find no basic evidence of what Coleridge called the esemplastic power of the imagination, we may have to deny his lines any place at all in the 'cabin of art'. Now in my earlier essay, 'The Very Gimbals of Unease', I proposed one kind of answer favourable to Webb's achievement — that the diverse images of his poems reveal a coherence and meaning extending through the entire *oeuvre* rather than individual works. While not relinquishing that position, I would now wish to argue the presence of an integrating force within single poems. The case can again be put by demonstration, in this instance the first stanza of 'Mousehold Heath':

Chapfallen acres; a pettifogging hierarchy of bushes
Rooted in this world's sand beneath turf impeccable,
Slavering no writ of shadow, extending their several arms
To divine, seduce the All of light collapsing:
Bare arms: winter grinds tribute of a token leafhood,
And into evening the last bird-mitre topples;
Bungalows wink, nose forward;
A simper and freckle of jazz;

Frozen orange lights are knotted on dead roads bounding
These acres untilled, this plaintiff colony, dust.   (*p. 175*)

While the immediate effect of these lines may be quite as unsettling
and bizarre as in the other passages I have quoted, a close familiarity
reveals several strong threads of connection running between their
apparently discrete loci of attention. From the very first word, 'chapfallen', for instance, there flows a whole set of facial allusions. The
'hierarchy of bushes' are 'slavering'; 'Bungalows wink', there is a
'freckle of jazz'. Simultaneously, the second element of 'chapfallen'
introduces a string of images all to do with anxious and uncontrolled
descent — the 'All of light' collapses; 'the last bird-mitre topples',
bungalows precariously 'nose forward'. At the same time, a
submerged pun in 'pettifogging' propels through the stanza a train
of references to the weather: the idea of fog leads to the 'All of light
collapsing', which produces in turn the grey nullity of winter with its
stripped trees and untilled acres.

Learning to read 'Mousehold Heath' in this manner provides a
method which can be applied quite extensively to Webb's poems —
including those I earlier quoted as examples of the seemingly random
abundance of his vocabulary. From this point of view, thus, the
opening of 'Gustav Mahler' is seen to have a texture quite as tight
and intricate as that of 'Mousehold Heath'. The core images of stanza
I of 'Gustav Mahler' are revealed as those of the prison house, with
associated allusion to punitive repression, forbidding architecture, the
shoddy squalor of the inmates of the jail which is this world. Associated allusion — here, of course, is the crux of the matter. For it
is the trick of association which unifies the *congeries* of images which
make up each and every one of Webb's poems. And, I think I am
right in saying, this habit of language is at least as familiar to the
psychiatrist as to the literary critic. To demonstrate the presence of
associative strings of words in Webb's writing, that is to say, still does
not complete the argument that that writing is something more than
symptomatic, that it is in fact poetry.

The argument is, however, capable of completion, and in a way
quite familiar to literary criticism. For the critic, an associative habit
of language is a certain indicator of creative potential though not
necessarily of creative achievement, is evidence that a writer may
possess the equipment of a poet without knowing properly how to
use it. The aesthetic test that will discriminate between potential and
achievement concerns the degree and kind of control which is exercised over the associative behaviour exhibited by the writer. In
adjudicating such matters, literary criticism has at its command an

enormous range of 'control situations' — all the documented practice of the acknowledged poets who have made the literary tradition. The practical difficulty is simply to select a 'control' appropriate to the case in hand. In the case of Francis Webb, and in relation specifically to the associative basis of his verse, there seems to me no more useful point of reference than John Donne.

One of the most celebrated descriptions of Donne's Metaphysical art occurs in Dr Johnson's *Life of Abraham Cowley*: 'The most heterogeneous ideas are yoked by violence together'.[3] Yet, as I have been at pains to suggest, the same phrase could be applied with almost equal aptness to the poetry of Francis Webb. It becomes, therefore, a matter of crucial importance to determine how, in what particulars, the twentieth-century Australian artist's habit of violent lexical association differs from that of the seventeenth-century Englishman. A useful aid in this necessary discrimination is the first stanza of one of Donne's well-known pieces, 'A nocturnall upon S. Lucies day':[4]

> 'Tis the yeares midnight, and it is the dayes,
> *Lucies*, who scarce seaven houres herself unmaskes,
> The Sunne is spent, and now his flasks
> Send forth light squibs, no constant rayes;
> The worlds whole sap is sunke:
> The generall balme th'hydroptique earth hath drunk,
> Whither, as to the beds-feet, life is shrunke,
> Dead and enterr'd; yet all these seeme to laugh,
> Compar'd with mee, who am their Epitaph.

The extravagance, the darkness and desolation of this writing seem in many respects akin to Webb's. Occasioned by the winter solstice, Donne's is a poem of deep mourning which confesses the almost total annihilation of his spirit because of the loss of a deeply loved woman. These quite piercing emotions are, furthermore, woven together by associative leaps which bear on the surface a marked similarity to Webb's. Under careful scrutiny, however, the similarity yields place to significant difference. Dr Johnson's famous phrase is part of his attempt to define Metaphysical wit. And even the sharpest transitions of 'A nocturnall upon S. Lucies day' are controlled by a supremely self-confident, ironical and witty intelligence. A proper defence of this assertion would, to be sure, demand a close analysis of all five stanzas of Donne's poem. I am confident, nevertheless, that the qualities I am imputing to 'A nocturnall upon S. Lucies day' are discernible even in the few lines I have quoted. They are brilliantly focused in the paradox, mingling amused self-deprecation with genuine grief, of the final epigrammatic couplet of the first stanza:

yet all these seeme to laugh,
Compar'd with mee, who am their Epitaph.

The qualities I have ascribed to Donne are among the most widely accepted commonplaces of twentieth-century criticism. The value of rehearsing them once again, and in this context, lies precisely in the fact that they do not inhere in Webb's poetry. Superficial similarities of associative practice, that is to say, are animated by what we must believe to be quite disparate needs and intentions. Whatever it is that motivates and moves within Webb's lines, it has little of what T. S. Eliot (also referring to the Metaphysicals) called 'a tough reasonableness beneath the slight lyric grace'.[5] Not, to be sure, that Webb's verse is wholly lacking in wit or ironic judgement. But when comedy is heard in his lines it is characteristically through the sardonic laughter of a Gothic kookaburra at the grotesque spiritual emptiness of Australia and the world. Webb's work, it must be said, lacks the mature self-awareness of which Donne's ironic wit is so convincing an embodiment.

To say so much by way of explicit comparison between Donne and Webb may seem to register a lesser judgement, perhaps even some denigration, of the modern writer. For the moment, however, I am not prepared to concede so much, preferring to prolong a little further my effort to describe as exactly as possible his imaginative character. I do so now by adopting a reverse procedure to the one I have just followed — by pointing, that is to say, to a phenomenon present in Webb's poetry but absent from Donne's. Thus, although one of the important lesser modes of seventeenth-century verse is what we have come to call emblem poetry, there is very little of Donne's work I am inclined to call emblematic; there are whole tracts of Webb's that are nothing else.

In literary criticism, an emblem is commonly understood as an object or the image of an object representing symbolically some abstract quality, and the supremely representative seventeenth-century emblem poet in English is Francis Quarles. It is to Quarles indeed that the Oxford English Dictionary attributes the statement that 'an emblem is a silent parable'. Now such a use of imagery is, I believe, fundamentally alien to Donne's imagination — as one of my undergraduate teachers, Alec King, used to say, Donne could afford to be so metaphysical only because in the first place he was prepared to be so physical in his language. On the other hand, the will to emblematize images drawn from the physical world seems to me to lie at the very core of Webb's art. The opening of 'Light' is in this regard prototypical; 'For a certain doctrine have sunrise' (p. 140). The urge to transmute sensory fact into some kind of abstract formulation underlies almost every descriptive poem Webb ever wrote. It can be seen, still fairly brief, simple and accessible, in 'On the Mountain': 'To climb a mountain is to seek out a view' (p. 65). In 'In Memoriam: Anthony Sandys, 1806–1883' aphorism is expanded into teasing assertion:

> Bird-song is your reverberating touch.
>
> But metaphor is the enormous second frozen,
> Reduced behind courtly glass, and laid in stores
> Out of the public view for certain years.   (*p. 206*)

The need for abstraction becomes alarmingly clear in 'The Horses':

> The vegetative soul is the dedicated rhetorician:
> Yellow knuckles of gorse are eloquent; motion
> Is the psyche entire whose fullness is a naked growing
> Ungirt with passion or reflection.   (*p. 201*)

Finally by way of illustration, this deeply ingrained pattern of Webb's imagination is sustained, at top pitch, through the first stanza of 'Canobolas':

> Love best of all the hour of that grave Wish:
> Colour elected, deposed: something is dying:
> Galahs parade in their circuit cheering and crying,
> Each flaunting his ruddied ceremonial sash.
> The sun goes down as an ancient broad-mouthed fish
> Whose blood asleep is alarum and defying
> Bent pins of usage, all the worrying, trying.
> It is now the unchevroned sentry puts on flesh.   (*p. 197*)

What is clear from such writing is that even in his most strikingly evocative descriptions of natural phenomena, Webb's deepest need was to evacuate his poetry of all sensuous delight, to see the world almost exclusively as emblem. This fact can be again brought home by comparison with another major poet — Gerard Manley Hopkins, for whom in at least one of his pieces ('Hopkins and Foster's Dam') Webb implied personal admiration through the simple technique of direct quotation. The opening words of Webb's poem, 'Look at the Stars', are openly borrowed from Hopkins's 'The Starlight Night'. A more useful general field for comparison between the two writers, however, lies in their treatment of nature. Both, for instance, return again and again to cloudscapes in their poems. Here is how they are rendered in three of Hopkins's well-known works — 'Pied Beauty',

'Hurrahing in Harvest', and 'That Nature is a Heraclitean Fire', respectively:[6]

> Glory be to God for dappled things —
> For skies of couple-colour as a brindled cow; . . .

> Summer ends now; now, barbarous in beauty, the stooks rise
> Around; up above, what wind-walks! what lovely
>   behaviour
> Of silk-sack clouds! has wilder, wilful-wavier
> Meal-drift moulded ever and melted across skies?

> Cloud-puffball, torn tufts, tossed pillows flaunt forth, then
>   chevy on an air —
> built thoroughfare: heaven-roysterers, in gay-gangs they throng;
>   they glitter in marches.
> Down roughcast, down dazzling whitewash, wherever an
>   elm arches,
> Shivelights and shadowtackle in long lashes lace, lance, and
>   pair.

Whatever else may be going on in these lines, they are firmly based on Hopkins's delighted perception of the textures, the shifting patterns, of cloud and sky. Hopkins characteristically went on to translate that perception into an assertion of dogma or principle, but Webb seems impelled to go straight to the abstraction without any intervention of the senses whatsoever. Here, thus, are three of his typical cloudscapes, from 'From the Cold', 'Socrates', and 'Gale Force':

> These puppet-states of water grinding and exploding together,
> This street corner crowd of cloudburst beating soiled wings,
> This coral, this weed, this man,
> Pray for the midnight sun, for the frozen myth.   (p. 138)

> Sisyphus heaves again at the sun: Furies huddle eastward:
> Watch that miry cloud working, glistering in a sweat:
> Thumping heart and lacerated hands.   (p. 133)

> With rumbling brilliant barrow-loads devise
> Temple and tower of cloud upon the sky,
> Let the brave arch, the column fall and rise
> With engrossed genius of your slavery.   (p. 139)

The same insistence that nature is most importantly emblem can be discerned in Webb's treatment of all his favourite nature motifs — sun, sea, landscape. He seems determined, as it were, to stand William Carlos Williams's famous dictum on its head and declare through his lines, 'No things but in ideas'.

Even Webb's own (comparatively few) utterances about image and metaphor support this reading of his work. In the sequence 'In Memoriam: Anthony Sandys, 1806–1883' he several times speaks of the value he finds in metaphor. In the lines quoted above metaphor is 'the enormous second frozen'; later it becomes a 'glass façade' (p. 206); later yet, in addressing the nineteenth-century painter, he avers 'Your metaphor is this picture' (p. 207). To put the case extremely, Webb consistently and deliberately declines to see nature for what it is, even to look through nature to whatever may be beyond; rather he insists on seeing it always as parable, the visible projection of abstract principle. Such a mode of perception is certainly singular, may even be accounted perverse. At least, however, we may say that where the rich tangle of Webb's verbal associations accounts for the difficulty of his poetry, his emblematizing establishes its uniqueness. In this poetry we encounter an imagination determined to locate its creative products as far as possible within the limits of conscious awareness and interpretation. It may be that from this fact we will wish to deduce a fear of whatever is lurking in the sub-conscious so great as to find every means possible of keeping it locked away. I shall leave such speculation, however, to my professional betters, and content myself with the observation that the quality of Webb's poems, as poems, bespeaks an imagination deliberately cut off from its sources of inspiration, self-limited by the demands of an imperious will. Webb almost certainly was writing better than he knew when, at the beginning of 'Inland' he coined the phrase 'The rich surplus of consciousness'. Against the background of the *Collected Poems* it reveals itself as an exact definition of the foundation, centre, and shape of his art. If 'consciousness', then, must join 'rich' in having a special application to Webb's poetry, it remains for me only to amplify and justify my use of 'surplus' in the same context. The idea of some sort of superfluity, excess, in Webb's art indeed raises perhaps the most important issue of all: whether Webb discovered poetic forms capable of containing and harmonizing the jostling richness of his emblematic imagery.

The necessary starting point to this last phase of my enquiry is Webb's prosody. I shall not offer any detailed technical analyses of rhyme and metre: merely the observation that the formal conduct of Webb's verse involves a paradox. What I have described as a singular feature of Webb's art — its drive towards abstraction at the expense of simple sensous delight — does not, nevertheless, drain it of energy. Indeed, I suspect that the first reaction of many of Webb's readers is likely to be one of simple exhaustion — it was certainly mine. And the exhaustion will stem not only from the difficulty of wrestling with his complex code of symbolic imagery. In some measure at least it derives from the very pitch and beat of the lines. The basic rhythms of Webb's verse transmit the most vivid sense of what he called in the 'Around Costessy' sequence a 'mind/ Fretting and hammering at itself' (p. 205). For all its minimal delight, there runs through the *Collected Poems* an eternal energy, a high-powered prosody which has the unusual effect of constricting the artist within his own field of force, as it were, rather than liberating him from it.

If I am right in thus describing the paradoxical result of Webb's prosody — of imploding theme and perception into a kind of critical mass — there is about his whole achievement a special poignancy. For insofar as his verse argues a precise role for the artist it is wildly at odds with the effects his poems actually achieve. Two pieces (one quite early) point unguardedly to Webb's sense of the poet's bardic role, his vatic responsibilities. 'To a Poet' begins with an image and an aspiration — 'Wayfarer, glorious one, / Heart fiery as a sun, lips stammering prophecies' (p. 2) — that are repeated in the much later 'Poet':

> I'm from the desert country — O, it's a holy land
> With a thousand warm humming stinging virtues.
> Masters, my words have edged their way obediently
> Through the vast heat and that mystical cold of our evenings. (*p.152*)

This image of the bardic poet must carry with it some idea of an audience to whom his prophecies may be addressed. It is, nevertheless, extremely difficult to reconstruct from Webb's poems the sort of audience he hoped to reach, though there are several important hints as to the mode of communication he most highly valued. In 'Self-Portrait' Webb imputed to the painter Anthony Sandys the 'mission / To sing the posture of reality' (p. 207). As it seems to me, this is a mission that Webb appropriated to himself. Throughout the *Collected Poems* and quite beyond the references to favourite composers like Mahler and Bruckner, one senses a desire, never quite fulfilled, to create a poetry that sings. Only rarely — in for instance 'Bells of St. Peter Mancroft' or 'Five Days Old' — does Webb achieve an unforced lyric tone. More usually one is aware of a harsh repression of the singing voice rather than of its easy release. It is as if the poet discovered through his stern technique the only means he knew to contain the rich abundance of material moiling and pressing against the bounds of his conscious mind.

Perhaps it is fairer, however, to say that we hear in Webb's verse an utterance that ears attuned to the main stream of English lyric poetry find extremely difficult to recognize as song. In 'Electric'

Webb wrote that 'Man must clasp to his soul / The sacred illness' (p. 173). It may be that we must fully understand the love implicit in that desperate embrace before we will hear, clear and true, Webb's singing. In proffering this suggestion I realize only too well that I am allowing my argument to stray close to that sensitive area which is properly the domain of psychiatry — the nexus between art and illness. I do so only because it allows me to venture on another comparison which may bring us yet closer to an understanding of Webb's creative achievement. If we accept that the inner music of Webb's verse tells of the passion with which he embraces his mortal condition, his sacred illness, then we may fairly ask if there is no other way in which that theme may be told. The answer, I believe, must be that there is. We have the example of a great contemporary of Webb's afflicted with a not dissimilar dis-ease of spirit, who found radically different means of singing the posture of reality. I refer, of course, to Robert Lowell, between whose work and Webb's Sir Herbert Read, writing in the Preface to *Collected Poems*, detected 'a close parallel' (p. ix). Except by way of the most general comparison, I am unable to share Read's view, least of all with respect to the methods each writer developed for absorbing his 'sacred illness' into his art. In pressing the relationship between the two poets, the most clearly pertinent of Lowell's books is *Life Studies*. From one of its well-known pieces, 'Man and Wife', I quote some representative lines:

> Oh my *Petite*,
> clearest of all God's creatures, still all air and nerve:
> you were in your twenties, and I,
> once hand on glass
> and heart in mouth,
> outdrank the Rahvs in the heat
> of Greenwich Village, fainting at your feet —
> too boiled and shy
> and poker-faced to make a pass,
> while the shrill verve
> of your invective scorched the traditional South.[7]

Even without full explication of the circumstances from which the poem arose, its very language cannot fail to convey its exact blending of wry personal amusement at youthful behaviour, clear-headed recognition of serious mental disturbance, the remembered intensity of an intimate relationship, and, most remarkably of all, an astute brand of cultural reportage and interpretation. Eschewing Webb's large orchestral flourishes, Lowell's poem runs along a melodic line of mingled clarity and complex evocative power. I am not often moved to quote from dust-jacket blurbs, but in this regard nothing finer has been said about *Life Studies* than the remark by Elizabeth Bishop which appears on the jacket of my copy of the poems:

A poem like "My Last Afternoon with Uncle Devereux Winslow", or "Skunk Hour", can tell us as much about the state of society as a volume of Henry James at his best.

Whenever I read a poem by Robert Lowell I have a chilling sensation of here-and-now, of exact contemporaneity: more aware of those 'ironies of American History', grimmer about them, and yet hopeful.

I make this point about the societal element in even the most 'confessional' of Lowell's poems precisely because it cannot be made about Webb's. From *Life Studies* and, say, *For the Union Dead*, it is possible to construct not only a very complete portrait of Lowell's personal pain but also a wide-ranging family history and, not least importantly, a most penetrating critique of the American way of life in our time. Clasping his sacred illness lovingly to his imagination, Lowell was rewarded with insights into the human condition seemingly denied to Francis Webb.

I hesitate to say absolutely that such insights eluded Webb, because we have no evidence (at least in his poems) that he ever sought them. We can, however, say this: that Webb's poetry forgoes the 'confessional' quality which has so engaged Lowell's many readers, that it confounds rather than encourages the construction of a biography, that it completely disregards the kind of cultural *aperçu* which recommended Lowell's work to Elizabeth Bishop, among many others. Anything like a political reference, indeed, is extraordinarily hard to find in Webb's pages; even the verse-play 'Birthday', which follows Hitler's last hours in the Berlin Bunker, is hardly to be construed as a work of the political imagination. If the candour of direct self-revelation has little place in Webb's art, any possibilities of cultural interpretation are metamorphosed through the expressive use of familiar places (Sydney, Montreal, Costessy) to ends almost entirely solipsistic. In effect, his poems are too firmly fixed within his own consciousness to follow connections outwards to the dimension of social history. 'Ages leap in your body', Webb wrote of Sandys, 'And flood into the unselfconscious soul' (p. 204). That kind of privileged communication was never accorded to his own imagination.

If, then, Webb found in the idea of an embrace between the soul and its sacred illness a means of sustaining his belief in his own poetic vocation, he did not easily find the means of translating that belief into poems. He certainly had to look elsewhere than Lowell's kind of verse to discover a workable nexus between his life experiences and the art he wished to create. In this respect it was his particular misfortune to be born Australian. For the cultural traditions of his native land offered no usable models for an imagination like his to turn to. Norman Lindsay, Webb's early patron, could offer little beyond superficial help and encouragement. The supremely confident author of *Creative Effort* could never meet at any deep level the creative needs of one so unhappily gifted as Francis Webb. Neither, it seems, could Webb find elsewhere in the Australian literary tradition any example of technique or substance to answer to his own troubled needs. By and large, indeed, it seems fair to suggest that he made little study and less use of his Australian predecessors. In the whole of the *Collected Poems* the single act of cultural homage is one piece addressed to Henry Lawson. Even that work conveys no sense of an exemplary lesson to be learned from its subject — Lawson is accorded immortality simply because he was an artist. The whys and wherefores of his art play no part in Webb's own poem. Nor is there any other evidence in his writing that he searched the record of Australian verse for other careers against which he might test, measure, shape his own. As far as he was concerned, Kendall's long struggle against inner demons might never have been, nor the tragic heroism of Brennan's pursuit of the predictive lights of his poetry to their end in nihilism and silence. His career, in effect, was constructed out of an elected loneliness.

A response to Webb's poetry, that is to say, is less likely to be illuminated by than to shed light back on his cultural heritage. Any account of his achievement, as I have tried to show, if only by demonstration, is more likely to be better served, in the short run, by reference to figures set in other poetic landscapes. Donne, Hopkins, Lowell — these are the names I have felt called upon to adduce in my own survey of Webb's accomplishment. And now that it is almost concluded, I find 'survey' to be a peculiarly apt term for what I have attempted to do: I see it now as a kind of exercise in critical triangulation, an effort to 'place' Webb's poetry by reference to a set of major landmarks whose positions, magnitudes, elevations are known and agreed upon. Against those trig points, Webb's own significance in the map of poetry stands out, I believe, both more sharply and in finer detail than before. His imagination is seen to be composed of singular harmonies and proportions, bent towards quite special creative ends. If, in the very longest run, it falls short of the greatest achievement, it is because it just fails of that splendid criterion for sanity and high art, joined in imaginative achievement, by which Arnold measured the genius of Sophocles: 'he saw life steadily and he saw it whole'. Webb's vision found its truths in its very limitations.

If, finally, I were required exactly to measure Webb's achievement against Arnold's strenuous ideal, I would have recourse to T. S. Eliot's notion of creative activity expressed in the essay on 'Shakespeare and the Stoicism of Seneca', when he spoke of 'the struggle — which alone constitutes life for a poet — to transmute his personal and private agonies into something rich and strange, something universal and impersonal'.[8] Webb's unique success, I am inclined to believe, lies in the fact that the effort to transmute his personal agony into universal truth became in itself the most compelling image of his poetry, his method became its own subject. Stalled as it were in his own illness, Webb yet made out of that tragic circumstance an image of humanity neither irretrievably caught in chaos nor yet fully delivered to wholeness. Between those two extreme possibilities, known directly by so few of his readers, he left us a moving and memorable emblem of the human mind struggling to make something of its rich surplus of consciousness.

Eve Langley

Oscar Wilde in the Blue Mountains
1984

Oscar Wilde died in June 1974 at Katoomba in the Blue Mountains of New South Wales, the death being discovered only because the police were called to the cottage where the body lay. In making this assertion I am not flying in the face of history and common sense but merely recording a sober truth. For we have it on the authority of some of her closest acquaintances that the writer Eve Langley had, perhaps as early as the 1940s, changed her name by deed poll to Oscar Wilde. To enquire into the true identity of the individual who suffered that lonely death in 1974 is, then, no idle matter: it takes me straight to the heart of my theme in this essay — the peculiar contribution that the author of *The Pea-Pickers* and *White Topee* made to our literary culture.

Beatrice Davis, her editor at Angus & Robertson, is among those who vouch for the fact that Eve Langley literally changed her name to Oscar Wilde.[1] Hal Porter, in *The Extra*, the final volume of his autobiographical trilogy, sheds a slightly different light on this astonishing annexation of one literary personality by another. Porter was the librarian at Bairnsdale in the 1950s, at a time when Eve made a nostalgic pilgrimage to the Gippsland which had been setting, subject and motive force for her two published books. In his recollections, Oscar Wilde emerges as less Eve's *alter ego* than an ever-present shadow to whom she referred everything that touched her, for inspection and approval. The first of these unsettling manifestations that he noticed was sufficient to unsettle even Hal Porter:

'New Zealand! So cold, so Nordic, fiords and crags. These relics of my beautiful Gippsland will warm me when the stars are freezing there.'
She says this sort of thing; and I know what she's saying. I'm uncertain of what I know when she adds something like:

'Oscar would completely agree.'

Throughout the day, not too often but often enough, Oscar Wilde thus flits into her lightest-hearted prattle or her repining the absence of some beauty sponged out of the picture as she last saw it.[2]

Later on the same day of this sentimental journey back to Metung, the propensity to see Oscar Wilde everywhere was repeated in even more startling circumstances. Hal and Eve were talking to the owner of Bancroft House, in the 1920s a boarding establishment where Eve had stayed. Suddenly the retarded daughter of the current owner appeared:

> Around the corner marches the child. At the same moment Eve Langley, one hand full of 'mementoes', starts to climb the steps from the garden. Her head just about level with the veranda floor she sees the child stalking by like Don Juan's Commendador.
>
> 'Oh, Oscar,' she cries out, but gently, happily, transfixed, 'I knew you'd be here. Dear Oscar!'   (*The Extra, p. 149*)

Not all who met Eve Langley were subject to these ghostly encounters with the long-dead *fin-de-siècle* poet and dramatist. Nobody who ever saw her, however, could mistake or forget her customary garb. Always it was some variant on the male attire she had adopted for her first adventure into Gippsland in 1926. Beatrice Davis gives a vivid account of her characteristic appearance:

> She had this massive dark fur coat to her ankles that she wore in summer with an athletic singlet and shorts, and in winter with a man's suit. But always a sort of topee and usually a string bag containing little pieces she had picked up that could be a stone, could be a doll, but they all meant something tremendous to her.   ('Shadows', *p. 23*)

Yet nothing of her recollected behaviour or appearance compels us more intensely to contemplate her elected metamorphosis of self than the climax of *White Topee*. The heroine is talking to her Italian friend Panucci:

> "I must tell you about the day I was 'born'.
>
> "It came about in this way. There was nothing; I was not. Then there was a huge blackness far away off in the earth and sky, and in this far-away blackness, which was a certain length of time, part of me was like a star. I came to myself in a buggy, at Manildra, in the Australian bush, sitting between a man and woman. I was Oscar Wilde, or I had recently been him . . .
>
> I made a great struggle to be once more, and at once, the always brilliant Oscar Wilde, beloved of London, or known of London, for the astonishing genius of his swift recoveries from the most severe attacks of Fate or man. But I could not. . .

And just then, to my horror, I saw the white ribbons fluttering from a baby's bonnet, and staring at them, saw a baby sitting on the woman's knee. The ribbons appeared to me to be waving out against a cold chill windy afternoon, and I exclaimed with the most dreadful despair and horror possible, '*Heavens, I'm the baby!*' I at once collapsed into deepest unconsciousness, while the horse moved on with us through the bush of Manildra.[3]

The metamorphosis of Eve Langley into Oscar Wilde (of which the lines I have quoted offer only the merest gloss) was not only the climax of *White Topee* but, as we can now perceive, the culmination of her whole career. Between the appearance of *White Topee* in 1954 and her death twenty years later, Eve published only a handful of poems. All her other attempts at writing petered out, it seems, in indecision or dissatisfaction. This sad decline forces us, more urgently than any other circumstance, to grapple with the mystery of why Eve Langley opted to become Oscar Wilde and how she effected so strange a transformation. The mystery is yet further compounded by our ignorance about her life. The biographical record is pitifully thin: a brief entry in the Miller–Macartney bibliography, a sentence or two in H. M. Green's *History*, a radio feature by Meg Stewart, an interview with Hazel De Berg,[4] and little more. What little more there is must be largely pieced together from hints and clues in her two books. And even that procedure is not without its difficulties. Both *The Pea-Pickers* and *White Topee* originally offered themselves to the public as novels, and were so received. It was as novels, I have to confess, that I treated them in my survey of Australian fiction from 1920 contributed to Geoffrey Dutton's Penguin *The Literature of Australia* in 1964.

I need scarcely rehearse the old truism that the materials of fiction must be treated with the utmost wariness as sources for their author's biography. Nevertheless, I find myself increasingly inclined to use Eve Langley's works exactly in this way, to deal with them as belonging to the department of autobiography rather than fiction. I shall not in the long run neglect the consequences for critical judgement attendant upon this shameless change of mind. In the short run I shall take the opportunity it affords me of presenting an account of Eve Langley's life which is an amalgam of the established facts of her career and the information she chose to set down (or perhaps invent) about herself in *The Pea-Pickers* and *White Topee*. For the life that she imagined through her heroine Steve is just as truly her own as any biography which scholarship will in its own good time produce. I shall call my character Eve rather than Steve, and shall hope to disclose how the inner narrative of her life is nothing less than a journey towards her transformation into Oscar Wilde.

Eve, then, was born in 1908 at 'The Honourable Killens', a cattle station near Forbes in central New South Wales. On her mother's side, her ancestry stretched back to the pioneering days of Gippsland; the Davidsons were for several generations highly successful horse breeders for the Indian remount trade. By the early years of this century they had established strong connections in Melbourne, some of the family's men being educated at Scotch College, one becoming a magistrate in the city; another, Boas, owned a large racing stable and was an *habitué* of Tattersall's Club.

Eve's own education began at Fifield school near Forbes. In her childhood she moved with her family to nearby Molong, and thence to Rokeby, Jindivick, the Tarago River, in Victoria, and later to the township of Dandenong, in the hills east of Melbourne. By 1926 she and her sister June were living at Dandenong with their widowed mother, at 'Laurel Lodge' in Walker Street. Eve had already held several jobs in Melbourne — as a printer's devil and in a commercial art studio. Early in 1926 the sisters embarked on the adventures that Eve would later transmute into *The Pea-Pickers* and *White Topee*. By New Year 1929 June was ready to marry and settle down; Eve's subsequent career is more obscure. Already called to the writer's vocation, she had begun jotting down material later incorporated into her first book, and in 1930 followed her family to New Zealand. There she contributed to magazines like the *New Zealand Mercury*, and discovered the fascination of Maori culture, made contact with the young Douglas Stewart. Stewart recalls one phase of her life in New Zealand:

I think Eve at that time was living in a town called Wanganui with a Maori faith healer and prophet called Ratana who had his own village there and a church full of the crutches thrown away by cripples whom he healed . . . She moved from Wanganui north to Auckland . . . she was living in a shack, in the backyard of a shack occupied by the Maoris in the Auckland slums and you really couldn't get anything more primitive than that. And she told me she was living on dirt or earth which she found very nourishing . . . there was nowhere to sit down, it was a dreadful shed, but she had with all this squalor around her — she was like a little dark flame in the middle of all that, she was so vital and lively.   ('Shadows', *p. 4*)

Some time during her years in New Zealand she married the painter Hilary Clark, and bore him three children. By 1939, and prompted by the outbreak of the Second World War, she was ready to write *The Pea-Pickers*. The whole book was finished in three months:

It was in 1939 when Great War II broke out and Adolf was marching across Europe straight into the heart of Russia, and I felt like that advancing army.

I sat down before that Remington typewriter with a great "Ilium" on it, that was enough for me, it was as good as Ilium, and with each pink page I wrote rapidly as though I were the advancing panzer into the heart of Russia. But within me I could sense also the great race of the Russians on the Don, trying to stay my advance, and really at the Don they did sort of turn me off, there was a sort of great Parisian blue midnight, Paris midnight blue, and that struck me back off. But I kept going. As the German army, I worked rapidly at the typewriter as though it were a machine gun, and I rapidly wrote and in three months' time I had completed the book, and I was awfully happy, too.   (*Hazel De Berg interview, pp. 5–6*)

Submitted for the *Bulletin*'s 1939 S. H. Prior Memorial Prize under the *nom de plume* of 'Gippsland Overlander', *The Pea-Pickers* shared first place with Kylie Tennant's *The Brown Van* and M. H. Ellis's *Macquarie*; it was published by Angus & Robertson in 1942.

Some time in the 1940s, seemingly, Eve's marriage failed. She changed her name to Oscar Wilde, continued to write verse, and to long for her native Australia. It was not, however, until after the publication of *White Topee* in 1954 that she was able to return. In late 1956 she sailed to Sydney, and during 1957 travelled extensively up and down the east coast of Australia — as far north as Cairns, as far south as Hobart. Mainly, however, her journeyings took her back to the places that had been important in her youth — Forbes, Manildra, above all, Gippsland. In 1959–60 Eve travelled again — briefly to the United Kingdom. It appears to have been after her return from the northern hemisphere that she settled permanently in Australia. There were seasons of hop-picking in Rutherglen, a trip to Greece in the latter half of 1965, some contact with the literary community in Sydney, attempts at further novels. By 1964, however, she was firmly ensconced in her cottage, 'Iona-Lympus' in Katoomba. In that year she was interviewed by the tireless Hazel De Berg, and thereafter virtually nothing was heard of her until her death a decade later.

I present this composite portrait of Eve Langley with no sense of apology, for even after the historical facts have been fully and accurately brought to light, my portrait, I believe, will continue to be the one that counts. In a career which reached its climax in the writer's personal transformation into Oscar Wilde, the inner life must take priority, for it is only in contemplating that inner life that we can hope to understand the meaning, the force, the imaginative necessities of the creative effort which gives her career its importance. From this point of view, even the sketch I have outlined above can be no more than a starting point. The exact contours, the strange textures of her imagined biography — what I shall presume to call her 'real' life — can be determined only if we attend to the innermost inventions of her art.

Many of the literary virtues of *The Pea-Pickers* and *White Topee* have been long recognized and acknowledged. Hal Porter, for instance, intersperses the shrewdly personal observations of *The Extra* with warm praise for just those qualities we might expect him to note most subtly and intensely:

The bravura of her style enthralls me, but most inspiriting is the stance she takes. Heroes of all sorts have come one's way . . . but never one without a tooth in his gums. Eve Langley's characters have the soupçon of literary unreality that intensifies their reality . . .

The White Topee . . . is about Gippsland in the 1920s. Like one possessed, she's apparently been taken over by the area and the era, snared for ever at the heart of an imperishable Gippsland summer. (*The Extra*, *pp. 141–2*)

Douglas Stewart's essay on *The Pea-Pickers*, collected in *The Flesh and the Spirit*, takes the form and title 'A Letter to Shakespeare'. In it Stewart speaks in glowing terms of the book's comedy, of its 'laughter leavened with understanding', its pity, its 'living truth . . . in its depiction of the agony and delight of young love',[5] the enormous gusto of its many and memorable picaresque scenes.

After such commendations, little further need be said about what I shall call the serial virtues of Eve Langley's books, those happy triumphs of insight and sympathy which are borne along on the flow of her narrative. It is the narrative itself, its inner drive and design, which, as it seems to me, still challenges criticism. A scrutiny of that time from February 1926 to New Year 1929 which took the person Eve Langley imagined herself to be to her re-creation as Oscar Wilde will alone answer the questions which still task our literary history: why and how did the writer who was Eve Langley so radically feel the need to imagine herself into another personality that in the end she condemned her own existence to virtual annihilation?

Any answer to these questions must start out from the element of sexual uncertainty which colours virtually every page of her two books. What began as a youthful, high-spirited adventure of 'dressing-up' in male attire was discarded by Eve's sister when she followed what was, for the time, the conventional path to marriage and a settled life. The trope remained a central feature of Eve's behaviour to the very end. In her writing, she comes back again and again — ruefully, humorously, defiantly — to her need to adopt the role as well as the garb of manhood. She offers only one fugitive clue to the psychological basis for her behaviour — in a passing remark to Macca in *The Pea-Pickers*: 'Tonight, Macca, I think of my father, that twisted moody failure, who despised me, and set in me the seeds of destruction'.[6] Whatever its genesis, however, the ambiguity about her sexuality must have been a potent contributor towards her final identification with Oscar Wilde, who was not only bi-sexual in his life, but in such a work as *The Picture of Dorian Gray* provided a compelling image of both the *doppelgänger* and the fascination of eternal youth.

The habit of male attire, moreover, contributes in many quite specific ways to Eve's discoveries about herself and the lines along which she must develop. The assumption of men's clothes, for instance, frees both the girls into a happy amorality, a freedom from convention, not infrequently expressed through acts of petty thievery. The pilfering of food and fruit and drink is less an index of actual want or hunger, however, than a kind of unformed, juvenile exuberance. For it must be remembered that Eve and June (or Steve and Blue, as they become) are no more than adolescent girls when they set out on their adventures. Kelly Wilson, Eve's first Gippsland love, is a stripling of sixteen, and Eve herself only two years older. Her whole personality is still at a stage of youthful plasticity, craving a shape, a form. She first goes to Gippsland, she tells us, in search of love and fame; no less, she might have told us, a formed identity. The great bell striking on the railway station at Moe, on the borders of Gippsland, announces that her journey is a quest whose principal goal is her as yet uncreated self.

Not yet knowing what the goal may be or what shape it will assume, Eve on her first trip to Gippsland goes through a series of extemporizations. Her passion for Kelly Wilson, suffused with the brevity as well as the intensity of youth, is soon put behind her. Macca, supplanting Kelly in her affections, comes to command an obsessional yearning beyond the powers of any sixteen-year-old to inspire; a yearning which will be the catalyst for the re-making of her personality:

Then without a word I loved him. I chained myself to him for all my youth. I set my heart down at his feet, and it became his. To me, in reward, after a long season, came the outline of my soul.   (*PP, p. 111*)

On first acquaintance, however, Macca is a most unlikely inspirer of such terrible affection:

As we stood on the jetty, watching the dark and glistening waters that murmured around the old wood, a youth came along with a peculiar ambling walk. Standing beside us, he lit a cigarette that gave us a glimpse of a large dreaming white face, full-lipped, heavy-eyed and stubborn-jawed.

"I meant to go to a dance tonight," he said slowly.

"What are dances like around here?" we asked for something to say.

"No — (shocking bit of profanity) good!"   (*PP, p. 68*)

We must believe that, beyond any young girl's desire for a love affair, there stirred more complex needs. They included the urge, defined by Eve's friendship with Edgar Buccaneer's wife, the Black Serpent, to be a wife and mother; the desire for companionship with the rural workers; delight in flouting social convention; the need to maintain the bond with her sister. They included, pre-eminently in the opening sequences of *The Pea-Pickers*, a love of Gippsland itself. Both Douglas Stewart and Hal Porter have paid ample tribute to Eve Langley's skill in capturing the sights, the sounds, the very feel of life in that faraway time and place. Yet something more remains in both *The Pea-Pickers* and *White Topee* than nostalgic glimpses of a vanished way of life. Eve Langley's Gippsland becomes, to her vision, both crucible and talisman. As crucible, it directs the purgative heat of an Australian summer onto the chemistry of her own being; as talisman, it makes the very syllables of 'Gippsland' and 'Australia' strike through the pages of her books like incantations. Gippsland in particular is the gateway to the world of the imagination because it is the home of her maternal ancestors, and ancestor worship is strong in Eve Langley. Steve and Blue go to Gippsland ostensibly to rediscover their roots among the pioneering Davidson clan, and they find sufficient relics of their past temporarily to assuage their hunger for a way of life larger than their own. From every encounter with Gippsland's geography and history, however, Eve retreats to the limited and unsatisfactory self she already knows. The talisman of race and place could turn no lasting key. Yet it held one other kind of magic — language itself. The very sounds of 'Gippsland' and 'Australia' proclaimed to her ear that the medium might indeed be the message; that the way to fame, fortune, and self-esteem might lie in the gaining of authority over words, in effect in becoming a writer. Far more profoundly than in its delight in word play and puns, *The Pea-Pickers* is an antipodean portrait of the artist as a young person. It is, quite literally, the story of Eve Langley's attempts to become a writer — Oscar Wilde.

Before her goal became quite so plain, being a writer meant for Eve being at least two things: a man and a poet. Somewhere in her tortuous understanding of her own sexuality rested the belief that poets were necessarily male. The sole exception that she was prepared to admit to this rule was Sappho — and that for reasons which, I suspect, need no further exploration. Otherwise, the poet most immediate to her was the young Chinaman with whom she struck up a conversation in the train returning home from the abortive excursion to Rutherglen and Tumut early in *The Pea-Pickers*. Known ever after as 'Borrelerworreloil', his letters to her and hers to him give Eve a means of communing with a poetic spirit at once conveniently close and safely held apart. She is in fact drawn much more strongly to the sensibility and ethos of the English and European Romantics. Verlaine and Keats she numbers among her 'old friends' (*PP*, p. 38) — Verlaine in whose 'Chanson d'Automne' she later finds consolation (*PP*, p. 150), Keats, the author of 'Lamia', and 'Ode on a Grecian Urn', whose lines could open magic casements onto the foam of perilous seas and faery lands forlorn. Francis Thompson, too, is to be found among that lengthy catalogue of poets she quotes with passionate adoration. Rupert Brooke is another favourite — the supreme representative of those doomed young English poets of the First World War who came to represent for Eve Langley and her generation all the glamour of youth, love, beauty and untimely death. And inevitably among this crowd of creative spirits towards whom Eve yearns throughout *The Pea-Pickers* Oscar Wilde appears more than once — but only tentatively, and with features not yet sharply enough defined to make him desirable above all the rest. He is merely an element in Eve's still generalized urge to lose her identity in richer, more challenging forms of life and experience.

These extemporizations with the lives of other poets are accompanied throughout *The Pea-Pickers* by an even more obvious sign of Eve's desire to assume the mantle of the creative artist: at moments of personal crisis or lonely meditation, she writes poems of her own. Composed, by and large, in the manner of those artists she most admired, they display not so much any major achievement as a poet as an intense desire to live and feel poetically. They are signposts along the way of her pilgrimage towards self-immolation. For, in spite of the seeming randomness of her adventures among other poetic personalities, in spite of the picaresque construction of her whole narrative, on at least one level the various episodes of *The Pea-Pickers* cohere into a pattern which may fairly be described as a pilgrim's way. In its use of place and season, the book moves to a rhythm of alternating commitment and withdrawal which gives its inside narrative the unity of a spiritual quest. The first visit to Gippsland, I have already said, is ritually announced by the ringing of the station bell at Moe; thereafter, every approach to or retreat from this land of heart's desire is accompanied by the same symbolic note.

The first excursion, of February 1926, is tentative, involving the less-than-serious affair with Kelly Wilson. The intensities of Eve's love for Macca can be fully developed only after the visit to north-eastern Victoria which is a necessary prelude to the second voyage to Gippsland in August of the same year. The second part of *The Pea-Pickers*, 'The Glitter of Celtic Bronze Across the Sea', is the longest and psychologically most important of the book's four sections. In it, Eve makes her most sustained attempt to achieve a conventional fulfilment of her desires by applying all her powers of feeling to the love of a young man. Her failure is all the more bitter because Macca is a Gippslander like herself; it must represent for Steve a personal defeat at the deepest levels of her self:

"It's true. The Gippslanders don't want me. Gippsland doesn't want me. I am despised because I work in her fields, and her sons cannot understand me. I bewilder them, and they weary of me."
I wept as I walked with him across the soil of Gippsland, and through my tears I saw the Southern Cross glittering, and the luminous fire of the Milky Way above seeming to roar aloud in the heavens, to be spuming and foaming over with light. My heart ached. O Time, how vast you are and how pitiless. Well, fly then with me to the end, and from these human eyes blot out the moon and the stars and the human faces I have loved. Surely I shall find escape in the spirit!   (*PP, p. 181*)

After such intensities, some relaxation of mood is both an emotional and a structural necessity; the need is perfectly met by the sojourn, through autumn and winter, in the alpine world of 'No Moon Yet'. Far away from her ancestral home, from the summer heat of Gippsland and its lakes, Eve can temporarily recapture the impish high spirits, the easy companionship, with which the two sisters had set out on their adventures. The long fallow months in the high country permit a refreshment of spirit in preparation for the new life and challenges of the springtime world in Part Four, 'Ah, Primavera!'.
The station bell at Moe once again rings out its greeting to this climactic sequence in Eve Langley's strange quest:

"O, who is this come again to seek sorrow in Gippsland? Clang, clang, clang on her heart who seeks for love in me. For, to her, I have none to give. Behold me . . . the door of death! My gates open out on Gippsland and a voice from the soul of the country cries that she shall perish who comes to it, crying for love."   (*PP, p. 284*)

The bell may welcome her back to Bairnsdale, Bruthen, Metung, but not to 'adventurous comedy like that of last year' (*PP*, p. 290). Macca is now definitely lost, and for all the camaraderie of Peppino and the other Italians, the chance of finding a new self through dedication to another in love has now entirely passed her by. Even that part of herself (better, more attuned to conventional happiness?) that Eve had recognized in Blue is now denied her with her sister's forthcoming marriage. At the end of the book she is left entirely dependent on her own resources:

> "No, Blue," I said calmly and coldly. "You must go home. Some day we'll be together again, perhaps. But you've given your word to marry, and you can't break it now."
> Poor Blue. She took my hand tightly in hers when I mounted the mare, and looked up into my face. "No Steve, we'll never go pea-picking again. Good-bye, Steve!"
> "Good-bye, Blue!"
> I touched the mare with my heel and rode away into the bush, riding aimlessly all day, anywhere, until night.
> When I came back to the gully, my heart ached. The owls hooted and the stars shone, and the galvanized iron walls of the hut went "Spink . . . spink" as they contracted after the heat of the day. I opened the door and walked in. I was alone.   (*PP, p. 317*)

There was, of course, no chance that Eve would rest in the diminished solitude achieved at the end of *The Pea-Pickers*. Many aspects of her personality remained unsatisfied by that conclusion — not least a mythic passion revealed in her remarkable interview with Hazel De Berg in 1964:

> I start off Australian, but behind that I've got a terrifically massive Scythian build-up, and as people don't know what Scythians are, well, I'm safe . . . as a Scythian, part a nomadic race and part a Tartar race too, I'm just like a caravan, I'm full of stories like a caravan and like a caravan I am born to wander across all the plains of fantasy.   (*Hazel De Berg interview, p. 3*)

A *wanderjahr* through the State of Victoria at the age of eighteen could scarcely quench the Odyssean desires of one 'born to wander across all the plains of fantasy'. She must move on, even from solitude, and still bearing her idiosyncratic emotional baggage. The fascination with cruelty hinted at by her identification with a barbarian people like the Scythians, openly admitted in the equation of composing *The Pea-Pickers* with the German panzers driving deep into Mother Russia, was by no means satisfied by the writing of her first book. Neither had she finished her accounting with the many non-Australians whom she so closely encountered in her wanderings — Borrelerworreloil, Karta Singh, and, of course, the host of itinerant Italian workers. Lurking behind the cheerful camaraderie, the good-humoured practical joking, is the shadow of something not quite racism but which revels in its sense of the Apollonian superiority of the sun-drenched Australian. If she is to meet Italian or Greek as equals, it is only on the mythic ground of the antique Mediterranean world.

Eve could not, to be sure, entertain these disquieting qualities within herself without some pain. Significantly, the only Christian allusion in *The Pea-Pickers* occurs twice and even the comic context of Rutherglen cannot disguise the seriousness of its import. Rutherglen, where the sisters were betrayed by the vignerons, becomes, in memory, Aceldama — the field near Jerusalem purchased with the blood money earned by Judas Iscariot. Despite the florid intricacy of the style with which she defended herself, Eve remained perpetually open to betrayal by a world of which she asked perhaps too much. Even the elected solitude at the close of *The Pea-Pickers* came to be seen as a self-betrayal which must be fled no matter what the cost.

The direction of her flight is recorded in *White Topee*. Why that book was delayed for over a decade after the appearance of *The Pea-Pickers* I can only speculate — it almost certainly had something to do with the intervention of the Second World War, and the failure of her marriage. Yet when *White Topee* did appear, it continued exactly the same subliminal metaphor which had supported the earlier book: that of a mythic quest through a fantasy land of ancient Mediterranean culture. 'I chanted lines from the *Aeneid*' (*WT*, p. 8) says Eve in the opening scene, as she mends fishing nets by the seashore. In every respect, indeed, *White Topee* is a direct continuation of Eve's efforts in *The Pea-Pickers* to invent an identity for herself which would be more ample, wider-ranging, than that of the adolescent girl she did not want to be. At the same time *White Topee* also narrows and intensifies its predecessor's themes. Its opening paragraphs, set in late 1927, insist more fiercely than ever before on the purgatorial heat of an Australian summer:

The Australian sun rose rapidly, blindingly; entered the lonely gully and began to scorch more easily the short dry grass around my hut. I heard the iron on the roof give an uneasy warning note at the sudden heat; I saw the light burn on the heads of the dry bracken. I flung open the door of the baracca, as I called it, and in white cotton pyjamas I stood for coolness on the hard dry dirt outside and stared up the gully.   (*WT*, *p. 3*)

The burning vision of summer wrings from Eve an unmourning farewell to her puppy love for Kelly Wilson, a harder abnegation of Macca, and a deeper commitment to her search for self-definition in and through the Australian earth. For all its comicality, her account of a punt crossing of the Snowy River symbolizes Eve's entry onto a new stage in her search for a new identity:

Clank, clank, went the punt chains, ringing out over the warm dark river, and the water seemed sweet on my lips. The smell of river weed and water-moistened wood made me feel an odd love for everything.   (*WT, p. 31*)

'Down Calulu Way', the first section of the book, hints at where this new identity may be discovered. The whole work takes its name from a white topee given to Eve by Jim McLachlan, her tea-planter employer, who knows her passion for such articles of headgear. The gift immediately provokes a sympathetic response to its imperial connotations:

I don't know how many Eastern mornings that topee reminded me of, and of the most terrific middays. And one always looked from that topee down, down, reflectively on the sharp, fine, impeccably laundered tropical kit beneath, the white straight wide trousers and white kid shoes; and the weight of the brazen sun was heavy above, and the faint, far dark leaves of some fragile Japanese bush waved in one's mind.   (*WT, p. 14*)

An internalized imperialism becomes one of the important shaping forces of *White Topee*, directly affecting Eve's further experiments in the modes and manners of her personal behaviour. More and more she shows herself attracted to individuals notable for creative authority, an aura of eternal youth, a rejection of conventional sexuality. Rupert Brooke occupies a permanent place in her imagination; the sound of Caruso's great tenor voice, heard on a scratchy phonograph, haunts her for days afterwards. Edgar Buccaneer recognizes in her tendencies as yet undefined to herself: '"Ha! Wilde," he said. For some reason or other he often called me Wilde' (*WT*, p. 6). Her determination to escape from loneliness by the assimilation of her identity into another's is potently realized in the second section of the book, 'A Vision of Clouds'. The clouds themselves appear to have for her the traditional Romantic symbolism of the power of the imagination to create infinitely new forms of art and experience. Under their canopy, she sees herself as a 'patriarch-cum-priestess' (*WT*, p. 55) offering a blood sacrifice to her own intentions.

A brilliant and disturbing paragraph at the opening of 'A Vision of Clouds' describes the complex pleasure she takes in shooting at the gut-hawks which nest in a tree by the foreshore of a lake. Eve identifies with these brilliant predators even as she seeks to slaughter them with her rifle. 'For each man kills the thing he loves' is the unspoken but appropriate gloss on the scene:

There was mystery, delight, and satisfaction in partaking of the day and the homecoming of the hawk. Afar they had been killers, over the paddocks they had ranged as slaughterers, without mercy, but at the sight of their tawny wings making tilted lights against the blue sky, a syllable formed between the element and the bird, a sympathy expressed to me that within sight of the nest the bird changed, and was no longer the killer but the solicitous parent. These contrasts had a strange enchantment for me. Between the wing and the sky and my vision a subtlety was spoken. My heavy rifle, too, was mysterious — first, in that it tied us all together in life and death; secondly, in that it couldn't have hit a house at a hundred yards. There was a fault in the barrel. I aimed for the breasts of the hawks as long as the bullets lasted. They were heavy-calibre .44. I took pleasure in the pain of the report, and the hawks' tearing one-sided flight.   (*WT, p. 55*)

Her fascination with rifles and firearms is only in part to be interpreted as a response to their male symbolism; it also involves the amalgam of power and violence she associated with artistic creativity and the drive to make one's self anew. Not surprisingly, *White Topee* records not only Eve's fascination with such weapons but also her growing personal collection of them. In 'A Vision of Clouds' she records that among her treasures were 'seven rifles and two Service revolvers' (*WT*, p. 60); that number is added to before the end of her tale, as her passion for firearms helps to shape those circumstances from which there was no way out except to become Oscar Wilde.

In 'A Vision of Clouds', however, her situation did not yet require so drastic a resolution. She could still entertain a myriad alternatives to her solitude, just as the clouds could take on an infinite variety of forms. The sense of hopeful experiment is splendidly conveyed in the description of Eve's springtime return to Gippsland after a temporary retreat to Dandenong:

When winter was ending I made ready to go back by train to Gippsland. Young, refreshed, poetic, I rushed, I flew, I fevered back to Gippsland . . . along the golden line, the olden line, the steam and dew and iron line, to live the last and loveliest springtime I should ever know.   (*WT, p. 61*)

Eve, new-born into the spring of 1928, could entertain the possibility of becoming virtually any *doppelgänger* her imagination might present to her: Ruskin or Keats, Adonis or Dante, Australian Lawson or English Wilde. Only when she meets Macca for the last time by moonlight, in the hut sacred to their former love, Rupert Brooke's is the sole existence worthy to absorb her own:

"Brooke, eh? You'll go around quoting that fellow and thinking about him, Steve, until you'll have us all turned into him. And then we'll be all Brooke."

"Yes."
"Or broke."
"Too right."   (*WT, p. 70*)

'A Vision of Clouds' concludes with that bitter-sweet meeting. The section which follows, 'The Rich Red-and-White-Zarro', records a further narrowing of purpose. The comparatively short episode chronicles Eve's companionship with her Italian friends — Domenic, Samozarro, Gabriello, Angelo and the rest. It is full of gaiety and good humour, yet the superiority of Eve, the wearer of the imperial topee, is never completely obscured by the fun; nor the fact that, in a way, she is using these dark Mediterranean men for her own ends. In particular, they bring her closer to the impersonal joys, pains, and pleasures of aesthetic creation, especially music and poetry. Of Samo she decides that he was 'part of my existence, and consequently a poet, or part of a poet's diet' (*WT*, p. 76). He and his friends provide a means of release to one who, looking at herself in a mirror, sees 'nothing but a painted tree' (*WT*, p. 74). To remain nothing but an artificial imitation of a natural object is an unendurable fate. Eve prefers to look into the face of Peppino, and there to discover a future infinitely to be preferred:

He was remarkably handsome; an oval Spanish ivory face with unusually noble lines in it. His hair was like black grapes; he was as ornate as Beardsley's illustration for Oscar Wilde's *Salome*; and his thick creamy eyelids were in a heavy Greek slant from the temple down. But he wore this beautiful mask of a face with such a splendid unconsciousness of it, that one was all the more struck by it.   (*WT, p. 87*)

An anonymous mask-like beauty, lush with a hint of cruelty: such was the *persona* towards which Eve was now clearly tending. 'The Rich Red-and-White Zarro' closes with a further insight which must have strengthened her perception that Wilde, with his ambiguous sexuality, was to be her necessary resting place:

I had to feed my art on diverse food. I had not the reasoning power of a man, whose summing up of his kind is based on humanity. Mine was based on femininity, and femininity must be fed with emotion and passion, the lesser things bringing pain in the backwash.   (*WT, p. 93*)

Before this final transformation could be achieved, however, there remained some last steps in Eve's rite of self-creation. In Section IV, 'Il Panucci', the pleasure of companionship with the music-making Italians is shattered when a letter arrives from Blue announcing her imminent marriage to Keith Wilson, the sweetheart of her schooldays. The irretrievable loss of the sister who two years previously had set out on the Gippsland adventure as a fairer image of herself, was almost beyond endurance. In her pain she temporarily becomes John Keats mourning for his Fanny Brawne. The change is fleetingly revealed to Billy Creeker:

"Your face as you were looking downward reminded me of Keats for a moment, Steve. I often wonder if you were Keats. You may have been. Sometimes, looking at you, I could swear you were John Keats."
"What?" I felt shocked and saddened. I had a very high opinion of Keats . . . Keats? Half asleep, I thought, Was I? Was I? Oh, no, it was incredible. But the suggestion enchanted me, for to be like him would have been a light thing, a pleasure, an awayness from myself. I slipped in and out of the thought as I pleased.   (*WT, p.118*)

That curious pleasure is to be only a passing one. At the end of 'Il Panucci', Eve takes another journey by water — on the S. S. *Burrabogie* — which brings her to a last trial by ordeal. In the heat of December Macca reappears; his mere presence precipitates the final stage in Eve's quest. Paralysed and alone, her Italian friends departed, she comes to the view that for her 'beyond literature there is nothing' (*WT*, p. 161), except perhaps the hope of ecstatic death:

When I leapt onto the horse's naked back it seemed the spirit of Argentina and Mexico sprang up out of the earth and rode with me, too . . . Over impassive soil I rode and found the horses in a torrid corner of a paddock. Lunging in amongst them, I sent them startled and brown, black and white, galloping down to the stockyard. God, one could live for ever among the silken hues of their downward piston-stamping hooves! Bitter moment when it would be ended — I longed to become part of death, if death were the endless stamping of horses and their nobility.   (*WT, pp. 203–4*)

This inner turmoil is resolved by the intervention of external authority, embodied in the person of Judge Box, retired from the Melbourne bench to the heart of Gippsland. He unwittingly ratifies the message that Eve's inner voices have long been whispering to her: that there is one *alter ego*, and one only, capable of satisfying and reconciling all the elements chaotically at war within her being:

day in and day out he wore no other dress than that worn by the great Oscar Wilde, knee-breeches and black silk stockings. And that in the Australian bush. It meant that he was devoted to and loved Oscar Wilde more than any other writer living or dead. And he believed Wilde to be as innocent as a babe unborn of any crime under the sun . . .
He sat among us, exactly as he did in the court in Melbourne. We felt very afraid of him; he had such an air of judicial authority about him that we

literally trembled before him. He was not interested in us at all, however, but sat there in a large chair, in his black silk, and began, after a while, to speak to Frank Foster of Oscar Wilde. If Wilde had been alive he would certainly have felt himself vindicated and his innocence established that day. (*WT, pp. 197–8*)

There follows a period of calm, when the wind blows up cool from the sea, and Eve prepares herself for a second journey to the high alpine country. Unlike that earlier one in *The Pea-Pickers*, this journey will be accomplished on horseback and alone. All that remains are some few acts of psychological preparation and farewell. Love and friends put behind her, she casts aside even that talismanic Australia which had first drawn her into her strange adventure: page after page of the closing sequence of *White Topee* is devoted to peopling Gippsland with characters and events from alien mythologies — those images of Greece and Rome and Scythia which had always most deeply supported her image of herself as a wanderer on the face of the earth. The last transformation of self, furthermore, demands a concomitant change in appearance. From a Bairnsdale tailor she acquires a grotesque parody of the outfit of an English gentleman abroad — 'a pair of Bedford cords of a sublime cut, to go with either golf socks, leggings, or riding boots' (*WT*, p. 235). And so, on a late summer day in the New Year of 1929, she unburdens her soul to Panucci in the sustained and eloquent passage which spells out the myth of her re-creation as Oscar Wilde:

"And to be born does not appeal to me. When they begin to talk about my extreme youth, I wish to rise up and say in a perfectly level and dignified fashion, 'I was forty-four years of age, and the compleat Englishman, the night I landed here on you . . .'"   (*WT, p. 241*)

A few loose ends of business are tidied up, a ritual farewell bade to the symbol which had expressed and sustained her violent, imperious, relentless effort to create an inner empire of the spirit:

The white topee! I saw down the years, from Khartoum to Calulu, the long line of solar helmets and the great minds dreaming in their cool curve, and out of their dreams making an empire. And joining themselves to that line, I saw our own dreams, and the toil we had given out of ourselves through this great ideal summer, the Australian summer that we had shared together and that now was ended.   (*WT, p. 250*)

At the end of *The Pea-Pickers* Eve had been left alone with her own troubled self; at the end of *White Topee*, troubles, self, even the magic lakes of Gippsland, all melt away in the presence of Oscar

Wilde, the *alter ego* which has now fully taken possession of her being:

> I touched with my shoe the black slumber of the racehorse into the bright angry fire of life, and, remembering deeply within itself some set goal of long, long ago, it set out with long striding strong impatient steps to carry me towards the far-off Australian Alps. The black-and-white staghound ran ahead, and Gippsland fell behind.   (*WT, p. 250*)

In moving into that elected privacy, which she inhabited virtually for the rest of her days, Eve Langley, it may seem, moved out of history as well as out of the personality she was born to. Yet such has not been her fate; *The Pea-Pickers* and *White Topee* remain a nagging presence in the minds of all those who seek to interpret the literary record of this country. They still tell us that their creator was something other than a cultural 'sport', a freakish product of circumstances quite tangential to the mainstream of our creative achievement. Indeed, I would suggest that it is only because we sense that she bears very hard upon that achievement that these two books have not sunk entirely into that limbo reserved for talents at once minor and eccentric. If, in presenting *The Pea-Pickers* and *White Topee* as I have, I have too rashly schematized their structure and intentions, it is because I have wished to insist on their relation to some of the great themes of our literature. The Eve Langley who moves through their pages is no less Ulysses bound than Dr Richard Mahony, no less a spiritual wanderer than Christopher Brennan. That same Eve Langley knew quite as much about self-definition through self-annihilation as the Kenneth Slessor who wrote *One Hundred Poems*, and stopped; could have read Patrick White's Theodora Goodman many a lesson in the meaning of 'the great fragmentation of maturity'; sensed as thoroughly as Francis Webb all the nuances and stresses of an internalized drive towards authoritarian power. Long before David Malouf imagined his way into the mind of Ovid on the barbarian frontiers of Roman civilization, she had appropriated to her own identity that of another poet no less extreme, no less in exile from himself and his native culture.

Nevertheless, her two books derive their abiding distinction not only from the fact that they unfold some of the pivotal themes of our literary culture, but also from the manner of their unfolding. In the second last section of *White Topee* Eve mourns for Macca and his whole generation of young Australian men in these words:

> Macca was to me the symbol of man in the year 1928 in Australia, and that symbol, and man as he was, they were both flying from me. Men who were

young at that time were in the melting-pot; theirs was to be a short youth only, for more than the years pressed on them. In those days so many were being born that they loaded the young with premature age, and hurried them onward that they might find a place for themselves. Hating change of any sort, I saw Macca and his kind changing before me and new men coming along of another age, and new songs to take the place of those they sang. (*WT, p. 223*)

This is not the easy nostalgia for a simpler past that has characterized much of our recent autobiographical writing, but a writer's acknowledgement that, as the chronicler of a vanishing society, she was uniquely pressed to find an appropriate form in which to embody it. Too early for the mode of unabashed personal reminiscence which became possible for Australian artists in the 1950s, she declined to take refuge in the full-blown symbolism of Brennan's Wanderer or fictional obliquities of Henry Handel Richardson. For a brief moment, in the late 1930s and 1940s, Australian literature hung suspended between the displacement of personal experience onto fictive verse and prose and its prideful display in explicit autobiography. Eve Langley, and perhaps she alone, was equal to that precarious moment. Her two published books are neither fiction nor autobiography, neither picaresque record of a *wanderjahr* nor deliberate sociography, neither wholly comedy nor wholly tragedy; they are wholly themselves. Into the studied intricacies of *The Pea-Pickers* and *White Topee* Eve Langley poured all that she knew and was with a most elaborate candour, a vulnerability that is anything but naive. Once those books were written, the historical moment past, the act of imagination done, there remained only twenty years of false starts and empty gestures. When Oscar Wilde, who had been Eve Langley, died at Katoomba in the Blue Mountains of New South Wales in June 1974, she left everywhere in her home, we are told, 'mysterious parcels, carefully made up of newspaper and brown cardboard and chicken wire which when unwrapped had nothing inside them' ('Shadows', p. 25).

Hal Porter and the art of autobiography

1984

> 'I'm not an animal given to introspection,
> and have a quaquaversal mind . . .'
> Hal Porter, *The Extra*[1]

The first part of this utterance is as seemingly preposterous in a literary autobiographer as the epithet in its second is *recherché*. Yet both the preposterous and the *recherché* are essential ingredients in Hal Porter's autobiographical art, the one, in a sense, directly related to the other. For, as we may come to believe, it was precisely because of his refusal to look deeply into his mind that Porter could let it go on happily pointing in every direction at once — continue, to borrow his own phraseology, in its quaquaversality. It was, further, the simultaneous possession of these two qualities which produced one of the special features of Porter's achievement — the close conjunction of his works of fiction and those of avowed autobiography, the trilogy comprising *The Watcher on the Cast-Iron Balcony*, *The Paper Chase*, and *The Extra*.

Much fiction, if not indeed all, has its basis in autobiography. Nevertheless, Porter seems to insist far less on the distinctions and distances between the two literary forms than most writers — at least after a false start in a book which was self-consciously novelistic to a degree. This is how, in *The Paper Chase*, he pictures himself at the beginnings of his writing career:

Out of work. Homeless. Practically penniless and, as it were, large with child, gravid with the novel which is to have twenty-four chapters, each covering an hour in one day's red-hot wedge sliced from the lives of a number of characters based on Williamstown people. Each character is to be dealt with in a signature-tune style which is to involve me in imitations of James Joyce, Conrad, Henry James, Thomas Mann, Kipling, Evelyn Waugh, Mary Webb, Proust, and others I forget. The result is, of course, to be the Great Australian Novel.[2]

If one were to concoct a second-rate novel derived from every experiment in style, structure, and technique fashionable in the middle 1930s the result would be virtually identical to Porter's first abortive, never finished and never published, venture into fiction.

After that ill-considered gesture towards the idols of the day, Porter continued to write prose narrative — but short stories only: he did not publish a novel until *A Handful of Pennies* in 1958. Among those early tales, as recorded in *The Paper Chase*, were 'And Nothing More', 'Café Samovar', 'The Two Bachelors', and 'At Aunt Sophie's' — published in the *Bulletin* some twenty years after their composition, when Ronald McCuaig recognized and fostered Porter's talent in a time and climate more attuned to it than the 1930s. These and the other early stories are unlike the aborted novel in that they draw very directly on Porter's personal observation and experience. Some were written while he was teaching school in the Strzelecki Ranges of eastern Victoria — an experience which would, in itself, provide material for later fiction. 'On the Ridge', for instance, collected in *A Bachelor's Children* in 1957, re-plays the episode of 1938 set down as autobiography in *The Paper Chase* (p. 111 *et seq.*).

Both *The Paper Chase* and *The Extra*, in fact, provide abundant evidence of how closely, from the beginnings of his career, Porter drew on his own life for the materials of his fiction. Many of the portraits offered in *The Paper Chase* of his life in Bairnsdale, his schoolmastering years in Adelaide, Hobart and Sydney, his excursion into Occupation Japan, had all been vividly rendered years before in the stories which fill up the pages of *A Bachelor's Children* and *The Cats of Venice*. *The Extra* sets down in detail the Sydney episode already presented as fiction under the title of 'Party 42 and Mrs. Brewer'; reports Porter's own participation in Writers' Week at the Adelaide Festival where it had previously been transmuted into fiction in the short story 'Festival'. It need hardly be insisted on that the abiding pain of his mother's death — the structural and emotional centrepiece of *The Watcher on the Cast-Iron Balcony* — was time and time again the *raison d'être* of his fictional narratives. I shall mention only 'Act One, Scene One', 'Francis Silver', 'Flag Race' and 'Gretel' to make the point.

The conclusion is inescapable: that from the first stirrings of his creative imagination, and no matter how florid, extravagant, startling in its execution, fiction had been for Hal Porter a special, if oblique, mode of autobiography. That conclusion leads in turn to further questions: when, how, and why he was moved to attempt, not fiction as disguised autobiography, but autobiography masquerading as nothing but itself. The short answer to the first of these questions — when did Porter first formally attempt the art of literary autobiography? — is between March and September 1962, the period identified on the last page of *The Watcher* as that of its composition. Issues of means and motive, however, demand more complex answers, and of at least two kinds. The first seeks an explanation of Porter's move from fiction towards autobiography in terms of his personal history, the second in an inspection of the larger cultural patterns of the Australian society to which Porter belonged.

In personal terms, 1962 was for Porter only twelve months on from two of the major landmarks of his life. In February 1961 he had turned fifty, and in the same year decided to become a full-time professional writer. I suspect that it is generally true that any author, unless he has been abnormally busy or is extraordinarily arrogant, will begin to see his own career as a subject of interest to himself and others only after he has experienced something like half a century's living. He needs that long to get his life's adventures into a perspective, a pattern. In Porter's case, however, I believe that something more than simply the arrival of his fiftieth birthday moved him to a head-on encounter with autobiography rather than to more of those sly, provisional skirmishes with what he had, up to that time, chosen to call fiction. There is evidence in some of the stories of the late 1950s of an urge to use his fictional narratives to inspect his own behaviour in a new, more detached and rigorous way. In 1959 and 1961 Porter had written, among others, two stories which patently draw their material from his private schoolmastering years, during the 1940s, in South Australia, Tasmania, New South Wales, and Victoria. Entitled 'Fiend or Friend' and 'Say to Me Ronald', they share the same protagonist, somewhat ironically portrayed, who bears the name of Perrot. This all too obvious anagram for Porter indicates, it is not unfair to suggest, that Porter was responding, in his writing, to a new need to include himself in his stories as actor and subject as well as shaper and observer.

Perrot reappears in at least one other tale, 'The House on the Hill', printed in the collection of 1970, *Mr. Butterfry, and Other Tales of New Japan*. 'The House on the Hill' opens with this sentence:

When, after twenty years, Perrot returned to Japan on a six months' sketching tour, he was braced for its transformation, for near-skyscrapers instead of *apres-guerre* ruins, for near-arrogance rather than *apres-guerre* mock-humility.[3]

Like all but one of the pieces collected in *Mr. Butterfry*, this story grew out of the visit to Japan that Porter factually recorded in *The Actors* (1968). As 'The House on the Hill' claims for Perrot, so it was for Porter: for both it was a second experience of Japan. Porter himself had first journeyed there in 1949 as a civilian appointed to teach the children of Australian officers in the Army of Occupation. That first collision with Japan, indeed, generated his first published novel, *A Handful of Pennies* (1958). Like so much of his longer fiction, this work tells a luridly melodramatic story, played out in this case by two main classes of character — the distinctly unlikeable and the pathetically inept. Apart from both these groupings stands Major Everard-Hopkins, an invention of particular interest in the present context. In his beaky, sardonic rejection of the values and vulgarity of the Occupationaires, in his love of what remains of pre-war, traditional Japan, he is, with one or two important qualifications, a version of Hal Porter himself. He is, too, a forerunner of the unnamed traveller in the much later novel, *The Right Thing* (1971) who teaches Gavin Ogilvie so much about himself in the course of a sea voyage from Australia to England. This enigmatic character even bears an unmistakeable physical resemblance to his creator:

Tall, striking in an aquiline and ravaged style, he had something of the upright rigidity of a scarecrow, something of the herring-gutted ranginess of a scarecrow, but one too faultlessly dressed for standing, and standing, all weathers, winter to summer, doing no more than signify, "Beware! The tremor of your wings I sidelong see! The glitter of your beak I note!"[4]

The final parting between Gavin and the mysterious stranger is a yet clearer betrayal of the latter's close identification with Porter himself:

He looked at his watch. "Four minutes to get to my bus. Good luck in London. No, no, not luck. I foresee your success. I never say 'goodbye'."
(*The Right Thing, p. 117*)

The terms of this salute derive straight from one of Porter's own habits of feeling and language to which he confesses in, among other places, *The Extra*: 'My mother's superstitions are mine, and even if I don't believe one of them, "Good-bye" still means "Never more"'
(*The Extra, p. 161*).

The fleetingly choric commentator of *The Right Thing* is a tougher, more disillusioned version of Major Everard-Hopkins in *A Handful of Pennies*, and both, one can guess with some confidence, are versions of their inventor. Whatever Porter had begun to learn about himself in the late 1940s, had, a decade and more later, hardened, solidified, set. The details of that learning process depend less, it seems to me, on the mere passage of the years than on the acquisition of new insights into himself and the world he inhabited during his first visit to Japan. The nature and quality of those insights are revealed unequivocally in the closing pages of *The Paper Chase*. That he has reached a point of mid-life revaluation is made decisively plain to Porter during a chance visit to Kure:

What, to me, seems clear enough is that until I reach Japan in October 1949 I am a shape that lacks some faculty, some key to the door of the maze . . .

It is unmistakeably true that, until Japan, I have laid hold on little except happiness of a dead-level sort, on trifling distresses, unsplendid victories, and the empty joy that lives in the sad and wonderful truths of others . . .

However much it is possible honestly to be dishonest, vigorously to denigrate or mock myself, however much it is possible wryly to pat myself on the back or wilfully to put myself on the rack or — most shaming of all — to make emotionally and socially profitable misunderstandings of myself, there is a point where the possible becomes impossible. In the smoke-charged and inferno-hot vastness of din, a cool silence gets to its feet, and stands up straight in the trampled and scorched paddock of mere words, and convictions in words, and love and hate in words, and — then — I know. I know that clumsy years have been spent in seeking to discriminate between the essential and the incidental, and that I have arrived at the time and place where the answer is ready, omnipresent, and mine for the asking, mine for the bare looking.   (*PC, pp. 274–5*).

The minute particulars of the answer to the riddle of his own self are discovered in his relationship with his house-girl Ikuko-san, and articulated to both Porter and his readers as the plane lifts away from Japan to take him back to 1950s Australia:

Teacher!

I have taught nothing except that I have to be taught! . . .

As the aeroplane carries me towards Australia and forty it comes to be [me?] that what lies between unavoidable entrance and inevitable exit — life, Ikuko Sakamoto, anyone, anything — is equally unavoidable and inevitable. This has not come to me so clearly before. Life has seemed avoidable. The knowledge that a child's sash and a purgee brother's pencilled letter can scarify the conscience, that soft silk and cheap paper can plough deep and bloody, proves otherwise.

Nothing is avoidable, not even one's own ignorance.

The farther I cross the wilder and deeper and blacker the water, the higher I climb the more perilous and tempest-bitten, the steeper the mountain.

Here, having seen more than I have ever seen, I know that I know less than I have ever known.   (*PC, pp. 304–5*)

Japan's gift to Hal Porter, that is to say, was his perception that he needed to see, define, and value himself anew. In the ten years that followed his return to Australia in 1950 he came to enjoy a steadily growing reputation and confidence as a writer of fiction; at least part of his success, I have suggested, stems from his willingness, learnt in Japan, to include himself as sufferer and participant in the snippets of oblique autobiography he chose to publish as fiction. By the time that he had reached and passed his fiftieth year, then, it had become possible, even necessary, for him to write autobiography direct — direct but not, to be sure, plain or simple.

The writing of *The Watcher on the Cast-Iron Balcony* between March and September 1962, was the outcome of ten years' creative discipline initiated in Japan; its publication in 1963 came at a fortunate moment in Australia's cultural history. It coincided, in effect, with the first flowering in our society of a major artistic form — literary autobiography. One might fairly date the beginning of this phenomenon from the appearance in 1955 of Alan Marshall's *I Can Jump Puddles*: it continued, in many manifestations, and with a most various and unabated power, for something like twenty years — Patrick White's *Flaws in the Glass* presented itself, in 1981, as one of the later successes in the genre. Between *I Can Jump Puddles* and *Flaws in the Glass* many of our leading writers added to the volume of successful literary autobiographies. Hal Porter provides a catalogue of some of the best known names in *The Extra*:

I wrote autobiographically because it seemed the most convenient way to record 'my generation'. In this I'm no Robinson Crusoe. For example, at that time, unknown to each other, Xavier Herbert and I are both on the same tack: our autobiographies appear in the one week. Tedious to list all the Australians who, in a decade or so, and as though a virus has infected them, attack this largely sociological chore, but the roll-call includes people as widely various as Jack Lindsay, Peter Hopegood, Katharine Susannah Prichard, George Johnston, Robin Eakin, Donald Horne, Graham MacInnes, Rose Lindsay, Alec Chisholm, Patsy Adam Smith, Roland Robinson, John Hetherington. (*The Extra, pp. 188–9*)

I am not enough of a sociologist or cultural historian fully to account for the movement that Hal Porter here catalogues in his characteristically exhaustive way. Several reasons for its appearance, however, cannot fail to present themselves. In the first place, by the middle and late 1950s Australians had had sufficient federal experience to feel some degree of confidence that they owned a real national identity. The nexus between the general national experience and the kind of cultural assuredness which permitted the appearance of literary autobiography was made emblematically as plain as it could be in the life of Xavier Herbert: born in 1901, the year of Federation, he insisted on the parallel developments of the Commonwealth and his own career. It was not until 1963 that he judged it appropriate to publish his account of his own early life, *Disturbing Element*.

Porter, then, and his contemporaries felt that by about 1960 the record of a single creative career could be both representative and interesting. They had also travelled far enough from the circumstances of childhood and youth to make the evocation of Australian life, *circa* 1910–1930, not only an exercise in personal nostalgia but an act of cultural piety. Porter's *Watcher on the Cast-Iron Balcony*, for all its elaboration of manner, transmits the sense of looking back on a more innocent (and mainly rural) Australia, a lost order of innocence we will never know again. In that fact, if in none other, it is deeply typical of the whole autobiographical flowering of which it is one of the most distinguished examples.

It must further be said that, perhaps without realizing it, Porter and his fellow-autobiographers were seizing their opportunity just in time. By 1960 Australia was developing a whole set of new and unfamiliar patterns of demography, industry, politics, culture — so new and unfamiliar, indeed, that had they not written their autobiographies when they did, they might have been unable to write them at all. The next wave of Australian literary autobiography would be epitomized by, say, Clive James's *Unreliable Memoirs* whose personal roots are in a national matrix as far removed from Porter's as Kogarah is from the metropolitan London to which James removed himself.

The publication of *The Watcher on the Cast-Iron Balcony*, then, represents a happy intersection of personal development and cultural circumstance. If I can fully explain neither Porter's individual development nor its relation to the whole complex pattern of Australian experience, I can at least say that the appearance of a substantial body of autobiographical writing confronted the indigenous critic with a new set of issues he could not in conscience shirk: the range and kinds of critical methods necessary to the proper interpretation and evaluation of this compelling literary form. Theoretical discussion of autobiography has flourished for many years in the northern hemisphere but seems only now to be acclimatizing itself to Australian conditions. Before I can take my account of Hal Porter's traffic with the art of autobiography any further, I must therefore turn, however briefly, to the critical issues raised by *The Watcher on the Cast-Iron Balcony*, *The Paper Chase*, and *The Extra*. If we are to consider literary autobiography as a form of creative writing as valid and identifiable as, say, the essay or the epic poem, the saga or the sonnet, what special tasks should we expect it to perform? Where should we expect to find its emphases placed? What should we demand of it by way of generic responsibilities? The answers to these questions, it seems to me, cluster around four main elements, some (but not all) held in common with any branch of autobiography. The literary autobiography, in particular, needs to be judged (1) as personal record, (2) as social record, (3) as the exploration of the processes of the creative imagination, and (4) as the creation, rather than the transcription, of a unique self. A creative artefact in its own right, quite as much as a mediaeval allegory or a Shakespearean tragedy, the successful literary autobiography must answer to the laws of its own kind just as strictly as the allegory or the tragedy.

If, in one light, a literary autobiography is a personal record, one unavoidable criterion of judgement must be the degree to which it tells the truth, the whole truth, and nothing but the truth. Too rigorous a critical expectation in this regard clearly must be tempered by the writer's unavoidable need to select, to cut his material to publishable shape and length. Equally, critical expectation must accept (in some cases) the autobiographer's reasonable concern for the laws of libel — Herbert's treatment of the nomenclature of key individuals in *Disturbing Element* is, I suspect, a case in point. On the other hand, critical tolerance need not extend to the recital of deliberate lies, the suppression or distortion of significant facts. In what measure is our assessment of Alan Marshall's *I Can Jump Puddles*, for instance, diminished when we become aware of misrepresentation of his father's occupation? Is Katharine Susannah Prichard's *Child of the Hurricane* crucially flawed because it breaks off just at the critical moment in its author's life — her husband's suicide? How well does Hal Porter measure up to the critic's simple demand for the truth?

In truth, I do not know. A fair and full answer must await a properly researched biography. But this at least I can say: that Porter tells a great deal more about himself in his autobiographies than any of his contemporaries, or seems to. D. R. Burns puts the point well in his essay, 'A Sort of Triumph Over Time':

Granted autobiography offers the facts of the writer's past, he aims in *The Watcher* and *The Paper Chase* to set forth, in a frenzy of reliving, *every* fact of that past, so that the hasty sentences all but overflow.[5]

What Burns is talking about here, of course, is the achieved effect of Porter's autobiographical writing rather than what might be called its archival base. I am confident that, in the long run, its impression of total recall will be shown to be just as much an admixture of cunning selection, creative shaping, and interpretation as that of any other work in the genre.

The same assertion can just as fairly be made of Porter's trilogy in its existence as social record. D. R. Burns is again worth listening to:

Porter's finest writing occurs in those narratives which celebrate victory over Time; in particular, certain of the short stories and sustained passages of the autobiography. Past experience, in these, makes a momentous impact upon the willing cells of memory. The narrator's memories are essentially of objects. The objects are quite solid, completely fashioned, 'blocky', immutably themselves . . . It is, indeed, a world of 'thingness'.   (*Burns, pp. 112–13*)

Porter's capacity to revivify the social past through the material phenomena in which it was embodied is matched only, in his generation, by George Johnston: and Johnston's fictional trilogy — *My Brother Jack, Clean Straw for Nothing*, and *A Cartload of Clay* — is as surely autobiographical as Porter's autobiographical trilogy is, in its 'realization' of a self-consistent world, fictional. Both writers, in effect, use the social data which cram their memories not merely to record the past but to re-create it. As Porter puts it in *The Paper Chase*, he was 'concerned with the truth rather than the facts' (p. 25). The exercise of that concern makes *The Watcher* in particular one of the most marvellously successful renditions of lower-middle-class, country-town Australia in the 1920s to be found anywhere in our literature.

The Watcher, that is to say, shares at least one quality with Donald Horne's *The Education of Young Donald* (1967); though he does not state it as an explicit intention, Porter, quite as much as Horne, is writing 'socio-biography'. The major difference between the two works lies in the role of the protagonist. Where young Donald is an exemplary figure in his society, and is seen to be, young Hal is the odd man out, or seems to be. I have specified *The Watcher on the Cast-Iron Balcony* in this regard because the success of the social record as social re-creation is much more intermittent, I believe, in the two later volumes of the trilogy. I certainly miss in my own reading of *The Paper Chase* and *The Extra* the sustained pleasure I draw from *The Watcher*'s mimesis of unfamiliar times, places, social circumstances in what is felt as their living entirety.

The success of autobiography as social record is, in the long run, as closely bound to its author's creative abilities — his capacity to 'realize' his material — as to its success as personal record — his willingness to set down the truth of his life experiences. Both social and personal record, are, that is to say, intimately associated with the processes of the creative imagination. These processes themselves, I have urged, we can properly expect to be a major subject of literary autobiography. For many, if not most, writers the most compelling aspect of their lives lies exactly in the struggle to produce their poems, plays, novels. The essential part of a writer's autobiography, we might go so far as to claim, what might pre-eminently recommend it to the interest of others, is what it can tell us about the creative imagination.

By and large, Australian writers have had very little of absorbing interest to say about the innermost patterns of their careers. The very fact that it does so defines, I believe, one of the major distinctions of Porter's trilogy. In *The Watcher*, for instance, he speaks of his youthful discovery of poetry:

> I see what poets are.
> Long shafts of light pour from them through the galleries of the years, and cohere in a single greater shaft. This shaft does not blind; it scarcely even dazzles. It is an illumination in which not only the years and the poets themselves are radiantly visible but also the poet's skylark or daffodil or ocean. I see that the poet's possessions are everyone else's, and that he is saying what everyone else cannot say or read or even think clearly of . . .
> The lit lamps thickly line the way I am to take; I cannot keep the fingers of my mind from their flames; the pain of the scorch is fresh and delicious and agonizing; but it leaves no scar; when I cry out, it is only in my heart, like a man.[6]

This introduction to the pleasures and passionate rewards of writing extends through the trilogy as one of the few idealized, romantic commitments Porter allowed himself to entertain: an undiminishing regard for the writer's vocation. *The Watcher* is dedicated to Kenneth Slessor, who becomes, in time, the focus of some of the most unstinted admiration in *The Extra*:

> Kenneth Slessor's poems, a few, scintillating and disturbing, come your way in the 1930s but you're not able copiously to baste your mind until his *One Hundred Poems* collection appears in 1944. Curious this wider, deeper, later acquaintance with his work doesn't modify one whit the image you have of the man himself. Doubly curious because you almost never give imagination its absurd head, and the image is formed from nothing except the fumes and flashes behind a poet's words. (*The Extra*, p. 85)

Even more curiously, this intense romanticization of a local idol was not dissipated when Slessor was encountered in the flesh. Porter's devotion to Slessor, indeed, however quirkily displayed, bespeaks a profound belief in the writer's vocation which is permitted only rarely to show through the prevailingly sardonic commentary on his trade. One such glimpse occurs in his account of the 'cultural circus' (p. 109) of the Adelaide Festival of the Arts:

Even if pursued in everyday life by cataclysms biblical in their capriciousness, as many a notable Australian writer has been, these Men and Women of Letters, the toughest of them, can still draw from within themselves images powerful enough to negate the trite worst, can still parse the stars and clouds above a situation with the intensity of Chaldean astrologers.   (*The Extra, p. 112*)

Having once accepted the writer's vocation as his own, Porter can tell us a great deal of what it is like to move around within it. The trilogy is replete with lists of books and authors read or put aside; more pointedly, it contains passages which bring home, as the work of few other Australian writers has, the very stress and flow of creative activity:

At night, late, alone, when lust has had its fill, or the visitor who talked too long about Thomas Wolfe has gone down the stairs into the starlight, or the late-night walk in the sea-lacerating gale is over, when filling-in-time is over, I write about these people. They glow in my mind with such an intensity that it seems the simplest of labours to get them down clearly, in glowing sentences, and as though I do really see them clearly, and glowing. It is, alas, a more brutal and ego-tripping labour than it seems when leaning on the gale, or abstractedly making love, or not listening to the garrulous visitor. I am not the panted-after crystal able to be seen through by myself, but a grime-clouded pane of glass — the pawnshop window! — on which my own reflection intrudes, with the grime, to defile the glowing images, and make them secondhand.   (*PC, pp. 60–1*)

Out of many such moments, Porter forged an absolutely disinterested attitude towards his art which is surely one of his major achievements, and whose cumulative revelation is one of the great distinctions of his autobiography: 'writing is not to earn money with. It is, like virtue, its own reward' (*PC*, p. 151).

As foil to this diamond-hard core of conviction, the trilogy offers many incidental insights into Porter's attitude towards writing, his methods of composition, his judgement of his own work and that of others. Increasingly in *The Paper Chase* and *The Extra*, however, his interest is not so much in literary activity in general as in the issues and problems he was forced to confront when he embarked on his own career as an autobiographer.

Early in *The Paper Chase*, for instance, he takes up exactly that problem to which, in the eyes of many of his readers, he has provided so personal a solution — that of selecting material for his autobiography which will be at once sufficient, adequate and appropriate:

An autobiographical writer, one who rides a horse to catch a horse, rounds up in half a century of jog-trotting, cantering, and outright galloping a limitless host of characters. He is compelled, therefore, severely to limit the number of them he lets out at one time from the overcrowded concentration camp crowning the ridge of his mind, from that Ark straining at the seams like a lunatic asylum or bargain-sale department store on the Ararat of memory. Were he to attempt to let all free, the avalanche would dance and roar over him, mouthing the unmouthable, scorching him to flinders, mashing him to silence and nothing beneath a torrent of flaming soles. Out of control, the cascade of square-open mouths and hyper-eager eyes, of hair streaming like a storm of oriflammes, of billows of ardent flesh and hot hearts, would hurtle operatically into the quicksands below, carrying optimism and cowardice, modesty and flattery, honour and menace, guilt and grace, forever out of hearing, forever out of sight.

The outlet must be kept narrow; a few figures beckoned into the flood-lit outer world; the gate slammed — oh, quickly. Even so he finds himself reeling back a little from the power of life left in these long-time internees, finds himself drawn into a frieze of posturing profiles, hemmed in by the inhabitants of that Wagnerianly bloated cliché, a Cavalcade of Humanity. (*PC, pp. 90–1*)

Nothing could demonstrate more convincingly that the effect of total recall so shrewdly noted by Burns is indeed just that — an effect, achieved by a fierce selectivity, an assimilation of the world of objects into the imagination of the writer.

An awareness of the technical centrality of the autobiographer to his autobiography is the foundation on which the whole of *The Extra* is constructed. On the second page of the final volume in the trilogy Porter commits himself to an overt definition of the very genre he is practising: 'An autobiography's composed of what its author's composed of'. Given that bald assertion, it becomes a matter of crucial importance to determine of what elements the author of *The Watcher*, *The Paper Chase*, *The Extra*, is composed, in effect the dimensions of the self which is dramatized in their pages. In this regard one of the most revealing of the many asides with which Porter laces his narrative is to be found in Chapter Three of *The Extra*:

A writer's composed of others, can only be a thread on which, like a barbaric necklace, are strung a number of experiences. Self, as one ages, becomes decreasingly interesting to a writer. That's why this autobiography, despite my intrusions as thread, is really less about me than about events I slip into as into the wrong room at the wrong time, and . . . oops! . . . quickly out of. (*The Extra, p. 79*)

Later in the same volume Porter pushes the idea a step further:

T. S. Eliot says a writer's progress is an ever-increasing 'extinction of personality'. You take it he means that, as a writer ages, he's progressively less curious about himself, more and more interested in clues to others' natures: their possessions, fads, frenzies, accents. It's certainly your position.   (*The Extra, p. 174*)

It is because he can make a claim such as this that Porter rightly describes himself as 'not an animal given to introspection'. It is when he makes a claim such as this that his intellectual concern with the theory of autobiography slides towards the fulfilment of the fourth of those responsibilities I imputed to the genre he practises: the creation of a self, in the pages of his autobiography, which carries the same kind of realized authority we expect of a created personality in any department of literature.

The Watcher on the Cast-Iron Balcony is, in my view, brilliantly and movingly successful in the dramatization of its protagonist-narrator. Nevertheless, Porter's theories of both self and autobiography produced a problem for his own writing which becomes progressively more severe in the course of the two volumes which followed. It may be most readily expressed in the form of a paradox: as Porter became more theoretically aware of his task as an autobiographer, the execution of his autobiography became more and more flawed. His increasing self-consciousness of himself as an autobiographer is manifest in many ways other than statements about his art of the kind just quoted and which, while strewn through *The Paper Chase* and *The Extra*, are hardly to be found in *The Watcher on the Cast-Iron Balcony*. It can be measured, for instance, in the very titles chosen for the three books. *The Watcher on the Cast-Iron Balcony*, as a title, is rich in implication, none more germane to my present purposes than the nexus it establishes between the writer's perspective and the kind of world-view embodied in the materials selected for inclusion:

These earliest memories are of Kensington, a Melbourne suburb, and one less elegant than that in which I am born between the tray-flat waters of Albert Park Lake and the furrowed and wind-harrowed waters of Port Phillip Bay. The memories are centred in a house then 36 Bellair Street, Kensington. Of this house and of what takes place within it until I am six, I alone can tell. That is, perhaps, why I must tell. No one but I will know if a lie be told, therefore I must try for the truth which is the blood and breath and nerves of the elaborate and unimportant facts . . .

The slope makes it necessary to ascend from the front gate of 36 along a path of encaustic tiles, next by eight wooden steps on to a front veranda which is therefore a long balcony balustraded with elaborately convoluted cast-iron railings. From this balconic veranda I look over the plane-trees towards a miles-off miles-long horizon composed of the trees of the Zoo, Prince's Park, Royal Park and the Melbourne University.   (*Watcher, pp. 10–12*)

The title of the second volume reveals not so much a deeply necessary principle of aesthetic organization or mode of perception as a colourful label by chance discovered and then conveniently imposed on the events of the author's life. The image of the paper-chase occurs in the course of Porter's description of his first change of address after the death of his mother:

I order the first taxi-cab I ever order and, feeling extremely polished, very man-of-the-world, set out on what is to be a longer paper chase than I could have foreseen. (*PC, p. 27*)

Thereafter it serves arbitrarily to impose a pattern on the tale of Porter's wanderings between early 1929 and his return from Japan in 1950. The title, finally, of *The Extra*, betrays a theory of the representation of self in autobiography which leaves nothing centrally to represent. The narrator has now become a bystander, a super-numerary in his own life's theatre. The practical consequence of Porter's application of the theory of 'the extinction of personality' is a scissors-and-paste job, in which some brilliant vignettes are strung together until they reach book length in order to justify the announcement on its dust-jacket that it is Autobiography 3. *The Extra*, it seems to me, is marred by an increasing use of self-consciously literary 'devices' (poems and allusory epigraphs), by the distortion into mannerisms of those sharply personal manners which are so much part of the delight of *The Watcher on the Cast-Iron Balcony*.

With the self deliberately excluded from the representational aims of the final volume of the trilogy, what is left is a repertoire of atti-tudes, prejudices, *idées fixes*, not all of which present Porter in an especially attractive light. The protagonist of *The Extra* revels in his dislike of the young, especially students. At the Edinburgh Festival 'the students surge about, as students do, like primitives unhinged by an eclipse of the sun' (*The Extra*, p. 133). Migrants are disliked because they come from foreign parts:

Foreigners are only truly entertaining in their natural habitat, and preferably in national costume making horrible local delicacies or hideous local knick-knacks, and giving picturesque imitations of themselves. The effect of these refugees from the Old World and a seedy way of life on the tone of Australian society is, you observe, already in the mid-1950s, regrettable and standard-lowering. (*The Extra, p. 59*).

Also numbered among Porter's targets are politicians, left-wing writers, 'the well-paid working class' (*The Extra*, p. 32), literary critics, and academics:

I've no illusions about the quality of my intelligence. I have only enough to be anti-intellectual, anti-academic, and much more than wary of Culture and its fringe activities such as Adult Education, Summer Schools, Discussion Groups, and Critical Seminars. (*PC*, p. 174)

Against these somewhat distasteful attitudes — deliberately paraded, I suspect, for our annoyance — stand some much more likeable qualities of personality and action. As *The Extra* makes abundantly plain, Porter has a deep and particularized love of place and places — houses, country towns, cities visited, even (perhaps surprisingly) Australia:

All's not stated but, to sum up, I love Australia beyond all other places even though, over the years and before my eyes, many of its unique and most estimable aspects have been needlessly tampered with, altered, or destroyed. (*The Extra*, p. 237)

The special flavour of Porter's love of homeland is related to a pervading and reasonable conservatism — a conservatism which manifests itself in some of his most characteristic and intimate gestures. They include his fastidious good taste, his respect for the 'right thing' in personal relationships, his sense of the value of good manners:

Of all life's rules, those of manners are the simplest and most satisfactory to act upon: no after-taste; ears can't be boxed; confession unnecessary. (*The Extra*, p. 104–5)

The Extra, of course, is not unremittingly devoted to displays of Porter the aristocratic observer exercising his talent to charm or annoy. It is just as full of the morally neutral idiosyncrasies of which any personality is largely composed. The astonishingly acute sensitivity to the ravages of time, so often remarked, is, for instance, the foundation on which the whole trilogy is erected. Contributing less to the structure of feeling on which the writing is based but equally part of its intricate design is a whole range of seemingly discrete psychological phenomena, ranging from agorophobia, through a fatalistic acceptance of events, to a fascination with the extravagant, the grotesque. This last is relished not least when it is discovered in Porter himself. One of the memorable images of *The Extra* is of its author playing for the Hobart ABC's School Broadcasts 'a Grandfather Koala given to fruity ho-ho-ho laughter and homespun truisms' (p. 30).

To such a *mélange* of gesture, feeling, attitude, the self which had been so fully realized in *The Watcher* is progressively reduced in the second and third volumes of Porter's autobiography. So much, indeed, of the essential self of its protagonist–narrator has been concealed or eliminated from *The Extra* that what remains is, at worst, a truculent recital of prejudices, a sour rejection of much of the kind of fact in which Porter had earlier rejoiced; at best, an unabated curiosity, an inquisitiveness hungry for any item of behaviour the world may cast before it. In effect, the watchful eye of the six-year-old child has become the quaquaversal mind of the sixty-year-old professional writer. Considered as either personal or social record, *The Paper Chase* and *The Extra* offer as much, by way of catalogue, as *The Watcher on the Cast-Iron Balcony*. As the creation of a deeply imagined self (which, to my mind, is the essential task of literary autobiography), the second and third volumes of the trilogy fall far behind their predecessor. Manner has become mannerism; art, artifice. There is, nevertheless, a kind of heroism even in that decline. One of the crucial episodes in *The Paper Chase* concerns the accident on 1 September 1939, which shattered Porter's hip, kept him out of the Second World War, and condemned him to lifelong bouts of periodic pain. Out of that trauma arose some new discoveries about himself:

The most discomposing paradox in my luggage of new information is that I prefer to live alone because I am too fond of those I love.
One wants to be alone, fundamentally, not to escape others but to escape oneself, the versions of self compelled into existence by others. It is safer for me to be mere wood than to be wood painted to look like wood. (*PC, pp. 148–9*)

Only Hal Porter, perhaps, would have had the nerve to take that dictum quite literally; to attempt an autobiography which would so deliberately and progressively exclude both *autos* and *bios* as to leave in the end nothing but the graph of his random encounters with people and places.

The emotional structure of
The Watcher on the Cast-Iron Balcony
1984

The narrative design of *The Watcher on the Cast-Iron Balcony* is successfully straightforward: the hero's life story is plotted from his birth to his eighteenth year, with illustrative episodes highlighting the crucial periods of his development. Informing this history, however, and converting efficient narration into imaginative distinction, is another kind of design — an inside narrative of personal relationships, a structure of emotions which give colour, point, perspective to the autobiography. To investigate the emotional structure of *The Watcher on the Cast-Iron Balcony* is the aim of this essay.

The most palpably important relationship recorded in *The Watcher* is that between Porter and his mother. Everything else that he tells us about his early life is framed between his contemplation of her lifeless body and his account of her death and funeral. So long sustained, indeed, is the closing sequence of *The Watcher*, and at such a pitch of passion, that it challenges comparison with that other great modern rendition of a son's agony at his mother's passing — Paul Morel's tearing grief which is the climax of *Sons and Lovers*. In at least two respects, however, Porter's experience, along with his representation of it, differs from Lawrence's. The measure of that difference is as much a measure of Porter's achievement as of the English writer's.

In the first place, Porter had turned fifty before he dared approach the autobiographical challenge of *The Watcher*; Lawrence, in the year when *Sons and Lovers* was published, turned twenty-eight. The difference, then, between the two books is partly of years lived, of maturity, producing in turn differing formal perspectives on similar material. Where Lawrence still needed to displace the pain of his grief onto fiction, Porter could face it direct as autobiography, as fact.

While commitment to autobiography rather than fiction need not indicate greater psychological honesty on the part of one writer rather than another, in this instance Porter's decision about the form his work would take arguably produced a more clear-headed understanding of his material than Lawrence's.

Secondly, the mother–son relationship recorded in *The Watcher on the Cast-Iron Balcony* is drastically different in kind from that which drives *Sons and Lovers*. The whole of Lawrence's novel betrays a relation between Paul and Mrs Morel disabling in its closeness and obsessive demands for love, so that his mother's death is, for Paul, as much an imprisonment as a release. The deeply ambiguous legacy the mother bequeaths her son is splendidly embodied in the famous closing lines of Lawrence's book:

"Mother!" he whispered — "mother!"

She was the only thing that held him up, himself, amid all this. And she was gone, intermingled herself. He wanted her to touch him, have him alongside with her.

But no, he would not give in. Turning sharply, he walked towards the city's gold phosphorescence. His fists were shut, his mouth set fast. He would not take that direction, to the darkness, to follow her. He walked towards the faintly humming, glowing town, quickly.

Hal Porter's experience appears to have been, in almost every way except the felt actuality of love, the reverse of that which Lawrence projected onto Paul Morel. In his case, the mother's love for the son, and his for her, were in no way disabling or diminishing; indeed, their deep mutual affection was in the long run a benison offered to the writer's life. Evidence that Porter's love for his mother was no curse demanding exorcism, no guilty burden to be borne, abounds on virtually every page of *The Watcher* — not least in its tone, so happily and consistently free of neurotic tension, in the regularly pleasurable tenor of his recollections of his mother, or in what, on the face of it, must seem a most curious erasure from an otherwise photographically copious memory:

Let me immediately reveal, in my largely visual recollections of this pre-six era, that my father and my mother are not visually alive to me as the young woman and young man they then are. I cannot see them . . . I remember exactly the pearls and rubies in Mother's crescent brooch but not her eyes. Except for Mother's singing, I cannot hear them; a mere little litter of words blows down the galleries of time, some of it aesthetically haunting, more of it unforgettably trite.[1]

The young Porter, it seems to me, was fortunate in storing up and assimilating such potent memories of a beloved and vital mother that, as the sharp and separate vignettes of childhood faded, they became a whole way of looking at and reporting on the world. His lifelong passionate recall of his mother did not produce, as it did for Lawrence, a debilitating and obsessional dependence but the happy exercise of gifts he learned from her and her alone.

This rare and fortunate transmutation had its foundations, perhaps, in the fact that Porter was the first of a large family — there were in all five siblings. This primal experience of kinship translates into Porter's autobiographical art as one of its pre-eminent virtues — a passion for fecundity, abundance, plenty, a quality in his imagination of which Porter himself was so keenly aware that he returns to it again and again:

Abundance! Plenty!
To me, now, the years between six and ten are cards of the same suit. The total impression remaining is this one of copiousness. Never for one second do I realize that what I count as such is not so to many . . . I see fecundity everywhere — the seed-boxes of poppies shaking out their pepper, the winter-defrocked trees blotted with nests, the summer trees bearing billions of leaves, the vast mushroom-rings, the grapelike bunches of blackberries overhanging the paths and ditches along the river. Mother's fingers and mine stained emerald with the green blood of uncountable aphides we have squashed from the buds of the rose-bushes.
Fecundity! Plenty! Abundance!   (*p. 63*)

This sharp awareness of cornucopian plenty at the heart of his emotional life and in every facet of the observable world produces a number of quite personal effects in Porter's writing. One cannot miss, for instance, the sense of inviolable inner security which under-pins the narrative of the *The Watcher*, no matter what specific bitchery, agony, ecstasy, or simple pleasure is being enacted. Nor can one easily pass by Porter's intense attachment to the more opulent manifestations of the natural world:

I am never so passionately aware of the power of the earth and the lavishness of it as on Gippsland midsummer days. Before eleven in the morning the bees are staggering drunk in the madonna lilies. The endless safaris of ants pass each other scarcely speaking . . . Out and farther out, beyond the Golgotha of the slaughter-yards, lies the cemetery like a spilling of shapes in marzipan, the cemetery and its abundant dead boxed down under the free-sias and sparaxis and periwinkle and briers and gorse more abundant than they.   (*p. 69*)

Given the sensibility revealed here, it is fatuous to inveigh against Porter's preference for the ordered richness of the 'Englished' landscapes of Australia over those which usually recommend themselves to the patriot's eye. Such a preference was an unavoidable expression of the deep emotional structure of his imagination; and without that structure there would have been no watcher on the cast-iron balcony alternately to soothe and irritate the national ego.

Without that structure, too, Porter would have been unable to exhibit in *The Watcher* one of the features of his prose which has been most widely admired: his masterly control of fact. Nobody realized more intimately than Porter himself the source of his skill in acquiring and utilizing facts. He was aware of it as early as his days in primary school: 'I love facts, and the excitement and processes of getting facts. In short, I love school . . .' (p. 89). The understanding of his love comes much later: 'In the nineteen-twenties, I am not, of course, really alive to the fact that heart-holding is a form of my old greed for abundance and information' (p. 205). The connection, once made, between abundance and information, fecundity and fact, illustrates whole tracts of Porter's autobiographical art. Single, isolated facts never held any sway over him. The most splendid, the most memorable pages of *The Watcher* are almost invariably those in which facts tumble over each other in brimming abundance. John O'Hara once said of Scott Fitzgerald (one of Porter's favourite authors), 'The people were right, the talk was right, the clothes, the cars were real . . .'; by which he meant, of course, that Fitzgerald knew how to select some two or three facts to light up a whole epoch. For Porter two or three were never enough. Secure in his management of the tidal wave of facts pouring out of his memory, he let them spread across his pages, creating the effect of total rather than selective recall. Where fastidious choice had been the trick at Fitzgerald's command, for the Australian writer success lay in the reconstruction of the whole weight and mass and density of whatever time or place was in his mind's eye: and not only its weight and mass and density, but the colour and detail as well. As his mother's exact image faded from the young Porter's vision, it was replaced by all the glowing tints and hues of the world around him; it was his artist's privilege to retain them, in imagination, for the rest of his life. The translation of a mother's love into a rich and detailed sensory appreciation of his surroundings is quite as important to the emotional structure of *The Watcher on the Cast-Iron Balcony* as its brilliant accumulations of fact and information.

The security afforded by his mother, indeed, with her perennial singing gaiety and her earthy realism, provides the emotional foundation for Porter's autobiography. Her influence extended into more specific modes of perception. When he was six, Hal, his parents, his brother, and sister left inner suburban Melbourne for Bairnsdale and the Gippsland countryside. Restored to her familiar rural surroundings, Mrs Porter resumed habits of living she would pass on to her writer son as specialized capacities for observation. One of the great sequences from *The Watcher on the Cast-Iron Balcony* is Porter's description of his mother's ritualized country week:

She is Monday as she helps the washerwoman whose hands are as pleated and bleached and sodden as some tripe-like fungus . . .
    She is Tuesday as she sprinkles pillow-slips, Father's shirts, my sister's starched sun-bonnets, and the boys' cotton sou'westers, for her flat-irons . . .
    She is Wednesday . . .   (*p. 57*)

And so the catalogue swells to Friday night late-shopping. The mother's stylized observances showed her son one of his most convincing means of interpreting his own experience. Little in *The Watcher* rings more true than its registration of the kinds of social ritual Porter first learned in his own backyard. The initiation rites of schoolboys, their organization into hunting packs or exclusive gangs, their ceremonious first steps in sexual awareness and sexual play; the descriptions of such patterned social behaviour are among the triumphs of, particularly, the middle sequences of *The Watcher on the Cast-Iron Balcony*. Indeed, it is almost at the literal centre of the book that is exhibited one of the supreme moments of its art: the gathering of the Porter clan for the Sale Show. In that sequence all Porter's passion for abundance, plenty, information, his ardent love of colour and detail, his unerring nose for social ritual, his ear for speech, are welded together to immortalize the kinship patterns of Australian country living half a century ago.

Porter found the power to confer immortality on that scene, it may be, because, for him, his mother's zest for life conferred immortality on her. There is nothing feigned or forced about the closing episode of *The Watcher*, but not even the pain of her dying could erase the vivid memory of her living. Whatever the similarities between the endings of *The Watcher* and *Sons and Lovers*, there is a passage towards the beginning of Porter's book one would expect to find nowhere in Lawrence's:

Nor do I believe for one moment in Mother's dying.
    She is clearly not marked down for death. She is too entangled in life, too busy, too lively, too noisily chatterbox, and has, altogether, too many imperfections disqualifying her from death.   (*p. 80*)

Because the mother was, in life, so alive she could remain, in death, the positive, liberating source of the son's autobiographical art.

I have thus far written only of the influence of Porter's mother on the emotional structure of *The Watcher on the Cast-Iron Balcony*. Yet it should not be forgotten that the image of the dead father shares the opening paragraphs of the book with that of the mother, and that the paternal presence is, in its own way, just as pervasive in all that follows. The memory of his father, however, had utterly different consequences from that of the mother. Where the one endorsed for Porter the brimming value of the actual, the other left a sour and more difficult legacy. His father's bland indifference is what he insists on before all else. Indifference, furthermore, breeds more than indifference in those whom it chooses to ignore. Porter came to find something sinister in his father's elected role, something subtly and finally destructive. The difference that he sensed between his parents is tellingly dramatized in his father's recollection of the young Hal's first day at school:

> It is not until over thirty years later, my mother nearly twenty years dead, that my father accidentally lets me know what has happened to brake her. As she adds milk to the tea for the cropped warrior son returned from battle, for the bright son from the muddy fields, for My Son the King from his tour of assassin-riddled streets, have I, pleads Mother without pleading, have I cried?
> 'Fuck', I say, 'fuck, fuck, fuck, fuck, fuck.'
> My sixty-odd-year-old father, relating this, chuckles with dirty reminiscence, his face meantime creasing itself older, and looking too humanly ugly like one of Hieronymus Bosch's. Mother, who dies long before she learns the despicable rules of frankness, that subtlest dishonesty and deputy for truth, has said nothing ever of this incident.   (*p. 39*)

Noting such slyness and cruel deceit, it was a hard perception for the mature artist that, just as much as those of his mother, his father's modes of living and feeling had been absorbed into his own creative sensibility:

> The danger in Father's simplicity is that . . . step by hidden ruthless step, it has transmuted itself to stubbornness, thence to simon-pure indifference, the final and most killing of self-treacheries . . . instinct, and observation of Father, warn me in time to give attention to my own inherited simplicity and indifference lest they shrivel me too down to an inhuman actor.   (*p. 20*)

If Porter evaded the ultimate self-destruction of emotional indifference to the world, he certainly acquired some powerful traits of feeling and sensibility from that older man whose faults he so dispassionately exhibited. Coexisting in *The Watcher on the Cast-Iron*

Balcony with the delight in nature's abundance is an often ill-concealed scorn for large sections of the human race. Just as the child Porter rejected cricket because his skilful father wanted him to emulate his skill, so the adult writer rejected and mocked virtually all the value systems which prevailed in the Australia of his time and place. Bourgeois culture is assessed at the same low rate as the ethics and aesthetics of the left. To be sure, in his dress and gesture, as in his writing, Porter sometimes strove to assume the pose of the aloof aristocrat; yet there was something defensive even in that pose, just as there was almost certainly an element of fear and envy (also inherited from his father) in his rejection of the intellectual life:

> The Australian form of self-respect . . . is, essentially, genteel, ingrowing, self-pitying, vanilla-ice-cream hearted, its central fear a fear of the intellect. Father simulates all this in such a *trompe l'oeil* manner that he convinces himself too.   (*p. 93*).

The paternal indifference which taught the son the mode of savage irony could also induce such qualities as treachery, the power to hurt. There are few more difficult episodes in *The Watcher* than Porter's encounter with middle-aged Miss Hart — the sexual novice using and being used by the sexually desperate. In the telling, it leaves one at a loss as to which of the two to dislike or pity the more. In the outcome, it seems to have left Porter forever wary of the emotional implications of any kind of sexual encounter.

One aspect of his father's indifference seems to have been more important for Porter than all the rest — his lack of imagination:

> I am able to sniff out many of my father's imperfections because he has passed them on to me from his own father. It is a heritage I have to keep my eye on for many years, a heritage including a blindness to the points of view of others that amounts to insulting indifference, a lack of imagination, a stubbornness, self-satisfaction, and bland selfishness.   (*p. 92*)

On the face of it, no assertion is less believable from the author of *The Watcher on the Cast-Iron Balcony*, *The Tilted Cross*, *A Handful of Pennies*, and the rest, than a complete lack of imagination. It seems preposterous that so extravagant a writer could fabricate such a claim.

Nevertheless, incredulity must give way to acceptance: this claim, no less than most that Porter made about himself, is absolutely true. Once we understand his usage of the term 'imagination', we must concur that he is utterly without it. For what Porter means by 'imagination' is what is more usually described as 'invention' — the ability to 'make up' original stories about imaginary people with a whole range of imputed motives and emotions. And that ability, as he recognized himself, is quite outside his repertoire:

I do not know because, having no imagination, I do not understand people. I understand no one, and never have, and never will. What they will *do* is too easily foreseeable; for me it is nearly always impossible to know *why*. (*p. 93*)

It is hardly to be wondered at that among his earliest essays in creative activity were 'two forays into the world of grease-paint and illusion' (p. 127); the theatre offered colour and movement, but it also permitted the construction of plots which could move towards their pre-ordained end with minimal attention to motive and the explanation of behaviour. All Porter's mature dramas are designed, in the most juicily melodramatic terms, to display characters acting, reacting, behaving, with no apparent penetration into their reasons for doing so. The well-made play, on which all Porter's theatrical texts are variations, was precisely calculated to free Porter from the need to exercise any analysis of subtly motivated behaviour.

It was not even in fiction that Porter's creativity, deprived of invention, found its happiest resting place, but in the telling of stories embedded in known, luxuriant fact — that is to say, in autobiography. In *The Watcher on the Cast-Iron Balcony*, his lack of imagination is as much a positive source of emotional and aesthetic strength as his feeling for abundance and plenty. In autobiography, his creative powers were able to play over the tangible world that he had seen and known, to convert it into prose narrative which needed none of the symbolic obliquities of fiction. His father's studied indifference became as rich a source of constructive power as his mother's sardonic delight in the actual. In *The Watcher on the Cast-Iron Balcony* the paternal capacity for sly deceit and dishonesty combines with the maternal love of sensuous surfaces to produce the mocking, passionate, complex tone of Porter's greatest work of autobiography.

Again, nobody knew better than Porter how much he owed to the mingled memories of two such different personalities: 'Forget my father and my mother? I am them' (p. 31). Yet there was also a component in his sensibility uniquely his own. 'He has Mother and Father', but 'He has, above and beyond all and everyone else, himself' (p. 23). The unique sensibility of that oddly separate child contributes as much to the emotional structure of *The Watcher* as anything learned from either parent. Much of Porter's own contribution to the emotional patterns of his life and writing resides in a special technique for reconciling the equally pressing but often contradictory demands placed on him by the memory of his parents. It is pre-eminently a technique of paradox. One of the most potent paradoxes of *The Watcher* has been often remarked: an awareness of transience, of mutability, so acute and wide-ranging that it has to be captured in the permanence of language. I shall here pass directly to two other paradoxes equally germane to my theme. One of them, Porter identifies quite explicitly on the opening page of his book: 'I am born a good boy, good but not innocent' (p. 9). This piquant assertion is repeated, like that about his lack of imagination, several times in *The Watcher*, and, like that other claim, must be subject to some semantic unravelling if Porter's meaning is properly to be construed.

By 'goodness', it seems to me, Porter understands a desire to please others, a willingness to conform, as a means of getting on more readily with his own life. It is in effect an extension of that capacity for indifference and deceit, acquired within the family circle, to his widest human relationships. 'Innocence', on the other hand, the active desire not to wound others, was something Porter, as he believed, neither was born with nor acquired young; it was something he had deliberately to strive for every day of his adult life. Actively uninnocent as a boy, he cultivated the arts of minor deception:

As an obedient son I almost never run against my parents . . . It is easier to be obedient to the grown-ups deft in the mechanical tricks of existence . . . than to be disobedient and wrong. I prefer being right.   (*p. 138*)

Porter's growing-up involved many such accommodations. As he approached adolescence and young manhood it was complicated by more intricate social relationships, by the discovery of sex and strong drink. His introduction to alcohol was a reasonably decorous affair in a local wine bar in Williamstown. Sex, after his initiation by Miss Hart, seemed increasingly to involve cruelty and the power to destroy:

. . . sex is not a game but something more dangerously exhilarating, more deadly, more victimizing, a disease of the feelings, an itch, a rage, a mania. (*p. 156*)

The search for innocence is a long one, and it was not until he was fifty, and writing *The Watcher*, that Porter could see its pathway clear:

1921 is the last year, for many years, of my early poise, and is, therefore, part of the design of me, the last year of unflawed non-innocence. I am soon to begin that long, tempting and often shocking journey through the experiences of others which is, year by year, to wear the soles of non-innocence thinner and thinner.

I should, ultimately, die innocent, if I live long enough to wear down, to have wrenched from me, to lose in a half-dream, to give wantonly away, the supply of non-innocence I brought on to earth with me. To assure myself of this desirable end, since half-way house is nowhere, I am constantly uprooting myself, climbing out of the cosy pockets, avoiding the insured cave, the bed-sitter in Babylon, the air-conditioned foxhole with T.V. In short, I do not and must not rehearse for death under the popular anaesthetics.   (*pp. 115–16*)

Wanderings and journeyings form much of the subject matter of the two later autobiographical volumes, *The Paper Chase* and *The Extra*. Even by the time he was eighteen, however, during the period of his life chronicled in *The Watcher*, Porter had discovered a second paradoxical mode of perception on which much of his later art would be erected. His description of the Porters and their relatives assembled for the Sale Show is prefaced by a remark which displays that paradox with incisive clarity:

It is difficult enough for me, an unmistakable Australian, albeit of the Awstralian rather than the Osstralian variety, to convey in words to other Australians the exact temper of the clan gatherings at Sale . . .   (*p. 106*)

The acute sociological observation which follows makes plain, as nothing else, Porter's capacity to be simultaneously solitary and representative. In so much that he said and did, in the manner of his speech and the set of his clothes, Hal Porter seemed to take pains to set himself apart from his fellow-Australians; yet one of the most oddly moving virtues of *The Watcher on the Cast-Iron Balcony* is that it offers one of the most penetrating records of a whole generation to be found anywhere in Australian literature. In order to capture the Dublin he knew so intimately, James Joyce had to fly by the nets of race, religion and language, and seek voluntary exile in Trieste and Zurich. By a more inward manoeuvre of heart and mind, Porter insinuated his way into the subtlest characteristics of his countrymen quite as surely as Joyce at the same time as he set himself apart from them. There is one telling paragraph in his book which, in its closing sentence, as clearly reveals the source of his power of understanding his fellow-countrymen as it judges them harshly:

. . . the possible strengths and certified weaknesses of the Australian character . . . laziness, vicious sentimentality, self-pity, genteelism, self-satisfaction and lack of self-discipline . . . intentions to nobility, unstinted Good Samaritanism, powerful and Puritanical stubbornness, courageous foolhardiness and a brazenly sardonic independence of outlook. These attitudes . . . belong to millions living in barbarian's luxury at the heart of many-faceted abundance.   (*p. 68–9*)

The observer of human folly and the Australian culture in which it was displayed, this 'canny and ruthless self-watcher' (p. 199) nevertheless placed his own experience at the centre of his field of observation. While *The Watcher* may be grounded in emotional skills derived from his parents, it is shaped by a psychological tactic uniquely Porter's own. There was nothing in his early circumstances to forecast his remarkable ability to be both spectator and actor in the theatre of his life. The presence of his composed yet divided self, this simultaneous watcher and participant, is perhaps the defining paradox of *The Watcher on the Cast-Iron Balcony*. Incorporated into the very structure of its syntax (' he . . . I'), it is the means by which the pressing inheritance of parents, kin, time and place, is converted into art.

The very language of *The Watcher*, as I say, its grammar, syntax, lexicon, reflects the oddly double mode of vision which integrates the crowded subject matter of Porter's life. Yet in the end, language is more than a means of expression; it becomes itself part of the autobiographer's subject. 'I am fundamentally more realistic than imaginative' (p. 118), he writes, voicing one of the surprising truths of the book; but, he goes on to add, 'inclined . . . to find words more convincing than anything else'. Whatever realities of feeling and sensibility Porter learned from his parents, language itself became his own innermost reality. Language in *The Watcher on the Cast-Iron Balcony* is relished, explored, delighted in, and displayed as fully and fondly as any phenomenon of the human or natural worlds; language, which commanded Porter's perennial enthusiasm because through and in it he could fuse and reconcile all the contrarieties of his life's experience. Near the middle of the book he allows himself a profoundly revealing aside:

. . . so deep is my pleasure in the work of the garden that, if there be a dimension after death in which grieving for the loss of the world of senses is possible, I shall grieve for no person however once agonizingly desired and passionately beloved, for no emotional adventure however uplifting, for no success however warming, no infamy however exhilarating, for nothing half so much as I shall grieve for the loss of the earth itself, the soil, the seeds, the plants, the very weeds. What this preference implies I do not know, and can only wildly guess. It is a love almost overriding my love of the words that could express that love. It is a less demanding love than the love of words which are more treacherous than plants, more corrupting than picotees, harder to control than a rosemary hedge.   (*p. 106*)

In *The Watcher on the Cast-Iron Balcony*, where for the first time he put his whole trust in autobiographical fact, Porter united his passion for nature's abundance, his mistrustful fascination with human complexity, his self-mockery and self-observation, in a language equally responsive to his love and to his artist's control.

Criticism and the universities
1967

My subject is the relation between academic critics and the rest of
the literary community, both critics and creative writers. I shall put
my thoughts on this matter in the form of three propositions and
accompanying commentary. I shall speak from the point of view of
an academic critic teaching within an Australian university English
department.

Proposition one: 'academics are awful'

I need scarcely indicate that my emphasis is ironic. The proposition
is intended to indicate not my own belief but one which, as it seems
to me, is genuine and widespread among non-academic writers in
Australia. I shall not proffer any statistical evidence to support this
view, though it is there, I am persuaded, waiting to be garnered. I
can, however, say that all the attitudes I shall review have been
expressed directly to me or in my hearing, at one time or another.
And I could trace a fairly continuous history of suspicion or
antagonism between writers and academics well back into the last
century. The classic statement of the case is, of course, Henry
Lawson's poem, 'The Uncultured Rhymer to His Cultured Critics',
addressed to his friend Jack Brereton, later Challis Professor of
English Literature in the University of Sydney.

> Must I turn aside from my destined way
>   For a task your Joss would find me?
> I come with strength of the living day,
>   And with half the world behind me;
> I leave you alone in your cultured halls
>   To drivel and croak and cavil:

Till your voice goes farther than college walls,
Keep out of the tracks we travel![1]

In our own time there continues, it seems to me, an unexamined
hostility between, on the one hand, creative writers and, on the
other, all kinds of critics, but especially those whose base of
operations is the university. The phenomenon is not restricted to
Australia, but it is, I believe, more intense and prevalent here than
in, say, the United Kingdom and the United States. Here in the
antipodes the word 'academic' is all too frequently invoked as a useful
and sometimes dishonest way of devaluing comment which, somehow
or other, is found displeasing. The peculiar irrelevance of this usage
derives from the fact that it has little or nothing to do with either
literature or criticism. The causes of its appearance are more probably
to be found in a socio-cultural study of the patterns of Australian
civilization.

If or when the grounds for the creative writers' dislike of academic
critics are articulated, they are likely to take on one or other of three
forms. The first is a claim that academic critics are parasites. They
are a collection of overpaid hatchet-men growing fat on the sweat and
labour of the underpaid novelists, poets and playwrights. Nobody,
naturally, could deny that the average annual salary of, say, the
university lecturer in English is far in excess of the average annual
earnings of the serious Australian novelist. Nevertheless, the charge
of parasitism seems to me to be among the less substantial and more
fatuous of those which are characteristically brought against
academics. The grounds for its refutation are, by the briefest count,
twofold.

First of all, the issue of relative monetary recompense opens up
the whole enormous question of the nature of culture; the way
Australian, or any, society should be constituted; the proper relation
of creative artists to their nutrient culture, the proper role of teachers
within an institutionalized and official educational system. As soon
as financial matters are permitted into any discussion, the relative
merits of competing activities can no longer be settled in terms purely
of intellectual value; they are inevitably absorbed into the socio-
political nexus. And there it does not always follow that activities of
the highest importance to the health of a culture can or should
receive the highest monetary reward.

It might be further argued that psychological considerations are
pertinent to the issue: the nature of the creative imagination and the
conditions under which it operates to the best advantage of itself and
those to whom it is addressed. There is an ancient and not easily
dismissible theory that it operates most effectively from a position of

estrangement, and exclusion from the highest kind of material recompense.

Even if that theory proves unacceptable, even if it is conceded that Australian writers could be rewarded at a higher rate without detriment to their art and that our society should be prepared so to reward them, the elementary point in logic still remains. Two wrongs do not make a right. The answer is not to deplore the level of academic salaries but actively to campaign for the financial better-ment of the creative writers. Some academics, I might add, have interested themselves in precisely that kind of campaign.

I cannot ignore the issues of intellectual dishonesty and subservi-ence implicit in the charge of parasitism, but I shall defer my discussion of those matters for a few moments. Immediately, let me pass on to the second kind of charge on which the awfulness of academics is posited: their feeble-mindedness. Academic critics write academic criticism, so runs the argument, because they cannot do anything else. They have tried to be the genuine article, a creative writer, and failed. Those that can do; those that cannot, teach and produce footnotes.

One might put up at least part of a pragmatic case against this view by reciting such names as A. D. Hope, James McAuley, Vincent Buckley, Chris Wallace-Crabbe, John Couper. The logic, however, would be shaky, and a stronger case can be argued in terms of general principle. What is essentially at issue here is, I take it, this: the need to be a demonstrably creative person in order to practise criti-cism. Clearly, some of the greatest critics in the English literary tradition have themselves been major creative writers. Nevertheless, the existence of Dr Johnson, of T. S. Eliot, of Arnold and of Lawrence does not preclude the possibility of important criticism being produced by non-creative minds. Indeed, criticism by creative writers tends to be of two kinds: either very sophisticated special pleading for the sort of art that the writer himself produces or tech-nical comment of an especially penetrating nature. And neither of these kinds, I believe, represents the limits of what criticism may be or aspire to, or even its centre. The basic role of criticism, its first responsibility, has no necessary psychological connection with crea-tive talent. That role, that responsibility, have been finely stated by Alfred Kazin in his essay, 'The Function of Criticism Today':

For the interest of criticism lies in itself, in the thinking that it practices. Criticism affects the artist only as the artist is himself a member of the educated public that reads criticism. A writer will often get better advice about a book from his editor or his wife, or his literary agent, than from a critic. But the critic, if he is interesting and deep enough, will affect the

writer far more profoundly than would specific technical criticism of his book
— by making him see the significance of his efforts. At its best, true literary
criticism may actually suggest new subjects, can enliven the imagination. This
is the great tradition of criticism, a part of the general criticism of established
values which must go on in every age.[2]

Informed discussion of values is not then peculiarly or necessarily
the talent of the creative writer; it is the talent of the critic, and his
responsibility. The responsibility of the literary critic is to derive the
material of his discourse from works of literature. The total absurdity
of denying him this right and possibility just because he did not
himself create the literature was succinctly demonstrated by C. S.
Lewis more than a quarter of a century ago, in answer to his question
'Is criticism possible?'

> It is for cooks to say whether a given dish proves skill in the cook; but
> whether the product on which this skill has been lavished is worth eating or
> no is a question on which a cook's opinion is of no particular value. We may
> therefore allow poets to tell us (at least if they are experienced in the same
> *kind* of composition) whether it is easy or difficult to write like Milton, but
> not whether the reading of Milton is a valuable experience. For who can
> endure a doctrine which would allow only dentists to say whether our teeth
> were aching, only cobblers to say whether our shoes hurt us, and only
> governments to tell us whether we were being well governed.[3]

Often to be found in close association with accusations of parasitism or hand-me-down feeblemindedness is the complaint that
academic criticism in this country is almost wholly destructive.
Academic criticism, the argument might run, is so minute, ruthless,
and desiccating in its analysis as finally to destroy the objects of its
scrutiny. The characteristic question to be heard in the corridors of
a university English department may be supposed to be, not 'Have
you read any good books lately?', but 'What are you working on?'.
Here I am constrained to admit that in the jargon of academic
criticism, 'working on' can sometimes mean 'working over' (though
more often, I am inclined to believe, in the United States than in this
country). But again one must point out an elementary but pertinent
distinction: that between minister and ministry. Without committing
myself to a sacramental view of universities, what I understand to be
at stake here is not the performance of certain academic critics but
the whole idea and process of academic criticism. Do we, after all,
condemn the whole of English poetry because Joyce Kilmer once
wrote 'Trees'? If criticism generally is to be thought of as the
informed discussion of values in the field of literature, the essential
question is simply this: what special contribution can academics make

to this discussion which is peculiarly their own? I shall defer my answer to this question to a later point in this essay. For the time being, the gloss on my first text being now concluded, I shall proceed to my second proposition.

Proposition two: 'academics should be encapsulated'

My tone continues ironical. My intention now is to examine that attitude towards literary academics which, permitting them some contact with literary texts, would isolate them from contact with any real literary issues. On this argument they should abstain from any kind of popular reviewing in the dailies or weeklies, even perhaps the monthly or quarterly magazines, and retreat where they belong — into the fastnesses of the ivory tower. There, leaving criticism to the professionals, they would do no harm to anybody as they went about their proper business of logic-chopping, footnote-grinding, and, of course, teaching. This prescription may or may not be kindly intentioned, but it seems no more genuinely helpful than that of those bitterer souls who think of academics as wholly awful.

Such a strategic withdrawal is rendered impossible by the necessary interlocking of scholarship and teaching on the one hand, and criticism, on the other. The relation between teaching and criticism, indeed, is arguably closer than that between criticism and literature. The point can be readily made through two obvious and unavoidable examples. In order to teach literature — English, Australian, whatever — somebody has to draw up some sort of a syllabus, however informal. A syllabus can be drawn up only by a process of inclusion and exclusion based on a rational judgement of the range of available works; that is to say, by repeated acts of discrimination, by the process of informed discourse about values which is the essence of criticism. Even if conceivably a set of texts, once decided upon, could be presented with absolute pedagogic neutrality, the very fact that these works and not others were being presented would soon convey to any moderately bright student that judgement and discrimination were inseparable from the teaching and learning of literature.

By way of a second illustration, one might consider an alternative suggestion that university teaching of literature should be confined to literary history — in particular, the literary history of periods prior to our own. The best of the American critics, men like Kazin and Lionel Trilling, are, I believe, peculiarly sensitive to the competing temptations of contemporary literature and that of the past. Passing over, however, the theoretical problem of deciding just what is literary as opposed to other kinds of history, it is an Englishman,

Graham Hough, whom I call upon to demonstrate the practical impossibility of teaching even the history of earlier literature without the exercise of critical discrimination. This is what he has to say on the matter, writing in *The Dream and the Task*:

> . . . a case is often put for literary history as a separate department, and it will be best to get it out of the way. The fact is that all literary history depends on previous critical acts. The mere choice of one set of works rather than another is a critical act. To give twenty pages to one writer, ten to a second, and two lines to a third is a critical act. If literary history were not informed by criticism it might well devote itself to tabulating the themes and conventions in the novels of Marie Corelli . . . On the other hand, the critic needs to be enough of a historian to know what works exist, in what chronological order, what material is relevant for purposes of comparison — and a dozen other things of the same nature. In fact the two activities are so intertwined that it is senseless partisanship to set up an opposition between them.[4]

The quarantine of academic critics within their lecture rooms, protected by sandbagged barricades of variorum editions, then, to my mind represents an unreal solution to the problem of their relation to the rest of the community of literature. Believing, therefore, that their current status and function in Australia are sadly misunderstood and misrepresented, and that any proposal to enclose them within a *cordon sanitaire* would be wrong-headed in both theory and practice, I am under some obligation to outline my own solution to the difficulty — which brings me to my third proposition.

Proposition three: 'academics are people'

The decidedly unironic aim of this proposition is to claim for academics the same range of rights, privileges and responsibilities as would be accorded to any group of adult and often complex individuals who have committed themselves to a reputable profession, a distinct and recognizable brand of intellectual and imaginative endeavour. I shall come straight to the point, and suggest that the role and function of the academic literary critic can with some fairness be described in terms of a fourfold duty — to the academy, to teaching, to literature and to society.

In speaking of an academic critic's duty to the academy I wish at least to touch upon a subject which, to the best of my knowledge, has been largely ignored in this country. I can perhaps best put the issue in the form of a question. Is the academic critic doing the same job as any other critic except that by some happy chance he is enabled to do it in the ease, comfort and security ensured by his university appointment? Or does he have an obligation to adhere to certain habits of mind and thought which are or should be the common property of all members of a university — academic critic, physicist, economist, philosopher, agricultural scientist?

In practice, I suspect, the former position has been adopted by most Australian academic critics and accepted by non-academic writers. It may well be that it is the proper one. For all that, even a cursory examination of the second possibility discloses issues too often ignored, I believe, by Australian university English departments. If any intellectual commitment unites all the members of a university, it is surely the disinterested pursuit of truth within a defined or definable body of knowledge. Now, disinterestedness as a value *per se* runs counter to a widespread tendency in our English departments to treat literary criticism as a means of imposing this or that value system on literary judgement. A result of our present practice is often to disregard any sort of philosophical effort to establish the nature of literature on the basis of the available evidence in favour of inculcating a set of value judgements about the major texts in the English canon in accordance with passionately held discriminatory principles. Nobody has pointed more uncompromisingly to this academic failure of academic English departments than Northrop Frye. Nobody has advanced a more austere programme of rectification than the one he adumbrates in 'The Archetypes of Literature', the lead essay in *Fables of Identity*:

Our first step, therefore, is to recognize and get rid of meaningless criticism: that is, talking about literature in a way that cannot help to build up a systematic structure of knowledge. Casual value-judgements belong not to criticism but to the history of taste, and reflect, at best, only the social and psychological compulsions which prompted their utterance. All judgements in which the values are not based on literary experience but are sentimental or derived from religious or political prejudice may be regarded as casual . . . . This sort of thing cannot be part of any systematic study, for a systematic study can only progress: whatever dithers or vacillates or reacts is merely leisure-class conversation.[5]

The academic critic does have an obligation, I believe, disinterestedly to inquire into the nature of literature, and let the chips fall where they may. Here, if anywhere, the complaint against academic destructiveness has its locus as a genuine issue. It may well be uncomfortable for writers to realize that within the ivory tower their works and they themselves are being subjected to dispassionate scrutiny. I would suggest, however, that they should feel no more ill at ease or outraged than when the literary academics, in their turn, find themselves the objects of enquiry by, for instance, their psychologist colleagues.

And, of course, the possible dehumanization of literature and the academic critics is prevented by the nature of literature and the full responsibility of academic criticism. For, if the literature is good enough it will survive and indeed be enriched by disinterested examination; and such examination does not by any means represent the academic critic's full responsibility. His responsibility is to criticism as well as to the academy; and criticism I have described as the informed discussion of values in the field of literature. These two responsibilities of the academic critic fuse in the humanistic concern of his teaching.

In the day-to-day encounters with his students, the literary academic in Australia characteristically carries out his tasks with competence and, not infrequently, with distinction. Nevertheless, in the general fulfilment of our duty to teaching we have, I believe, no reason for complacency. Sincere personal practice cannot have its fullest effect when it is carried on in an outmoded system. And, to put the point extremely, the theory which underlies the practice of Australian university English departments is, if not obsolete, in some important respects obsolescent.

In general terms, we may say that the characteristic orthodoxy of our English departments is Cambridge, approximately 1917. Such a state of affairs in Australia in 1968 does not seem to me good enough. If we are failing, it is because we do not often enough ask the simple but hard questions — what are we teaching? whom? when? where? why? We are, in fact, teaching a large segment of the eligible population in a country which is steadily moving away from its British origins and connections. I am not sure that a system appropriate to a British socio-economic élite of fifty years ago was ever appropriate to this country. In 1968 I am almost convinced that it is not. I am encouraged in this heresy by an Australian and an Englishman — Manning Clark and, again, Graham Hough. In a recent review of Donald Horne's *The Education of Young Donald*, Professor Clark spoke of 'a decision made in the Australian colonies in the 1840's and 1850's — namely, to transplant to Australia an education system designed for the education of a governing class in England'. He went on to suggest that 'This may explain why the universities of Sydney and Melbourne, unlike the state universities in America, became billabongs cut off from the mainstream of life'.[6]

Graham Hough, again in *The Dream and the Task*, argues that the British system is probably breaking down even in Britain. He sees a hiatus between the great monuments of the literary past and the contemporary world — a hiatus that can be spanned only by some radical rethinking and reorganization of our university programmes in literary education. After speaking of the two competing approaches to English literature current in British universities he proposes his own remedy:

. . . we can best effect a fruitful reconciliation by abandoning the purely literary and the purely English in favour of a general literary education on a wider base.

But on this system the school of English, as our universities would understand it, would disappear? Yes, it would; and I think it is about time. So for that matter would the school of modern languages. What would take their place would be a school of literature, with many options, many varieties of choice. Classicists, philosophers, historians and divines would also have to leave the prison-houses of their expertise. The shutting of English higher education into watertight compartments has been a calamity, and we shall not get rid of the spiritless *accidia* that so often afflicts the arts departments of our universities until it is broken down.[7]

Even in my wildest fantasies, I cannot see Australian arts faculties adopting Hough's recommendations this year, or even next. Nevertheless, I submit that all academic teachers and critics of English in this country — a country wherein social conditions are shifting with marked rapidity away from the system of literary education that they support — should at least be prepared to pay serious attention to what he has to say.

The kind of changes that Hough suggests, even if only partly implemented and within an existing departmental structure, would have a number of important consequences for English department syllabuses. They would almost certainly be re-shaped to include more Australian literature, more literature in translation, and more contemporary literature. The first possibility I welcome, the second I regard with equanimity, the third I greet with a slightly wary exhilaration. If it is objected that Australian literature has too much that is minor, I will reply with Randall Jarrell that I cannot hope properly to value the major works until I have learned to appreciate the minor. If it is objected that great works cannot be fully appreciated in translation, I will agree but claim the right to try to appreciate them in part. If I am told that responding to contemporary literature is the most difficult and dangerous of critical activities, I will concur, insist that in order to go on living I must from time to time stick my neck out and have it chopped off, and go on to quote Frank Kermode:

I have often wondered why people who think English literature a self-sufficient discipline do not see the need to discuss, in class, the very latest things, before there has been time for anybody to 'place' them. It is after all implied that the discipline will facilitate accurate placing of just such works; why we don't, from time to time, sit with our students and discuss work on which there is as yet no received opinion — the latest Fulcrum Press publication or, for that matter, a new novel chosen at random — I cannot think.[8]

You will begin by now, I hope, to see that in my view of things the academic's duty to teaching is not only important in itself but has the further value of holding his duty to the academy and his duty to literature in dynamic engagement. If he is to operate adequately as a teacher, he will never be able to forget that criticism is the informed discussion of values in the field of literature, he will never abandon his advance post in the world outside the ivory tower. His duty to literature must involve him in issues as well as texts, issues which have their existence in actual human experience; it must involve him in personal judgement. Remembering Kazin's notion that criticism is 'concerned explicitly, fightingly, with an ideal of man, with a conception of what man is seeking to become, with what he must become';[9] remembering that his subject is literature, he will put his properly academic disinterestedness to the service of society, to the service of man.

In practice, this means he will not withdraw from such activities as reviewing for the weeklies, or writing for the monthlies, preparing educational scripts for radio, even making occasional television appearances, or, when protest is needed, writing a protesting letter to the editorial columns of a responsible newspaper. He will, however, engage in these activities only in moderation; he will be entitled to do so at all only if he is first of all true to his university duties. A judging criticism springing from wide knowledge and tenacious thought can, I believe, work nothing but good in our society; it is a kind of criticism the literary academic is peculiarly fitted to make. It is, too, a kind of criticism which other writers dismiss only to their own detriment. I could devoutly wish that all our daily reviewers had the benefit of a university training, which they were able and willing to recall in the practice of their art. If, as I have tried to argue, academic critics have a positive duty towards society, society (in which I include creative writers and non-academic critics) has a positive duty towards them: to pay attention.

I am not proposing the dissolution of that antagonism whose actuality was the starting point of my remarks in an orgy of mutual backslapping and bonhomie. I am contending for its replacement by a lively intellectual tension from which all parties could derive profit. If this recommendation has a latter-day Arnoldian ring, I cannot confess to any dismay. For, in reviewing the ideas I have been trying to set down, I find that I have been moved most urgently to quote from pieces which bear such titles as *Is Criticism Possible?*, *The Function of Criticism Today*, *The Age of Criticism*, *A Programme for Literary Education*. Perhaps in the end, then, I should come out into the open and conclude with a quotation from the inspiration and source of them all:

It is the business of the critical power . . . 'in all branches of knowledge, theology, philosophy, history, art, science, to see the object as in itself it really is'. Thus it tends, at last, to make an intellectual situation of which the creative power can profitably avail itself. It tends to establish an order of ideas, if not absolutely true, yet true by comparison with that which it displaces; to make the best ideas prevail. Presently these new ideas reach society, the touch of truth is the touch of life, and there is a stir and growth everywhere; out of this stir and growth come the creative epochs of literature.[10]

Criticism and the individual talent
1972

> . . . all human beings are the products of their culture to a much greater degree than we ordinarily imagine, and . . . cultures appear to grow in patterns and to fulfil or exhaust these. Why cultures so often behave in this way, especially in their intellectual, aesthetic, and nationalistic aspects, is not clear; but it seems to be one of their most distinctive properties.
>
> A. L. Kroeber, *Configurations of Culture Growth*[1]

I

Brian Kiernan's *Images of Society and Nature: Seven Essays on Australian Novels*[2] would have been a better book had its title and sub-title been transposed; at least such a metathesis would have brought its most valuable features into clearer focus. As things stand the main title, *Images of Society and Nature*, promises rather more than it delivers; epitomizes rather than resolves what I take to be certain problems current in literary criticism.

In fairness to Kiernan, I should say that this back-to-front reaction was prompted by some of the preoccupations at present in the foreground of my own mind. That a reading of this book did not remove those preoccupations into the background is in itself a kind of judgement on it, but a judgement which, let me hasten to add, has more to do with critical theory than any adverse sense of Brian Kiernan's practice. Indeed, had I read his several commentaries under the title of *Seven Essays on Australian Novels*, I am sure that my admiration for his achievement would have been cordial and unqualified.

For, taken one at a time, the individual studies of *Images of Society and Nature* offer much that is both worth saying and well said. Chapter 1, devoted to Furphy's *Such is Life*, might serve as a model for Kiernan's characteristic achievement. There seems to me nothing startlingly new or revolutionary here; the strength of the essay resides in its careful refinement upon what have by now been firmly established as the major critical issues generated by *Such is Life* — the relation of Tom Collins to Joseph Furphy, the limitations of Collins's understanding, the distinctions between appearance and reality, and so on. Giving fair acknowledgement to the charter work carried out by such a critic as A. D. Hope, Brian Kiernan makes his particular contribution through his discussion of the aesthetic status of Furphy's novel, the operations of its structural conventions.

The other particular studies of *Images of Society and Nature* maintain much the same kind and level of performance as Chapter 1. The account of Herbert's *Capricornia* (ch. 4) is especially useful in its treatment of the novel's Dickensian symbolism and comic distortions, while there is a fine and just responsiveness in what Kiernan has to say about Christina Stead's *Seven Poor Men of Sydney* and *For Love Alone* (ch. 3). Easily the best in the whole book, Chapter 5 is also the longest. This sympathetic survey of Patrick White's achievement is notable for its commentary on *The Vivisector*, a commentary which is likely to become an essential reference point in future dealings with that novel. Chapter 5 is also noteworthy for the development of Kiernan's pervasive interest in the structures of fiction into some very engaging ideas about White's use of 'parodic form'. I regret, indeed, that these ideas were not further developed to become the unifying *motif* of the whole book.

If Kiernan is at his best on Patrick White, he falls a little below his characteristic level in his treatment of Henry Handel Richardson (in ch. 2), and especially in his remarks on *Australia Felix*. In this instance, it seems to me that he was somewhat unfair to his chosen author, perhaps because too little sympathetic to the mode of fiction she was attempting. In the general Introduction, Kiernan speaks rather slightingly of 'the reportage of manners and morals' (p. vii) and, categorizing *Australia Felix* in this class of writing, he can find little good to say for it. To be sure, for Australian readers who have been touched by the Gothic splendours of White's symbolic fictions, it is all too easy to relegate any other kind of novel to a necessary inferiority. Yet we need only think of, say, 'Yo lo vi' scrawled on one of Goya's *The Disasters of War* etchings to be thrust back into sympathy with the direct human passion which can make 'reportage' the basis of great art. Something of that passion (not certainly, at Goya's intensity) is, I believe, to be found in *Australia Felix*.

Yet a single disagreement of this kind would scarcely justify my suggestion that *Images of Society and Nature* 'exemplifies . . . certain problems current in literary criticism'. To make good that claim I must refer to some of the larger attitudes and procedures of the book, especially those laid bare in the Introduction and in the final chapter, 'The Australian Novel and Tradition'. It is through the ideas expressed here that Kiernan seeks to give his book its conceptual coherence and unifying framework. He sanctions his choice of texts, thus, by an appeal to, among other matters, 'relevance': 'The relevance of a novelist's vision of our society to our own experience of it is something that concerns the readers of all Australian novels' (p. vii), and again, 'The key critical criterion should be the relevance to us now of the works examined *as* novels' (p. vii). Few vogue words in twentieth-century criticism seem to me to have outstripped their usefulness faster than this one. Too often, 'relevance' now stands for little more than its user's socio-cultural prejudices: 'what is relevant is what I like (or have read)'.

I will not do Brian Kiernan the discourtesy of imputing that kind of usage to him. Nevertheless, his advocacy of the criterion of 'relevance' seems to me seriously weakened by a failure to give the idea any kind of concrete actuality. For all its appeals to relevance and contemporaneity, *Images of Society and Nature* nowhere transmits any real sense of what Australian society is like now or has been in the past, or why some works should be more pertinent to contemporary Australians than others. Anybody who appeals to 'relevance' in the way that Kiernan does is under the obligation to make his chosen texts say to us, in an unmistakable way, *'de te fabula'*. This he conspicuously fails to do.

But the demand that major works of art manifest an immediate and practical application to contemporary behaviour is, if not misguided (and it isn't), at least limited in its rewards. The 'relevance' of the permanently important works of art is guaranteed as much by their permanence as by their malleability in the hands of a committed commentator on contemporary culture. A central part of the critic's task is not merely to enumerate the items of modernity exhibited by his chosen text but to demonstrate the inherent and continuing value of its own structures and strategies. Kiernan clearly has a grasp on this principle, and attempts to put it into practice (if there is a model for *Images of Society and Nature*, I would guess it to be F. R. Leavis's *The Great Tradition*). Yet still I find that his book stands as a symptom of rather than a solution to the problems of criticism.

Perhaps I may put the point in the form of a question which presented itself to me with greater and greater insistence as I read through *Images of Society and Nature*: for what kind of audience was Brian Kiernan writing? Certainly not one of professional scholars. The approach is 'critical rather than biographical or historical'

(p. viii), and the text eschews the niceties of scholarship. On the other hand, if he were aiming at the amateur of literature (who presumably should be the prime target of one who advocates 'relevance') he has again missed his mark. In this respect, reading *Images of Society and Nature* reminded me of John Wain's article, 'The Disappearing Critic'.[3] Wain's basic premise is, quite bluntly, that 'the age of criticism is over' (p. 165), and a good deal of his article is concerned to contrast the present diminished importance of literary criticism as a social and cultural force with the prestige it enjoyed in England in the period 1945–60. He writes of the attitudes he and his young contemporaries brought to literary criticism in those years:

We tended to assume that the actual engineering of social change, by means of legislation and so forth, could best be left to professionals; we believed that what a civilisation needs is the right quality of *feeling*. To respond to life with one's emotional priorities in the right order — that was the ideal . . . when asked where this wholeness [of life], this honesty, were demonstrated our answer was: 'In major literature — in the great books, past and present, which make up our tradition . . .'

To us, then, it seemed that literary criticism was a truly central activity, relevant to every area of human life. It was serious, it was constructive, and because of its gladiatorial element it was also exciting. (*p. 166*)

I am fairly sure that literary criticism did not, during the post-war years, enjoy quite the prestige in this country that it did, on Wain's evidence, in the United Kingdom. But I am fairly confident that it has shared in the same decline, the same shift towards the periphery of cultural significance. The causes of this changed state of affairs must be complex, including as Wain argues, the advent of new information technologies, altered attitudes towards the past, the rising status of the social sciences. They also include, I suspect, a failure on the part of criticism itself. The trouble with the profession of criticism today is that it has become, in a sense, too skilled, too expert, too professional. Its techniques are manipulated with such competence and confidence that there seems no further possibility of surprise, nothing with which it cannot cope, no text whose grandeurs it cannot contain.

In this situation of critical over-efficiency, it seems to me that the audience for *Images of Society and Nature* is most likely to be other critics. At home with its vocabulary and methods, they will be able to appreciate its many and real insights into the novels it discusses. The common reader — even, I am afraid, the young enthusiast in search of vivid contact with either society or nature — will most probably pass it by.

It may be, of course, that criticism will rest content with its codified techniques and diminished impact, and simply go on talking to itself. If, however, it wishes to regain something of its lost power and prestige, it must find some way of incorporating into its expertise the capacity for astonishment — find, that is to say, some way of rejuvenating its language. An alternative (or complementary) means by which criticism might re-establish its contact with vital human experience, without degenerating into either propaganda or impressionism, could be through a rigorous and thorough-going attempt to understand the relationships between the individual literary talent of the present and those of the past. Towards the end of 'The Disappearing Critic', John Wain writes of an attitude towards the past which, I suspect, is as prevalent in Australia as in England:

It is quite common to meet people in their twenties, often well-read and highly intelligent, who genuinely feel that the present age is so different from anything that went before that the bridges have been dynamited and nothing can come over to us from the past . . .

As long as this attitude prevails, criticism will inevitably stay out in the cold.   (*p. 167*)

The definition of criticism that Wain takes over from Frank Kermode — 'the medium in which past work survives' — indicates an important way in which criticism can bring itself back into the warm centre of cultural life. One of the great tasks for criticism at the moment is a disinterested investigation of the principles of literary historiography. When the profession of criticism has demonstrated an intimate and necessary connection between, on the one hand, the individual work of literature and the society in which it exists, and on the other, contemporary literary activity and that of the past, it may once again be listened to with the respect it once enjoyed and still rightly hopes for.

What is at stake is, quite simply, the nature of literary tradition. Now, as Brian Kiernan quite properly states at the beginning of Chapter 7 of *Images of Society and Nature*, 'We are constantly being assured that there is an Australian tradition' (p. 159). And the whole of the chapter is devoted to the theoretical problems connected with defining that tradition, along with some of the phenomena which may be deemed to characterize it. Some of Kiernan's substantive conclusions seem to me interesting and useful: his stress on Romantic and counter-Romantic themes in Australian literature is of a piece with his more particular analyses, i.e., refinement upon ideas already current. His demonstration of the generative force of European models is valuable, and would be worth developing further. What is for me the final disappointment, however, is the theoretical case which is argued in Chapter 7 in order to justify the generalizations and to unify the six preceding commentaries.

Kiernan thus opens a chapter on 'The Australian Novel and the Tradition' by asserting the inadequacy of the 'socio-literary approach' to literary tradition as exemplified in, for instance, Vance Palmer's *The Legend of the Nineties* — an accumulation of data treated as an inert background to literature conceived of as a report on the environment. He then proceeds to develop his own position by contrasting the difficulties of the Australian literary historian with those of his English and American counterparts.

The problems met with in considering 'the Australian tradition' are peculiarly different at the theoretical level from those met with in considering 'the English tradition' or 'the American tradition' within the contexts of English and American literatures, and it is instructive to consider the uses of 'tradition' in the writings of critics of these literatures. (*p. 164*)

I must say I do not find what follows convincing as either a demonstration of the 'peculiar difference' of the Australian tradition or a theoretical basis for considering literary traditions in general.

It is not so much that Kiernan's chief references are now such well worn ones: T. S. Eliot's 'Tradition and the Individual Talent' (1919) and F. R. Leavis's *The Great Tradition* (1948). It is rather that, in turning these references to his own uses, he seems to accept such a complete hiatus between what one might call Arnoldian high culture and the social anthropologist's culture as to make his sense of literary tradition quite unreal. The crux of the matter is to be found in two sentences on p. 171:

If we are going to seek an Australian tradition of the novel . . . we will seek it amongst our finest novelists first of all and ask if they have anything in common beyond their being related by their birth or their art to Australia. Whether each was influenced by his predecessors or experienced the same social milieu as his contemporaries are questions irrelevant to the primary concern of locating the best novelists; only in them will we find any meaningful basis for considering whether there is an 'Australian tradition' of the novel.

Now this, so far as it goes, seems to me unexceptionable: one clearly must begin any attempt to discern a literary tradition by looking for it among what practical criticism tells us are the master-works rather than the quantitatively dominant ones. But I find it difficult to accept Kiernan's further working assumptions: that because certain novels are master-works, their themes and appeal are 'universal' and should not, therefore, indeed cannot, be referred to the conditions of a specific culture to account, not for their merit, but for their particular quality.

In other words, it is my view that Australian (or any other) culture offers defining contexts of possibility which have a great deal to do with the concrete universals that its major writers seize upon as their themes and the forms and language through which they turn them into literature. Among these contexts of possibility must be included (as measures of understanding not of judgement), precisely those matters of social *milieu* and influence which Kiernan rules out as irrelevant. If they are not conceded to operate upon a national literature, that literature may be allowed to exhibit certain characteristic phenomena but scarcely a tradition — which is certainly a matter of cultural continuity though not necessarily of conservatism (a view which Kiernan imputes to Vance Palmer and Arthur Phillips on p. 163 of *Images of Society and Nature*). The idea of a literary tradition must accommodate some understanding of how it is in fact transmitted. Otherwise we may fairly speak of a literary heritage, but not of a tradition.

From the view that I have been adumbrating, it might seem that the delineation of a literary tradition would be best left in future to the historian and the sociologist. The literary critic would indeed be foolish to refuse their aid if his interests turn to the idea of an Australian tradition; but he need not leave the task entirely to them. One particular skill of the practical critic, in fact, seems to me notably pertinent to the investigation of a literary tradition: his skill in analysing and handling image and metaphor. There is one pregnant sentence from T. S. Eliot's essay on 'Shakespeare and the Stoicism of Seneca' which, in this regard, is probably just as useful as the whole of that on 'Tradition and the Individual Talent': 'the great poet, in writing himself, writes his time'.[4] He does so, surely, when and if the images that he accepts into his art well up from so deep a level of his own imagination that they illuminate and touch upon the culture in which he participates. No writer invents his metaphors *ex nihilo*; in the long run he finds them somewhere in the range of possibility that his culture makes available to him. The metaphors of great art may perhaps be defined as the point at which the thrust of the individual imagination intersects with the profoundest myths by which a given culture lives.

The means of utilizing such a theoretical dictum must be diverse, but at least one is immediately suggested by *Images of Society and Nature*. Brian Kiernan frequently speaks of the need to locate and respect his authors' 'deepest concerns'. Now, among novelists who have created figures such as Voss, Maurice Guest, Phelim Halloran,

Tom Collins, among novelists who may be interpreted against the pattern of Romanticism, these 'deepest concerns' will often manifest themselves in dream work, undertaken at various levels of consciousness, and under various degrees of control. Kiernan's studies of the Romantic element in selected Australian novelists do not, in the end, solve the historiographical problems they confront, but they do hint at some useful lines of advance. In contemplating the dreams recorded in Australian literature, it may be that we will come to a fuller understanding of its heritage and the processes by which that heritage has become a tradition.

II

Freud was right, profoundly right, when he showed 'that the dream is a compromise between the expression of and defence against the unconscious emotions; that in it the unconscious wish is represented as being fulfilled; that there are very definite mechanisms that control this expression; that the primary process controls the dream world just as it controls the entire unconscious life of the soul, and that myth and poetical productions come into being in the same way and have the same meaning. There is only one important difference: in the myths and in the works of poets the secondary elaboration is much further developed, so that a logical and coherent entity is created.' It is hard to exaggerate the importance of this difference, of course; yet usually we do exaggerate it — do write as if that one great difference had hidden from us the greater similarities which underlie it.

Randall Jarrell[5]

As a prolegomenon to the kind of enterprise I have been recommending, I offer here only the sketchiest comments on three exhibits, chosen not entirely at random.

The first is Les Murray's poem, 'An Absolutely Ordinary Rainbow'.[6] This representation of the public panic caused by the spectacle of a weeping man is on the face of it a highly idiosyncratic fantasy, created in response to what personal impulse it would be impertinent and irrelevant to enquire. The first responsibility of practical criticism is rather to discover whether the utterance has been brought under the kind of stabilizing control which will transform it from indulgent daydream into poetry.

The approved and expert skills of criticism will, I believe, very readily demonstrate that such a transformation has been effected. The rhetoric of the poem's development, in the first place, bespeaks an aesthetic authority beyond the reach of uncritical wish-fulfilment. The opening stanza makes the point sufficiently well:

> The word goes round Repins, the murmur goes round Lorenzinis,
> At Tattersalls, men look up from sheets of numbers,
> The Stock Exchange scribblers forget the chalk in their hands
> And men with bread in their pockets leave the Greek club:
> There's a fellow crying in Martin Place. They can't stop him.

The balance of the first two clauses, the reverse balance of the third, the careful weighing of the last short sentence against the rest of the stanza: this sort of syntactic discipline very clearly brings narrative order to the dream. At the same time the colloquial diction ('The word goes round Repins') is ironically played off against the distinctly extra-ordinary event as a means of making the poem's content accessible to the judging intelligence. The tonal fusion of amused contempt, disbelief, and the beginnings of unease in the fourth line indicates a complex emotional relation to the subject alien to the needs of fantasy.

Similar controls can be seen at work throughout the poem. While the narrative itself undergoes that swelling distortion so characteristic of unquiet dreams there is irrefutable evidence, stanza by stanza, that this is the ordered utterance of a very considerable poet. Part of this order is the sense, built into the very bones of the poem, that the unreal experience it relates has significance for its readers as well as for its author. The assertion of shared responsibility for as well as participation in the daydream stems in particular from the rhythms of the verse. 'The crowds are edgy with talk', Murray writes in Stanza II, and there is a sustained metrical edginess in the poem which forbids any passive reception of it.

We may, then, say of 'An Absolutely Ordinary Rainbow' that it focuses the normally distorting perspectives of daydream–fantasy on to some of the great commonplace themes of poetry which have become platitudinous and inert in other forms of verse statement. The simple universality of the poem's meaning is rendered transparently clear in lines like these:

> But the weeping man, like the earth, requires nothing,
> The man who weeps ignores us, and cries out
> Of his writhen face and ordinary body
>
> Not words, but grief, not messages, but sorrow
> Hard as the earth, sheer, present as the sea —

If this universality of meaning needed any further reinforcement, it would probably be fair to relate the central image of the poem, a man weeping, to one of the most famous verses in the New Testament, John 11:35, 'Jesus wept'. Christ, seeing Mary's grief at the death of

Lazarus, was, like Murray's weeper, giving expression to inerodible human feeling.

If allusion to the Bible may strengthen our sense that 'An Absolutely Ordinary Rainbow' transforms a personal fantasy into a statement of universal compassion, it is nevertheless my contention that the minute particulars through which that universality is realized are peculiarly a function of Murray's cultural context. Indeed, the images of the poem offer a very fair example of that intersection of personal impulse and profound cultural assumption out of which, I earlier suggested, literary traditions arise.

It is necessary, thus, to point to the fact that the poem is located in Sydney and that its narrative depends upon a very precise exploitation of the topography of that city. While this is arguably a superficial point, I would not want to dismiss it as a negligible one. (How far can one ignore the geography of London in discussing the universal significance of, say, Pope's *Dunciad* or the Prophetic Books of William Blake?) More difficult because less tangible, cultural issues, however, begin to appear in the third stanza of the poem:

> The man we surround, the man no one approaches
> Simply weeps, and does not cover it, weeps
> Not like a child, not like the wind, like a man
> And does not declaim it, nor beat his breast, nor even
> Sob very loudly —

It seems to me significant that the poet here associates himself with the crowd rather than the weeper (he does so again in a later stanza: 'Ridiculous, says a man near me, and stops/His mouth with his hands'). In that association, it may be, is revealed the essential Australianness of Murray's poem. One can certainly find elsewhere among the best works of contemporary Australian writers supporting evidence for such a view. One thinks of Alf Dubbo helplessly watching the crucifixion of Himmelfarb, of Le Mesurier observing Voss's fatal pilgrimage. One thinks of Hal Porter, self-styled Watcher on the cast-iron balcony. In 'An Absolutely Ordinary Rainbow', it appears, Les Murray may have drawn from his inmost imagination an image which illuminates and sums up a phenomenon crucial to Australian culture. Is the role of the artist in Australia, we may be led to ask, peculiarly spectatorial? Is he moved to creation less by experiencing suffering than by observing it?

And what, too, of the crowd with which the artist is identified? Can 'An Absolutely Ordinary Rainbow' offer us, in this connection too, some image wherein the private imagination and its cultural matrix meet on equal terms? The crucial feature of the poem, here, is surely the transformation of a 'crowd' into a 'concourse' in the disturbing presence of the weeper. The Australian spectators of this awful display of feeling are drawn together into psychological solidarity as they draw apart from the solitary individual who is unabashed by emotion. Only rare exceptions — a woman, a child — are capable of receiving the weeper's gift of emotion. All the rest stand aside. Even the police, those in authority, are withdrawn and subdued, powerless to touch the stranger they had initially tried to arrest. Does not Les Murray's daydream begin to take on a peculiarly antipodean outline?

And what, in the end, of the weeper himself? He is certainly a charismatic figure, and the consistent images of magic and extra-rationality might seem to impute to him some religious authority — 'Only the smallest children/And such as look out of Paradise come near him'. Yet at its literal centre, the poem insists on the complete secularity of the weeper's behaviour. The lines will condone no appeal to either a human or a natural sentimentality: the fellow 'weeps/Not like a child, not like the wind'. They will countenance no false religiosity:

> Some will say, in the years to come, a halo
> Of force stood around him. There is no such thing.

This is simply (and the irony of the fact is enforced by the title) a man weeping. And the precise concatenation of social hysteria and gritty humanism may open up understanding of far more in Australian life than the apparently isolated phenomenon of a single poem; as, indeed, may the final laconic refusal of cult-worship by Les Murray's weeper; 'Evading believers, he hurries off down Pitt Street'.

Surmise about the relation between the daydream images of a single poet and the patterns of his nutrient culture must, I suppose, remain largely in the area of surmise. Such images will be more useful to the literary historian if they can be associated with evidence of a more solid kind — of the kind, perhaps, to be found in the Proem to Henry Handel Richardson's *Australia Felix*, which Brian Kiernan, as I have noted, is inclined to treat somewhat dismissively. What gives the Proem its special significance for a theory of literary tradition is the status that Richardson herself assigned it. 'This dream it was' begins its penultimate and climactic paragraph. And the dream which Richardson is concerned to make actual in her prose is of a very different order from that which forms the basis of 'An Absolutely Ordinary Rainbow'. What in effect she is portraying is an antipodean equivalent to an idea widely familiar in the northern context: the 'American Dream'. The Proem to *Australia Felix* presents a microcosmic image of the social aspirations, motives, drives, of mid-nineteenth-century Australians, as Richardson consciously understood them.

This elevation of personal insight and intuition into deliberated social comment may usefully be referred to as a technique of controlled vision, a vision which has its origin in the image-making capacity of the writer's imagination but which is tested against the actuality of the social and phenomenal world. But — and this is a major consideration in arguing the critical case for *Australia Felix* to be considered among the major works out of which we must discover our tradition — the Proem is not an excrescence, an unintegrated historical set-piece tacked on to the front of a trilogy which is solely concerned with the private tragedy of an individual. The Proem, a necessary part of Richardson's fictional structure, stands as an emblem of Mahony's fate as it is determined by and worked out in relation to the Australian cultural dream. It is the first active demonstration of the point made quite explicit in the epigraph from Sir Thomas Browne's *Religio Medici*:

Every man is not only himself; . . . men are lived over again; the world is now as it was in ages past; there was none then, but there hath been some since, that parallels him, and is, as it were, his revived self.[7]

If one is prepared to read the Proem as an ordered and tested vision of some of the wellsprings of Australian life and a forecast of Richard Mahony's place in it, the theme of burial alive, as argued by F. H. Mares and accepted by Brian Kiernan (p. 46), becomes only one strand in a highly complex piece of cultural symbolism. For instance, the view expressed by J. G. Robertson, Richardson's husband, has quite as much to recommend it:

The Fortunes of Richard Mahony is then a book about the *auri fames* with which the great southern continent attracted to herself her first settlers; from first page to last it is a book about money; and with more justification than Zola's novel, it might have borne the little word money as its title.[8]

These words have their suggestiveness to cultural interpreters as well as to practical critics. They point to a line of enquiry which might investigate Australian life as organized around, deeply deriving from, a hope of unearned, suddenly acquired wealth. The Australian Dream would then be seen as radically different from the American phenomenon so tellingly represented in, say, Scott Fitzgerald's *The Great Gatsby*, the closing pages of which project a cultural vision in many ways comparable to Richardson's Proem.

The dream of wealth that is set out in the opening of *Australia Felix* arguably was transmitted both as theme and attitude into the mining trilogies of Vance Palmer and Katharine Susannah Prichard; was transmuted into, for instance, John Morrison's fascination with the consequences of sudden wealth or Frank Hardy's obsession with gambling; was perhaps even absorbed into Brennan's map of the imagination which figured forth the highest treasures of the spirit as 'rich Cipangos of the mind'.[9] For, in spite of what is often described as its dully photographic prose, the Proem is alive with cultural hint and implication, many located in the figure of a weeper quite other than that of 'An Absolutely Ordinary Rainbow'. To be sure, the first paragraph of the Proem describes the death of Bill, the young miner buried alive in the shaft. Thereafter, however, Richardson's interest is concentrated on Long Jim, weeping for his own hard destiny. He weeps out of self-pity, for the solitariness of life on the diggings, for the lonely anonymity of life in Australia. Literally an important connection between the Proem and the narrative of Richard Mahony, in his tearful desolation Jim forges an important symbolic link between Richardson's opening panorama and the inward-turning life of her protagonist.

If Jim's defeated emptiness of spirit suggests vital connections between the personal psychology of Richard Mahony and the social dynamics of mid-nineteenth-century Australia, his very occupation affords its cultural revelations. The immigrant miners, of whom Jim is a representative figure, swarm over Ballarat like ants over an antheap. In their lust for gold, they are themselves de-humanized, and the landscape violated. The large-scale description of the gold-fields to which the whole of the Proem builds is, I take it, not merely an act of historical recreation but a concentrated vision of the quality of Australian life as a major literary imagination conceived it to be. In that vision, vicious human acquisitiveness, at first despoiling the land, finally becomes the captive of an Australian mother earth taking her revenge for the incestuous rape wrought upon her:

Such were the fates of those who succumbed to the 'unholy hunger'. It was like a form of revenge taken on them, for their loveless schemes of robbing and fleeing; a revenge contrived by the ancient, barbaric country they had so lightly invaded. Now, she held them captive — without chains; ensorcelled — without witchcraft; and, lying stretched like some primeval monster in the sun, her breasts freely bared, she watched, with a malignant eye, the efforts made by these puny mortals to tear their lips away.   (*p. 16*)

The abiding force of Richardson's vision as cultural *aperçu* is attested in the twentieth century by, for instance the novels of Brian Penton or even Patrick White's *Voss.* The continuing value of vision as a mode of cultural understanding could be argued from, say, the first chapter of Palmer's *Golconda*, the first and last scenes of George Johnston's *My Brother Jack* — even in a way, the whole of Brennan's *Poems 1913*.

But the centrally significant fact about the Proem to *Australia Felix* is that its cultural insights are related, all of them, to the career of Richard Mahony. The point is made no more powerfully than in the closing paragraph of the trilogy, wherein Mahony's body is finally absorbed back into the same earth-mother who takes hold of the lives of the miners in the Proem:

All that was mortal of Richard Mahony has long since crumbled to dust. For a time, fond hands tended his grave, on which in due course a small cross rose, bearing his name, and marking the days and years of his earthly pilgrimage. But, those who had known and loved him passing, scattering, forgetting, rude weeds choked the flowers, the cross toppled over, fell to pieces and was removed, the ivy that entwined it uprooted. And, thereafter, his resting-place was indistinguishable from the common ground. The rich and kindly earth of his adopted country absorbed his perishable body, as the country itself had never contrived to make its own, his wayward, vagrant spirit. (*p. 928*)

To conceive of tragedy — and the history of Richard Mahony is an Australian tragedy — as a passage through the trials and disturbances of a competitive male world towards final acceptance by a dominant maternal spirit may be a uniquely Australian response to the human condition. To pursue the implications of that conception would almost certainly tell us a great deal not only about the development of formal drama in this country but about the widest and most intricate ramifications of personal relationships.

It would probably tell us something about the motivation of the weeper who is my third and last exhibit — the protagonist of Charles Harpur's poem, 'The Tower of the Dream'.[10] Composed in blank verse with two interpolated songs, 'The Tower of the Dream' is divided into five parts, which, after some introductory comment on the nature of dreams, recount a dream actually experienced by the poet. In his dream Harpur gradually becomes aware of a threatening landscape dominated by a tall, illuminated tower. At the top of the tower a beautiful young woman appears, with whom after some hesitation, the poet is united in mutual joy:

How long I knew not, but the thrilling warmth
That, like the new birth of a passionate bliss,
Erewhile had searched me to the quick, again

Shuddered within me, more and more, until
Mine eyes had opened under *two* that made
All else like darkness; and upon my cheek
A breath that seemed the final spirit of health
And floral sweetness, harbingered once more
The silver accents of that wondrous voice,
Which to have heard was never to forget;   (*pp. 24–5*)

Delight, however, soon gives way to nightmare with the arrival of a vague and terrible figure who snatches the woman away ('This/Is Love forbidden!', p. 33), leaving the poet under the guard of a winged dragon. His incarceration within the tower lasts for a week, until the second intrusion of the dark and threatening presence. He now sees the woman fly away into the skies, and escapes through the base of the tower to the world outside, there to be left with a sense of inconsolable loss.

No modern commentator would need to be aware of Charles Harpur's seven-year courtship of Mary Doyle in order to interpret 'The Tower of the Dream' as an amalgam of erotic wish-fulfilment and anxiety induced by sexual frustration. And, if that were all the poem amounted to, it need scarcely occupy the critic any further. Its significance as an individual work of art would be negligible, its value in delineating a literary tradition non-existent. While Harpur almost certainly did not recognize in his lines the meaning so apparent to post-Freudian readers, his own intentions are nevertheless sufficiently well-executed to give 'The Tower of the Dream' some merit on its own terms. Basically, it seems fair to say that, for Harpur, his dream afforded a glimpse into a kind of platonic reality, in which the woman embodied the highest virtue of Romantic idealism in personal relationships. The qualities embodied by the woman, however, had to operate in an imperfect world, constantly under the threat of those dangers symbolized in the tyrannical lord of the tower. The woman herself has some awareness of what these dangers are, as evidenced in her song:

Wide apart, wide apart
In old Time's dim heart
One terrible Fiend doth his stern watch keep
Over the mystery
Lovely and deep,
Locked in thy history,
Beautiful Sleep!

Could we disarm him,
Could we but charm him,
The soul of the sleeper might happily leap

> Through the dark of the dim waste so deathly and deep
>   That shroudeth the triple divinity,
> The three of thy mystical Trinity:
> Gratitude, Liberty,
> Joy from all trammels free,
> Beautiful Spirit of Sleep!   (*p. 28*)

Sleep here is represented as the human experience which most closely approximates the perfection of immortality. The fiend, then, who threatens the tower is partly the principle of mutability in a mortal world, the embodiment of Time's eroding power. The life of man is to be figured forth as a perpetual striving towards the beautiful perception of the woman in the face of the subversive attacks of the monster. Such an allegorical statement of man's fate is commonplace enough; the woman's song, however, does find its measure of originality in the concatenation of qualities which it postulates as making up perfection: Gratitude, Liberty, Joy. Here, we may think, is one of the points at which Harpur's personal impulse towards poetry intersects with some of the basic myths of his culture. How much of the subsequent history of Australian literature and social experience was Harpur forecasting in conceiving of human perfection precisely as he did?

The same question poses itself in relation to Harpur's sense of the present world as a paradise lost. In no rigorous sense is 'The Tower of the Dream' a religious poem, but it clearly refers its understanding of human behaviour, ideal or actual, to images of Eden, pre- or post-lapsarian. Herein, too, it seems to me that Harpur was predicting one of the great recurring themes of Australian poetry.

The substantive meaning that Harpur discovered in his dream, that is to say, has made frequent reappearances in Australian writing. In its presentation as well as in its substance, 'The Tower of the Dream' can also lay claim to symptomatic importance. There can be no doubt that, in terms of the verse itself, some of the most impressively achieved sections of the poem are those which involve the ruler of the tower, who becomes not only a projection of Harpur's personal anxieties but a figure from the world of myth:

> With deafened ears and looks aghast I turned
> Towards the harsh noise, there to behold, between
> The mighty jambs in the strong wall from which
> The door swung inward, a tremendous form!
> A horrid gloomy form that shapeless seemed,
> And yet, in all its monstrous bulk, to man
> A hideous likeness bare! . . .   (*pp. 31–2*)

Here we have a male (and paternal?) figure full of repression and menace. Biographical investigation might well track down the genesis of this image to Harpur's infantile experience but what is more significant to us is that 'The Tower of the Dream' generated a myth of repressive masculinity damaging to erotic and emotional fulfilment, a myth complementary to that pattern of ambiguous maternity woven into the Proem of *Australia Felix*. Both myths could provide useful starting points for a discussion of family dynamics and social values in the Australian socio-literary tradition.

Even more impressive than the depiction of the nightmare monster is the representation of the poet's emotions during his captivity. Weeping in his privation, he adds to our understanding of *homo australiensis* a further dimension beyond those revealed by Murray's charismatic figure of compassion and Richardson's self-pitying miner:

> Utterly blank I stood
> In marble-cold astonishment of heart!
> And when at length I cast despairing eyes —
> Eyes so despairing that the common gift
> Of vision stung me like a deadly curse —
> The dungeon round, pure pity of myself
> So warmed and loosened from my brain, the pent
> And icy anguish, that its load at once
> Came like an Alp-thaw streaming through my eyes;
> Till resignation, that balm-fragrant flower
> Of meek pale grief that hath its root in tears,
> Grew out of mine, and dewed my soul with peace.   (*p. 34*)

Surely this must be one of the first authentic accounts of an Australian dark night of the soul. Its special horror is not one of action or of pain, but of absolute, frozen despair, and it recurs in the lives of, among others, Richard Mahony, Maurice Guest, Phelim Halloran — indeed in most of the fictional lives studied in *Images of Society and Nature*.

Harpur's experience of profoundest horror in 'The Tower of the Dream' offers, that is to say, an archetypal episode for Australian literature. Like all the other dreams, visions, fantasies to be found in our major writing, it provides evidence of singular importance in assessing the nature and quality of our literary heritage. Yet 'The Tower of the Dream' has a further importance. Standing almost at the beginning of our literary history, it became necessarily one of the determinants of that range and context of possibilities out of which our tradition could be made. Indeed, there is ample evidence that not only this poem but a large part of Harpur's canon was transmitted, largely through the agency of Henry Kendall, down the nineteenth century as an element in the usable past, a visible ingredient in the cultural matrix out of which poems might be made in the present.

Thus 'The Tower of the Dream' can remind us more readily than either 'An Absolutely Ordinary Rainbow' or the Proem to *Australia Felix* of the truth that, where a literary heritage may be simply a *congeries* of excellences, a literary tradition is made out of the continuous transmission of complex possibilities. 'In dreams', Delmore Schwartz once wrote, 'begin responsibilities'.[11] And acquaintance with the manifold dreams recorded in our literature will certainly enrich our understanding of its heritage. Only when we have acquired a thorough and disinterested knowledge of how each writer 'was influenced by his predecessors or experienced the same social milieu as his contemporaries' will we truly be able to see how that heritage has shaped itself into a tradition.

The criticism of Arthur Phillips
1980

I

The year 1958 was a good one for Australian publishing. It saw the appearance of first novels by Hal Porter, Thea Astley, Christopher Koch; of further work by newcomers like Elizabeth Harrower and Randolph Stow; of continued output by such established writers as Geoffrey Dutton, Dal Stivens, Peter Cowan and E. O. Schlunke. Sir Robert Garran, one of the founding fathers of the nation, published his recollections under the title of *Prosper the Commonwealth*. Russel Ward brought out his highly influential piece of historical interpretation, *The Australian Legend*. In the long run, however, the importance of 1958 may be most closely associated with the publication of A. A. Phillips's *The Australian Tradition*.

By the middle decade of the twentieth century Australian literary culture had fostered a considerable body of prose and verse of quite genuine merit; what it had pre-eminently failed to produce was a concomitant achievement in criticism. Dutiful gestures could be made towards A. G. Stephens, a passing nod directed towards a handful of other figures. But the Australian scene had, by and large, few first-rate products of the critical intelligence, actively devoted to mediating between an indigenous literature and an indigenous audience. *The Australian Tradition* offered no massive corrective to the prevailing situation — it is massive neither in actual size nor in intellectual intention. But if the successful application of a finely discriminating, sympathetic analysis to a thoroughly understood set of circumstances is a mark of first-rate criticism, then *The Australian Tradition* was clearly first rate. To have been so at all in the context of Australian culture, especially to have been so in 1958, confers on Phillips's book an enduring historical importance.

Even historical milestones, however, are part of the distances they measure. And, if I am to claim a peculiar historical importance for *The Australian Tradition*, I must do so by appeal to some criterion more specific than the failure of criticism to keep pace with our creative development during the first 150-odd years of our national experience. The specific place that *The Australian Tradition* occupies in our cultural chronology is announced, in fact, in its title. Even in the 1950s there was a certain temerity in claiming for what (to some) appeared to be the miscellaneous accumulation of our literary records the honorific term 'tradition'. Phillips himself was aware of the hardihood of his enterprise:

At that time, it was pretty generally assumed that the Australian community was too young to have any traditions. That had long seemed to me a nonsensical view. Certainly our culture lacked mellowness; but to infer that it was therefore not influenced by indigenous traditions was to ignore plain facts. I was prepared to insist that the then generally received view was false, to nail the skull-and-crossbones to my masthead by declaring a contrary opinion upon the cover of my book.[1]

The slightly pugnacious stance which can be detected here was focused in the phrase which has bestowed on Phillips's book something beyond historical importance — a minor intellectual notoriety. I refer, of course, to 'the cultural cringe'. By that term Phillips was referring to the unthinking admiration for everything foreign (especially English) which precluded regard for any excellence that might be found at home. That the cringe still existed in 1958, was indeed a ripe target for criticism, there is ample evidence outside Phillips's own essay. The continued currency of the phrase even in the 1980s may indicate that we have not yet rid ourselves of the attitudes it was designed to highlight and debunk. There have certainly been great changes in Australian society during the past quarter-century. Even in 1966, introducing the second edition of his book, Phillips could voice the hope that those changes were sufficiently advanced to give his coinage a slightly *passé* air: 'Today I believe — at least I hope — that younger readers of my essay may wonder what I am talking about' (pp. vii–viii). Were he to rewrite 'The Cultural Cringe' today, however, twenty-eight years after the first appearance of *The Australian Tradition*, he might still find pockets of cultural sycophancy waiting to be mopped up, might still accept the need to retain the sub-title of his book, 'Studies in a Colonial Culture'.

The idea of tradition, nevertheless, must have greater intellectual cogency than that of a polemical catch-cry if it is to provide the unifying framework for a collection of ten[2] critical essays on diverse subjects. It must be the means of discovering order, pattern, continuity, in the literary phenomena under investigation. Again, there is no doubt in my mind that Phillips's general concept of tradition provided him with a powerful instrument for analysing his Australian materials. It was not, to be sure, a concept entirely of his own invention; on the contrary, it was a summation and a synthesis of the many loosely grouped attitudes and values which had made up the prevailing orthodoxy of Australian literary criticism in the two or three decades prior to 1958.

That orthodoxy and Phillips's distillation of it were founded on certain fairly clear ideas, including a number about the proper writing of Australian literary history. Two of the longest essays in *The Australian Tradition* are in fact exercises in literary historiography: 'The Democratic Theme' and 'The Family Relationship'. Both attempt to arrange the details of our literary record in accordance with a set of ruling values and beliefs. Phillips thus stresses the importance of Australian bush life as a seed ground for all that is best and most characteristic in Australian literature; draws attention to the pervasive and insidious influence of English language and literature especially on our nineteenth-century writing; locates the first great advance towards literary independence in the 1890s; notes a kind of regressive timidity in the early years of our century; postulates a renewed drive towards mature self-reliance behind the best work of the 1930s and 1940s, and so on. In sum, the history of Australian literature, as either expounded or implied in Phillips's essays, is based on the translation of the bush ethos into the social-democratic code of mateship, and the effort to express that code in an adequate aesthetic form.

In *The Australian Tradition*, however, Phillips shows himself to be a dynamic rather than a descriptive critic; he consciously endorses in the life and literature of the present those values which he has used to explain the past. Historically derived as they are from a sympathetic understanding of the bush ethos, of mateship, they appear in their relation to the contemporary world as a commitment to the idea of liberal democracy. Phillips's beliefs, of course, do not spring out of *The Australian Tradition* as Athena fully armed from the head of Zeus. They were many years maturing, just as the various essays were a decade or more in writing. As early as 1946, in the preface to his anthology, *An Australian Muster*, he had written of 'the one great tradition that our young country has had time to develop — the tradition of the "Dinkum Aussie", the standard of character that we have set up as our national ideal'.[3] In ensuing years and in accumulating essays he was to refine both the idea and its application — often finding publication in that most congenial of forums, *Meanjin Quarterly* under the editorship of Clem Christesen (perhaps our first great literary editor since A. G. Stephens). Or the introduction to his collection, *Five Radio Plays*, of 1949, vividly exemplifies the impact of European political history in the 1930s and 1940s on even Australian critics born, like Phillips, in or around 1900.[4] In that Introduction Phillips writes feelingly of 'one of the central problems of the present crisis of our civilisation: the problem of equipping democracy with a dynamic, of arming it with the alert integrity and fortitude necessary to its survival'.[5] Whatever the source of his socio-literary beliefs, wherever previously expressed, they had taken on by 1958 and the publication of *The Australian Tradition* the earned authority of experience.

General beliefs are only as good as the particulars in which they can be shown to operate, and from this point of view the writers that Phillips chooses to enshrine in his literary pantheon are fairly predictable. Probably the two best-known essays in *The Australian Tradition* are those on 'The Craftsmanship of Lawson' and 'The Craftsmanship of Furphy'. That Phillips should have made Lawson and Furphy two of the most important measures of our entire literary achievement should, as I say, be no matter for surprise — it would have been astonishing had it been otherwise. What is of rather more interest is the terms in which he praises these two great pillars of the democratic theme. If in the choice of *The Australian Tradition* as a title Phillips had nailed the skull-and-crossbones to his mast-head, in drawing attention to the skill and originality of Lawson and Furphy as craftsmen, he was unmistakably carrying the battle to the enemy.

The proponents of Australian literature even in the 1950s felt (with some justice) that one of the conspicuous examples of the 'cultural cringe' was the failure of university English departments to take a serious interest in Australian writing as a subject for either research or undergraduate instruction. Those same English departments, furthermore, were in the 1950s largely under the dominance of the kind of criticism represented in England by F. R. Leavis and *Scrutiny* and in America by the 'New Critics'. That criticism, founded on the close analysis of individual texts, eschewed biographical information and historical comment in favour of aesthetic–moral judgements based on such criteria as metaphoric complexity, verbal irony, significant form, organic unity — in a word, on controlled technique. In demonstrating, then, that Lawson and Furphy were master technicians in full control of their craft, Phillips was insisting that the best Australian writers could (and should) be approached on exactly the same terms as any of the important writers in the English tradition. The two 'Craftsmanship' essays were, in their time, direct blows aimed against the kind of double standards of critical judgement which all too often were applied to English and Australian texts.

In the patterns that he attributed to our literary history; in the authors he placed at the forefront of that history; in the nexus he made between his social and literary values; in the very methods of his criticism; in all these matters, it may be argued, Arthur Phillips summed up and distilled in *The Australian Tradition* not only the dominant orthodoxies of the previous quarter-century but also some of the most debated issues of the period. It is not uncommon, however, for the appearance of a *summa* to coincide with the incipient decline in power and prestige of the value system it synthesizes. Such, we may now begin to see, was the case with *The Australian Tradition*. In 1958 stirrings could already be felt which within a decade would work immense changes not only in Australian literature and criticism but Australian society at large. At a quite obvious level, the distribution and composition of the Australian population were moving it further and further away from the bush experience and Anglo-Saxon influence which were the fountainheads of Phillips's historiography and criticism. That shift in perspective, further, was filtering through to critical interpretations of Australian literature and society.

Since 1958 Phillips's notion of the Australian tradition may not have been completely abandoned, but has certainly been subject to some radical modifications; his version of the 1890s has suffered equally severe questioning; the whole issue of the influence of English forms and conventions has been reassessed; almost every one, in effect, of the assumptions and conclusions of *The Australian Tradition* has been challenged with more or less rigour and good sense. In retrospect, the transitional quality of the later 1950s is well symbolized by the death in 1959 (the year after the publication of *The Australian Tradition*) of Vance Palmer, who through decades of unremitting application and concern had laid down the foundations of the edifice of which Phillips's book was the capstone. Fittingly, it was Phillips who spoke the final words at the funeral of the man who had not only been his good friend but who for much of the first half of the twentieth century had been the doyen of Australian literary culture.

The sense of a culture in flux was further reinforced in 1959 by the publication of James McAuley's *The End of Modernity*, as it had been two years earlier by Vincent Buckley's *Essays in Poetry, Mainly Australian*. Both works, in their several ways, challenged the supremacy of the nationalist–democratic view of Australian literature so ably represented by Arthur Phillips. A number of the new novels of 1958, the very year of *The Australian Tradition*, also pointed to new emphases and loyalties in Australian writing — Thea Astley's *Girl with a Monkey*, for instance, or Christopher Koch's *The Boys in the Island*, or Randolph Stow's *To the Islands*. The most massive impetus towards, and evidence of, changed patterns in Australian writing had, however, been given in 1955 with the publication of Patrick White's *The Tree of Man*. That Phillips was thoroughly aware of the consequences of White's fiction for his own reading of the Australian tradition is indicated quite clearly in the footnote appended to the essay on 'The Family Relationship':

Since this passage was written, Patrick White, in *The Tree of Man*, has succeeded in reconciling a sensitive interpretation of Australian life with a keen feeling for the spiritual mysteries.   (*p. 111*)

That footnote appeared in the original edition of *The Australian Tradition*. When the revised version of the book appeared in 1966 there was even stronger testimony of Phillips's positive response to the changing circumstances of Australian literary culture. Much of the 1966 Preface, for example, is given over to a discussion of those changes:

No sane observer would today claim that our cultural outlook is as clear, mature and vivid as it should be; but at least we have come a long way in the last two decades. Re-reading the earlier written of these essays, I am happy to observe that some parts of them now seem dated.   (*p. vii*)

The very selection of essays for the second edition provides further proof of the fact that Phillips's allegiance to the Lawson–Furphy tradition of Australian writing was flexible and dynamic enough to confront the challenge of new conditions. The omitted essays are 'Culture and Canberra' and 'Two Anthologies and Some Generalisations'. The additions: 'Lawson Revisited', 'The Short Stories of Vance Palmer', and 'Barbara Baynton and The Dissidence of the Nineties'.

'Culture and Canberra' is a direct plea for greater governmental aid to the arts. While the enormous increase in precisely that area of activity since 1958 may suggest that the essay argued its case well enough to justify its later omission, it still has value as an illustration of Phillips's abiding concern for an immediate relationship between literature and the way people actually live. The absence of 'Two Anthologies and Some Generalisations' is, I think, of less consequence. Like all Phillips's criticism, it is pithy, intelligent, to the point; yet it reveals no general critical principles unavailable from the other, more substantial pieces.

The additions to the 1966 edition are of very great interest indeed. Maintaining the general view of Australian writing which had animated the original text, they nevertheless add some important new dimensions and perspectives to those assembled in the 1958 collection. 'Lawson Revisited', for instance (placed directly after the 'Craftsmanship' essay), offers a generalized impression of the writer which would have been quite out of place in the earlier, technical commentary. In the same way, 'The Short Stories of Vance Palmer' celebrates not only some of the major virtues of Palmer's shorter prose fiction but also some of the most attractive and sympathetic qualities of the imagination behind the prose. Perhaps, however, his account of Barbara Baynton most tellingly demonstrates Phillips's ability to accommodate to a changing cultural and literary scene without relinquishing his basic values. An acute exposition of some of the deepest motifs in Baynton's fiction, the essay attempts what was for Phillips a novel explanation of the phenomena he identified. Baynton's mastery of the details of bush life, it was easy enough for Phillips to praise; his entire critical career had prepared him to pinpoint that virtue, to give it its due weight:

You can feel the Australian bush — a certain kind of Australian bush — about [the stories], shaping them into the forms which they assume. Baynton obviously knows bush-life with a deep intimacy and something of an insider's pride. Only an insider with a mastered knowledge could have devised Scrammy 'And's strategy with the sheep. More than that, one can sense that she belongs to the freemasonry of the bush. One can feel her giving the lodge-grip as she writes "the hospitality of the bush never extends to the loan of a good horse to an inexperienced rider". (*pp. 77–8*)

Probing beyond Baynton's acquaintance with occupational detail, Phillips discovers other elements in her fiction which his established critical beliefs might have been less apt to deal with. Notably, he finds a 'terror and revulsion' (p. 78) in Baynton's writing, a 'savage distaste that almost smothers the comedy of [her] stories' (p. 79). These qualities, located in certain 'recurrent symbols' (p. 75), frequently have little or no narrative justification for their presence. Looking beyond an exclusively Freudian explanation of their presence (Phillips's kind and generation of critic maintained a healthy scepticism towards psycho-analytic criticism), Phillips finds his own explanation in external sources as well as internal pressures. He accounts for the oddly subjective elements in Baynton's fiction in two ways, the first well within the habits of thought which had led up to the 1958 edition of *The Australian Tradition*:

The force of the anger arises from the writer's feeling that the peasant element shouldn't be there [i.e., in the Australian bush]. It is a denial of the Australian legend; one of the articles of faith of that legend was the belief that Australian rural life was not a peasant life, that the free and self-reliant Australian had broken loose from the peasant's humilities and humiliations. (*p. 79*)

Phillips's second explanation of 'the sense of terror and revulsion' in Baynton's stories is offered as the culminating insight of the whole essay. Baynton's seemingly most personal feelings are ascribed to 'a sense of spiritual darkness emanating from the land itself, a feeling of primeval cruelty fed by the sunlight which glares instead of glowing, . . . by the guilty sense that man has forced his will upon the earth without the hallowing of ritual' (p. 81). In the following paragraph, this *aperçu* into Baynton's art is widened into a generalization about the entire tradition of Australian writing:

That sense of spiritual darkness emanating from the land itself touches Australian writing again and again; and almost always it comes from a deeper layer of the mind than the easy optimism, the simplicity of faith which are more constantly present. There is a sense in which Patrick White is more traditionally Australian than is generally supposed.   (*p. 81*)

The concessions articulated in those lines are the surest indication in the whole of the second edition of *The Australian Tradition* that Phillips's creative response to the movement of literature in the previous ten years had brought him to accept that the view of Australian literature and the Australian tradition expressed in the 1958 text, while not untrue, was incomplete. They provide, in themselves, ample warrant for our finding in the first and second editions of *The Australian Tradition* one of the most sensitive registers of the great changes that occurred in our life and literature in the years between them.

II

The re-issue of the second edition of Phillips's essays in 1980, however, did more than remind us of the importance of its predecessors as historical barometers; it showed us the contours, the shape, the specific gravity, of permanently excellent criticism. That excellence begins in the individual essays. Exactly calculated as to length, organization, use of exemplary illustration, they all enjoy a splendid harmony between form and substance. When the substance is rich and penetrating, they take on the authority of canonical utterance. It seems to me unlikely, for instance, that serious readers of Lawson or Furphy will ever be able to dispense with the 'Craftsmanship' essays.

Both these essays gain their strength through close and sustained attention to one or two crucial issues — Lawson's controlled irony, the structural unity of *Such is Life*. Richly responsive to the nuances of language, Phillips was yet never a critic of the minutely analytic kind; indeed he had a lively suspicion of the worst (often academic) excesses of exhaustive stylistic analysis. Essays like 'Lawson Revisited', 'The Short Stories of Vance Palmer', and 'Barbara Baynton and The Dissidence of the Nineties' are thus quite as characteristic of Phillips at his best as the 'Craftsmanship' essays, which owe their method (as I have already suggested) to a particular polemical purpose. On his second look at Lawson, in his encounters with Palmer and Baynton, Phillips takes a more comprehensive view of his chosen subjects, conveying with real success something of the writer within the work. What he especially aims at doing in these essays, it seems to me, is to make us feel the human qualities, the human worth of those authors who have uniquely attracted him.

Where the essays on individual writers have one kind of interest and value, the larger excursions into literary history have another. It may be that 'The Democratic Theme' and 'The Family Relationship' seem less wholly convincing now than they did twenty years ago (beyond competing interpretations, a wider and more detailed range of evidence has been adduced); yet the fact remains that in both essays Phillips has put his finger on key issues for *any* interpretation of our literary development. And, within their limitations, his own readings still retain a real air of authenticity. The historiography of *The Australian Tradition* is all the more cogent because it is not merely a pragmatic consideration of our own particular case; it derives from a general philosophy of history posited on a firm understanding of the organic relation between all societies and the literary culture they support. His particular comment that the change in tone in Palmer's stories 'is dictated by a change in the tone of the Australian life which Palmer was interpreting' (p. 127) is altogether typical. But the assertion that 'the spirit of a time somehow finds the voice which is suited to express it' (p. 63) catches the pervasive Hegelian undertones of all his literary history.

His critical judgements, likewise, are grounded in general principle; in, for instance, his belief in a direct nexus between aesthetic value and truth. 'The success of the device . . . depends on the wisdom of the content' (p. 13); 'it is a truth of life that sometimes a fine-hearted woman will be unflinchingly true to love through all discouragements' (p. 45); 'The strength and truth of many of his portraits . . . remain unchallengeable' (p. 90) — again and again, Phillips couches his estimates of writers, books, particular scenes, in terms such as this. The necessity of an appeal to 'truth' is plainly one of the undebated assumptions of his criticism. While others might (properly) feel the need to debate it, in *The Australian Tradition* it is applied with such consistency and conviction as to give the work much of its distinctive intellectual tone.

Criticism in general, however, tends to take its tone at least as much from the critic's personality (actual or created) as from his system of intellectual belief. Such is certainly the case with *The Australian Tradition*. Here, as so often in work of the highest order, the art of criticism becomes implicitly an act of self-portraiture. One might begin to characterize the portrait of the critic which emerges from *The Australian Tradition* by appealing to the profession which Phillips followed for so long. For many years he was the senior English master of one of Melbourne's distinguished private schools. And when I describe the prose of *The Australian Tradition* as, in a sense, schoolmasterly, I must hasten to add that my intention is honorific. Occasionally, to be sure, his habit of using the imperative ('Consider, for example . . .', p. 98) can suggest the wagging of a pedagogical finger. More usually, however, what I would call the schoolmasterly qualities of his writing derive from the genuine virtues of a great profession. Phillips, for example, possesses the splendid gift of clarity in both organization and statement — the lucidity of his prose can make the whole process of arriving at and recording critical judgements seem far simpler than it actually is. His habit, too, of easy and enlightening generalization probably derives from long classroom experience in clarifying and explaining. This trick of generalization is seen perhaps at its best in 'The Australian Romanticism and Stewart's *Ned Kelly*'. Accepting straight away the necessity of defining terms, Phillips launches his essay with a definition of Romanticism:

I define Romanticism, then, as the protest against the gap which yawns between the felt potentialities of the human spirit and the limitations of human circumstance. It is Man's outcry when he finds the straight-waistcoat of civilised living impeding the expansion of the lungs of desire.   (*p. 129*)

As definition, this may invite disagreement or qualification. But it is a definition, and it is applied clearly, consistently, and always with an eye to illuminating the main subject of Phillips's essay. Further, it leads on to another generalization — this time an allegorical personification. Phillips's distinction between the Ulyssean and

Telemachan impulses in human behaviour has a value for understanding tracts of Australian literature far wider than Douglas Stewart's verse drama.

The figure of the enlightened schoolmaster, however, does nothing like full justice to the personal quality which informs *The Australian Tradition*. An equally suggestive image is the one that Phillips so often invoked in praise of other writers: that of the craftsman. In 1946 (near the beginning, that is to say, of the decade's effort which culminated in *The Australian Tradition*), Phillips collaborated with A. Boyce Gibson, then Professor of Philosophy in the University of Melbourne, on a commonsensical guide to clear thinking entitled *Thinkers at Work*. Its opening paragraph finds the value of craftsmanship in exactly those qualities which would be later exhibited in the pages of *The Australian Tradition*:

Every craftsman, be he cook, carpenter, or thinker, goes through the same essential process; he takes certain raw materials and from them fashions something new and whole — a pudding from butter, flour, sugar and the rest; a chair from pieces of wood, screws and varnish; a conclusion from observations and information — and argument.

Two things are necessary for a piece of good craftsmanship. The raw materials must be reliable; and they must be put together in the right way.[6]

The craftsman as cook, carpenter, or thinker: such homely images are entirely appropriate to the modest, down-to-earth confidence of *The Australian Tradition*. As the essay on 'Lawson Revisited' approaches its climax, Phillips breaks off to observe, 'The abstractions of the critical vocabulary are too flavourless to convey this point expressively' (p. 27). And his prose is characteristically larded with images of a quite literally flavoursome kind: 'such phrases have a relish of Jane Austen' (p. 42); 'The connoisseur of literatures, rolling that paragraph round his palate, might confidently pronounce "Australian — probably a nineties vintage"' (p. 54); 'If, with a firm free hand, the *Bulletin* writers shook the naked tomato-sauce bottle over their plain roast mutton, it was because they shared the national taste in cookery' (p. 54). When Phillips walks out of the kitchen, it is likely to be into the carpenter's workshop. The essay on 'The Craftsmanship of Lawson', in particular, is crammed with images relating Lawson's virtues to solid workmanship in natural materials: 'It is a delicate problem . . . which Lawson had set himself — to find the minimum weight of framework which would hold the story erect' (p. 3); 'the last triumphant clap of the hammer on the nail driven home, would not do either' (p. 9); 'The device is no more than a piece of machinery which distracts us by its preliminary whirr and its final hiccough' (p. 15).

The critic as pedagogue and craftsman — to these qualities we must add at least the critic as humorist and ironist. *The Australian Tradition* is regularly punctuated by a deflatingly colloquial, comic turn of phrase. A salty verbal humour is, in Phillips's hands, a powerful weapon for defeating any possible pretentiousness in himself or his readers. In that, it is closely related to the purpose served by the ironic tone which can enter into his prose style. Now irony, as I have argued earlier, was a modish element in the critical repertoire of the 1940s and 1950s which, in several of his essays, Phillips turned against its champions. His own irony, however, is rather more than a technique (however masterful or subtle) of aesthetic control; it provides the means by which his vision of Australian writing is kept in clear and unvarying perspective. In the essay on 'The Australian Romanticism' he speaks of the 'puncturing ironic realism of the Australian temperament; . . . that quality which provides the check-and-balance in the Australian psychologic Constitution' (p. 143). With irony so understood, Phillips's own prose is thoroughly imbued.

To pedagogue and craftsman, then, add ironist — but in the end no combination of nouns or epithets will do exact justice to what I take to be the qualities of the critical intelligence unfolded in *The Australian Tradition*. In the end, I find myself driven to the kind of direct human statement about the author of that book which he so candidly makes about the subjects of his commentary. The Arthur Phillips who can be felt within *The Australian Tradition* is, quite simply, a singularly honest, gritty individual whose criticism assumes its authority because it is so consistently submitted to the service of something other than itself. Never of the pyrotechnic variety, never vainly exhibitionist, Phillips's criticism suggests above all else the image of an advocate, passionately convinced of his cause, arguing the case for the liberal imagination with a paradoxical combination of civilized moderation and wild energy. He is an advocate who stands mid-way between his own Ulysses and Telemachus — between energy and order — because that vantage point affords him the clearest view of the power of art to assimilate the contrarieties of human life.

It would be false, however, to leave the author of *The Australian Tradition* poised between two allegorical figures — even of his own contriving. To bring him back to his native ground, I must allude to the one essay of the collection I have so far passed over — 'Dolia Ribush and the Australian Theatre'. This tribute to a migrant European producer might be thought, in relation to the main theme of an indigenous tradition, to be among the least significant of the book. And, indeed, the piece bespeaks both the localness and the limitations of Phillips's performances. The locale, the ground, of all his criticism is Melbourne; its limitations include its readier application to prose fiction than to drama or even poetry (I make this latter assertion in full awareness of the many fine things that Phillips has said about our verse, of his finely demonstrated taste in the selection of *Australian Poetry 1956*).

Even the portrait of Dolia Ribush tells us less about Australian drama than about the practical activities of a particular artist of the theatre. Few Australians outside of Melbourne and Phillips's generation would have been able to experience Ribush's productions. Nevertheless, the evocation of this remarkable theatrical talent is touched by at least one quality which binds it tightly into the texture of the book of which it is a part: a recognition of certain virtues which belong as much to Arthur Phillips as to the subject of his essay. 'Because the theatre was the passion of his life', Phillips writes of Ribush, 'he wanted to see the richness which he found in Australian life translated into a play' (p. 155). I can summon up no better tribute to the author of *The Australian Tradition* than thus to paraphrase his own words: Because his passion is as much for experience itself as for ordering it into aesthetic forms, he wants to see Australian literature based on the richness he finds in Australian life. The permanency of *The Australian Tradition* rests in this: it is criticism practised for the sake of a literature which in turn is seen to be created for the sake of life.

5 April 1984

The two Winstons

1985

After we came out of the church, we stood talking for some time together of Bishop Berkeley's ingenious sophistry to prove the non-existence of matter, and that every thing in the universe is merely ideal. I observed, that though we are satisfied his doctrine is not true, it is impossible to refute it. I never shall forget the alacrity with which Johnson answered, striking his foot with mighty force against a large stone, till he rebounded from it, "I refute it *thus*."

Boswell's *Life of Johnson*, 6 August 1763[1]

The fifth of April 1984 is, or ought to be, a momentous date in the history of twentieth-century literary criticism. Twenty-four hours earlier Winston Smith had put pen to paper, inscribing the opening words of his diary: '*April 4th, 1984. Last night to the flicks*'.[2] By the following day George Orwell's most famous work had moved from the future into the past; the prophecy of future shock had been transformed into a narrative fantasy of questionable import and in dubious relation to its readers.

For thirty-five years after its publication *Nineteen Eighty-Four* had stood as a frightful warning of the fate that might overtake us all, did we not heed its injunctions; it had become part of the millenarian mythology of the latter half of the twentieth century. In the early years after its appearance many intelligent readers had found its impact so daunting and immediate that they could scarcely find that equilibrium of heart and mind which is the usual pre-condition of literary criticism. Orwell's image of the future — 'a boot stamping on a human face — for ever' (p. 268) — was so harrowing and, seemingly, so possible, that his entire text came to occupy a canonical place among contemporary works of political literature. It spoke, probably to uncountable millions, of their worst fears about modern politics, economics, technology.

Yet after 1949 the years rolled on; the advertised date of Orwell's Armageddon came steadily closer. The early months of 1984 itself were characterized by a spate of articles in the international press comparing Orwell's forecasts of things to come with the (alleged) state of things as they were. Unavoidably, a major film was made with two great international stars in the leading roles. What struck me most about the film, however, the star performances apart, and even beyond the determination to deepen and darken every last detail of Orwell's text, was something akin to wistfulness that the day of its prophetic flourishing was almost at an end.

The fatal day arrived on 5 April 1984. From that moment on we have had to discard *Nineteen Eighty-Four* from our imaginations as one of the great works of homiletic prophecy, offering visions of the future still capable of fulfilment. We have had to begin to find new ways of responding to what (some might say) is the same title but a different text. All Orwell's polemical ideas — about class, language, sex, power — must now be seen and judged from a different perspective. His prophecies must be read as fantasy, his forecasts as fiction. What was once topical commentary must be converted into timeless satire, the allusions to Hitler, Stalin, wartime London, and the rest, increasingly to be explicated by scholarship and learned footnotes. In effect, Orwell's vision of future horror is well on the way to becoming 'problematic'.

Along with this change in perspective on its formal status may go a corresponding loss of esteem for its achievement. As we adjust to reading *Nineteen Eighty-Four* wholly as a work of fantastic fiction, we may find that it holds less real power of intellect and imagination than we had, all those years, believed it did. For my own part, I believe that we will (or should) not value Orwell's book less highly than in the past. Nevertheless some immediate decline in its reputation would merely repeat a pattern which has often been the lot of texts which, in their time, have held great immediate sway over their contemporary readers. Beyond, however, our inevitably changing perceptions of the formal status of Orwell's text or of a possible diminishment in its reputation, there is one other general issue raised by the transition of *Nineteen Eighty-Four* from the future to the past which is the central and urgent concern of this essay.

The issue is, quite simply, that of the stability of all literary forms and genres, indeed of virtually any piece of discourse, literary or otherwise. If literary criticism is, as the very title of John Docker's recent book insists, in a critical condition,[3] the crisis displays itself exactly in a range of disagreements about the status and nature of the literary text itself. As Docker presents the case, the contest is (or should be) between post-structuralist theories flowing from the work of Jean Barthes and sociologically-oriented contextualist studies which (I take it) Docker accords his personal approval. Unfortunately, what should be clearly distinguishable battle lines are distorted and confused by the intervention of some ageing Leavisite New Critics who still seek to impose their views and their will by the exercise of intellectually disreputable methods. They continue to enforce their discredited notions of 'levels of meaning', 'tension', 'paradox' and so on, on the rebellious inhabitants of their feudal domains. I have elsewhere indicated that I find Docker's historical argument (at least insofar as it concerns Australia) to be largely ill-informed nonsense.[4] I am here much more concerned with the conceptual map he draws of contemporary criticism, and especially in the way so many of its features are reflected in the curious fate of *Nineteen Eighty-Four*.

It does seem to me true that much of the theoretical effort of the criticism of the past twenty years has been directed towards demonstrating the instability, the illusoriness even, of literary discourse. Meaning inheres, if anywhere, in the transaction between the reader and the text; significance may be dissolved and reconstituted in accordance with the present 'situation' of either text or reader. Literary discourse itself, so the theory goes, as an element in a language system, merges into, becomes indistinguishable for purposes of analysis, from any other kind of discourse. Such a set of basic assumptions must produce a plurality of interpretations (or reconstructions) of any given work, each as valid as the other, must at least encourage the elimination of value judgements from the critic's task, will certainly absorb any distinctions between 'high' and 'low' culture into a single sociologically-perceived context. For all of his evident dislike of Jean Barthes and his tribe, Docker's own favoured contextual approach has this in common with post-structuralist criticism: it offers no explanation as to why one text should be chosen for analysis and commentary and not another.

In such a climate of opinion, the critic's task defines itself all too clearly. He may, on the one hand, busy himself with endless and equally 'interesting' glosses of whatever text passes before his gaze, or he may take up the challenge of literary history. The challenge is likely to be met by the 'contextualization' of every piece of archival evidence that can be rescued from the past. Literary history so practised may have, in my view, a great deal of sociological and anthropological interest, but it very soon becomes a history of almost everything but literature. Whichever approach he elects, the contemporary critic runs the grave risk of emulating that aspect of Winston Smith's personality which the true critic in him strove to restrict:

Winston's greatest pleasure in life was in his work. Most of it was a tedious routine, but included in it there were also jobs so difficult and intricate that you could lose yourself in them as in the depths of a mathematical problem . . . (*p. 46*)

The grand cant phrase which both describes and legitimates the transactional concerns of modern criticism is 'the death of the author', coined by Jean Barthes. John Docker makes the point like this:

The deconstructionists, using Derrida (and Saussure) for their own formalist purposes, wish to view literature not as a product of an author or of a time (society, history), but as part of language. They want to release literature from author and society/history into language as the infinite play of difference . . . (*p. 189*)

This is well said, but with only a little rearrangement it would be equally well said, and apply to the kind of criticism that Docker promotes (but does not practise) in his book: 'The contextualists wish to view literature not as a product of an author or of a language, but as a part of society/history. They want to release literature from author and language into society/history as an infinite interplay of cultural determinants . . .'. The premises may be different, but the author is just as dead for Docker as for Derrida.

There is no point denying the agility, skill and even cogency of much of the argument that emanates from both sides of the debate that Docker makes a focal point of in *In a Critical Condition*. Yet a nagging doubt gnaws away at the whole range of this elaborate, self-confident theorizing. 'The author', one feels prevailed upon to repeat, 'is dead . . . But (one continues *sotto voce*), long live the author!'. It is particularly perhaps in reading a book like *Nineteen Eighty-Four* that such a response becomes imperative. In his Introduction to *Homage to Catalonia* Lionel Trilling recalled the oddly direct judgement that one of his graduate students made of Orwell — 'He was a virtuous man'.[5] Orwell was certainly that, but the anonymous student was driven to his remark not by first-hand acquaintance, nor by assiduous biographical research into the facts of the writer's life, but by a recognition of the imprint, the personal signature that Orwell, in word and phrase, in tone and style and realized presence, had placed indelibly on his published texts.

In his way, the nameless young man was asserting the life of the author in his own texts in a manner closely analogous to Dr Johnson's refutation of Bishop Berkeley outside the church at Harwich that morning of 6 August 1763. The vehement force of Johnson's foot against the stone may be crude as argument, may indicate a confusion between the sense of solidity and the fact of matter, may indeed betray some philosophical naiveté. But it has an undeniable, common-sensical effectiveness: it makes a real point about the way men and women experience the world they live in. Equally, it is impossible, it seems to me, to read Orwell's *Nineteen Eighty-Four* and not feel that one has encountered an experience as actual as that known by Johnson when his foot met the stone. Orwell simply phrases the argument in the language of mathematics: $2 + 2 = 4$. It is possible, I am sure, that each of us has his own O'Brien, his own Room 101; but should we ever encounter them and be persuaded that $2 + 2 = 5$, then we shall have passed into a sphere where criticism of any kind shall have ceased to exist. So long as we can hold that $2 + 2 = 4$, we must also accept that there is a hard core of meaning and value in every literary text which will resist every last attempt to deconstruct and reconstruct it, to dissolve and reconstitute it.

A belief in the final inviolability of a work of literature will be most surely confirmed by acquaintance with the great masters of the art — Shakespeare or Cervantes, Dickens or Dostoevsky. The belief, however, need not rest entirely on one's experience of the master-works nor even on an appeal to Johnsonian common sense. One line of argument in defence of the position might very well start out from a linguistic base. Familiarity with the major writers from, say, Shakespeare to Joyce clearly demonstrates that literary artists are not only elements within a cultural context but also may help to change and create that context through the inventiveness of their language. Since 1949 terms like 'Doublethink', 'Newspeak', 'Thoughtcrime' have been part of the common currency of socio-political discussion, but only because Orwell, not entirely the product of cultural determinants, invented them, and used them with enough force to make them stick.

Few writers have rivalled Orwell's scrupulous sensitivity to the power of words. 'Politics and the English Language' remains a classic essay precisely because it recognizes the nexus between language, culture and personal morality. Orwell knew that language is not only a neutral system of signs but a vehicle of values, the repository of the accumulated wisdom and experience of, in his case, the English-speaking people. In *Nineteen Eighty-Four* the sense of a yawning hiatus between the human values embodied in Shakespeare's tragedies and the texts produced by Pornosec is more than a neat narrative and thematic device; it is an item of belief on which the whole book is posited.

In one sense, the best creative literature is always dedicated to discriminating between what is valuable and what is perverse, dishonest, tawdry in any language at a given stage in its history. Criticism, equally, must attend not only to the prevailing patterns of linguistic usage at any given time and place, along with the speed and direction of linguistic change, but also to those few individuals who make a lasting impact on the practice and possibilities of language. In other words, while literary critics clearly must concern themselves with literary history in all its complexity and detail (socio-political as well as linguistic), they have an equal obligation to recognize how and why certain works of literature actually make the history which is their study. Literary histories may depend on literary archives, but they are not the same thing; the first are written out of a selection from the second, and selection, in turn, necessitates the exercise of some kind of discrimination.

One kind of discrimination, I have suggested, will involve an awareness of a core of linguistic idiosyncracy in major works of literature; another derives from the ineradicable presence of the author in his own work. John Docker draws attention to the New Critics' insistence on the autonomy of the poem, to the post-structuralists' reconstitution of the text into a myriad different designs; he seems to favour, for his own part, the assimilation of the work of literature into a total cultural context — all versions, we might say, of 'the death of the author'. Yet just as surely as Johnson felt pain when he struck his foot against a stone, so too does any intelligent reader feel the presence of a uniquely composing imagination when he reads *Nineteen Eighty-Four*, or *Lear*, or *Moby Dick*, or *Voss*, or *While the Billy Boils*. Those readers who, from whatever standpoint, assert the death of the author, simply cannot have read the master artists of language or must wilfully have closed their eyes, ears and minds to what is there. When L. C. Knights asked as long ago as 1933, 'How many children had Lady Macbeth?' he may have closed debate on a significant critical issue for a whole generation, but he did not annihilate it. In recent decades it has come back in sophisticated new forms. Yet neither Knights nor his successors, I take it, would retract from the view that the presence of an author in his own work drastically disrupts its autonomy.

Nevertheless, some way of adjusting critical theory to literary fact must be discovered if criticism is to find its way out of the crisis we may suppose it is now in. Some way must be found of permitting the author back into the work for which he was responsible. A start (perhaps unwitting) has, I believe, already been made in the wide-ranging and sophisticated discussions of autobiography that have been published over the last ten or fifteen years. Much of that discussion has dealt with the status of the protagonist of autobiography, that invented verbal construct who happens to bear the same name as the author. Many of the insights orginally directed towards the art of autobiography could be fairly and profitably broadened out to include virtually every literary form and mode. The verbal imprint of a personality which in autobiography seems to be that of the protagonist could, in other forms and modes, readily be seen as that of the author himself — not the author as he is in life, or as he might like to idealize himself, or as he might reveal himself to his most learned biographers, but as he is he is caught, realized, examined and judged in and through the language of his own choosing. 'Style', Susan Sontag once remarked, 'is the principle of decision in a work of art'.[6] 'Style', she might just as easily have claimed, 'is the imprint of a writer's personality'. In every work of literature, in every word and phrase, in every trick of idiom, tone and syntax, the writer leaves the signature of his identity as surely as a thumb print transferred from an ink pad. Every work of literature — autobiography, novel, lyric poem, or five-act farce — bears, within its thematic and technical bounds, a version of the writer's self realized with all the complexity and integrity the writer is capable of.

A thorough-going new theory of the author's right to be present in his work would, as it seems to me, go a long way towards disentangling criticism from the limitations, dilemmas, errors, heresies, which currently beset it. On the one hand it would free it from the solipsisms of much structuralist and post-structuralist analysis; on the other, it would relax the constricting demands that every last effect and triumph of major literature be accounted for by its cultural determinants. With luck, it might allow criticism to go back, unembarrassed, to the kinds of basic questions with which it has been uncomfortable for too long: what is good and what is bad? What are the qualities of literature that make it worth bothering about in the first place?

An adequate theory of authorial presence might even clarify the proper responsibilities of criticism in relation to literature. Criticism must certainly continue in all its rich variety of textual studies, continue to emulate that side of Winston Smith whose greatest pleasure in life was work composed of 'jobs so difficult and intricate that you could lose yourself in them as in the depths of a mathematical problem'. At the same time, and conceding that in every work of literature one is ultimately dealing with an individual intelligence, an individual imagination, it might just be prepared to risk judgements, evaluation, discrimination. In other words, criticism might embrace those qualities of mind which, beyond his technical efficiency, moved Winston Smith to commence his diary. Until criticism is once again prepared to risk such activity, with confidence that it is a proper part of its function, it may as well put up its shutters and leave the whole business to the sociologists and cultural anthropologists.

I have no easy recipe for converting these ideals into action. I shall, however, conclude by setting down a sort of modern decalogue — ten not-so-easy rules without which criticism will never regain the ground it has lost:

1 The critic must be clear in his own mind, and make clear to the minds of others, what his own dogmatic convictions and prejudices are. He will exclude them from the processes of criticism until the last possible moment.

2 He must strive to have the fullest possible acquaintance with the literary tradition which is his concern — its genres, forms, techniques, and conventions, as well as its social matrix.

3 He must respect intelligence as a major virtue in a work of literature, and conversely be prepared to adjudge a book bad if it is muddled, illogical, confused, or merely stupid.

4 He must learn to detect cynicism or dishonesty or opportunistic manipulation in the objects of his regard. Such qualities may excite his technical admiration, but must always operate adversely in his final judgement.

5 He must be prepared to discriminate between works of literature on the basis of their capacity to contain more or less of human experience.

6 He must make similar discriminations on the basis of their power to penetrate deeply into human life.

7 He must always hope (but not too often expect) to find some heuristic force in the books he reads — when he does, he has probably discovered greatness.

8 He must appreciate, as fully and subtly as he can, how any work represents its age — not in any superficial, monolithic way, but through the deepest designs, the complexities, even the unresolved tensions, of its language.

9 He must try to measure in what degree each work he reads escapes from the limitations of its time and place.

10 He will accept that the final test of a work of literature is the quality of its imagined life, and will hold with Wallace Stevens that 'the best definition of true imagination is that it is the sum of our faculties'.[7]

If the critic cleaves to these ten commandments he stands, I believe, a fair chance of avoiding all those errors of theory and application which John Docker represents as causing the current crisis in the profession. There is, too, one golden rule that he should constantly apply along with all the rest — he should recognize his own talents, sensibilities and perceptions for what they are, and adjust his own approach to works of literature accordingly. In so doing, he will produce, with luck, a criticism that is truly personal at the same time as it welcomes the inviolability of its object, a criticism that invites agreement or dissent through the amenity of its conduct rather than any shrill demand for compliance, a criticism that combines the technical dexterity of Winston Smith with the spirit of undogmatic enquiry that moved him to open his diary and start writing on 4 April 1984.

Notes and references

The uncertain self: Notes on the development of Australian literary form

1   Christopher Brennan, *Verse*, ed. A. R. Chisholm and J. J. Quinn (Angus & Robertson, Sydney, 1960), p. 105.
2   Chris Wallace-Crabbe, *Selected Poems* (Angus & Robertson, Sydney, 1973), p. 28.
3   The standard reference work, providing a comprehensive and fair-minded survey, is H. M. Green, *A History of Australian Literature, 1789–1950*, 2 vols (Angus & Robertson, Sydney, 1961).
4   H. G. Kippax, 'Australian Drama Since *The Doll*', *Meanjin Quarterly* XXIII, 3, 1964, pp. 230–2.
5   Leslie Rees, *A History of Australian Drama*, 2 vols (Angus & Robertson, Sydney, 1978).
6   Charles Sturt, *Two Expeditions into the Interior of Southern Australia* (Smith, Elder & Co., London, 1833), vol. I, pp. xiv–xv.
7   Edward John Eyre, *Journals of Expeditions of Discovery into Central Australia* (T. and W. Boone, London, 1845), vol. II, pp. 1–2.
8   Frederick Sinnett, 'The Fiction Fields of Australia', quoted in John Barnes, *The Writer in Australia: A Collection of Literary Documents 1856–1964* (Oxford University Press, Melbourne, 1969), p. 9.
9   John Barnes, *Henry Kingsley and Colonial Fiction* (Oxford University Press, Melbourne, 1971), pp. 3 and 25.
10 Manning Clark, *In Search of Henry Lawson* (Macmillan, Melbourne, 1978).
11 Quoted in Barnes, *The Writer in Australia*, p. 128.
12 Quoted in J. Normington-Rawling, *Charles Harpur: an Australian* (Angus & Robertson, Sydney, 1962), p. 50.
13 Mitchell Library, MSS A89.
14 Brennan, p. 165.
15 Kenneth Slessor, *One Hundred Poems* (Angus & Robertson, Sydney, 1944), p. 122.
16 Quoted in Barnes, *The Writer in Australia*, p. 326.

17 R. D. FitzGerald, *Forty Years' Poems* (Angus & Robertson, Sydney, 1965), p. 242.
18 Vance Palmer, 'Frank Wilmot', quoted in Barnes, *The Writer in Australia*, p. 175.
19 Patrick White, 'The Prodigal Son', *Australian Letters* I, 3, 1958, pp. 37–40.
20 Donald Horne, *The Education of Young Donald* (Sun Books, Melbourne, 1968), Foreword.
21 Hal Porter, *The Paper Chase* (Angus & Robertson, Sydney, 1966), pp. 148–9.

The metamorphoses of Henry Kendall

1 Barry Oakley, *Great God Mogadon and Other Plays* (University of Queensland Press, Brisbane, 1980), p. 86.
2 See the following: Donovan Clarke, 'Henry Kendall — A Study in Imagery', Part I, *Australian Quarterly* XXIX, 4 (December 1957); Part II, *Australian Quarterly* XXX, 1 (March 1958); Donovan Clarke, 'New Light on Henry Kendall', *Australian Literary Studies* II, 3 (June 1966); Leonie Kramer and A. D. Hope, *Henry Kendall* (Sun Books, Melbourne, 1973); Adrian Mitchell, 'The Radiant Dream: Notes on Henry Kendall', *Australian Literary Studies* IV, 2 (October 1969).
3 Frederick C. Kendall, *Henry Kendall: His Later Years* (Simmons Ltd, Sydney, n.d.), p. 13.
4 Henry Gyles Turner and Alexander Sutherland, *The Development of Australian Literature* (George Robertson and Co., Melbourne, 1898), p. 247.
5 Mitchell Library, MSS C199. Unless otherwise indicated the originals of all the letters quoted in this essay are held here.
6 Charles Harpur, 'A Storm in the Mountains', in Adrian Mitchell, *Charles Harpur* (Sun Books, Melbourne, 1973), p. 60.
7 All quotations from Kendall's poems are drawn from T. T. Reed, *The Poetical Works of Henry Kendall* (Libraries Board of South Australia, Adelaide, 1966), and page references are incorporated in the text. I am also indebted to Reed's edition for information about the first printings of Kendall's works.
8 The original of this letter is in the possession of Bishop T. T. Reed. It is reproduced as no. 86 in Donovan Clarke's unpublished edition of Kendall's letters (originally submitted to Sydney University as an M.A. thesis) where the date November 1867 is assigned to it.
9 See Clarke, 'Henry Kendall — A Study in Imagery', Part I, for some further suggestions about the relationship between Kendall's life and his work.
10 See Hope's Introduction to Kramer and Hope, pp. xxviii–xxix.
11 Turner and Sutherland, p. 248.
12 See Clarke, 'New Light on Henry Kendall'.

13   The original of this letter is in the possession of Bishop T. T. Reed. It
     is reproduced as no. 197 of Clarke's unpublished edition.
14   The original of this letter is in the La Trobe Library, State Library of
     Victoria. It is reproduced as no. 210 in Clarke's edition.

Between living and dying: The ground of Lawson's art

1   Manning Clark uses the phrase 'knew what life was all about'
    repeatedly in *In Search of Henry Lawson* (Macmillan, Melbourne,
    1978). I cite Colin Roderick's view from his Introduction to *Henry
    Lawson: Short Stories and Sketches 1888–1922* (Angus & Robertson,
    Sydney, 1972), p. xiii. This judgement was registered, of course, prior
    to the Clark–Roderick controversy, but it does seem to me to be
    representative of the highest kind of value that Dr Roderick
    characteristically assigns to Lawson's work. All future page references
    to Clark and to Lawson's stories will be, unless otherwise indicated,
    from the editions cited here, and will be incorporated in the text.
2   Denton Prout, *Henry Lawson: The Grey Dreamer* (Rigby, Adelaide,
    1963), p. 94.
3   Henry Lawson, *Autobiographical and Other Writings 1887–1922*, ed.
    Colin Roderick (Angus & Robertson, Sydney, 1972), p. 10. The italics
    are Lawson's.
4   See Colin Roderick's note in *The Bush Undertaker and Other Stories*
    (Angus & Robertson, Sydney, 1970), p. 256.
5   For this information I am indebted to Dr Roderick's notes to *The
    Bush Undertaker*. All other information about dating in this article is
    drawn from the same source, or from *Short Stories and Sketches
    1888–1922*.
6   *The Bush Undertaker and Other Stories*, p. 251. See the whole of Dr
    Roderick's notes on 'The Bush Undertaker' for the textual difficulties
    it poses.
7   The original title was 'A Christmas in the Far West; or, The Bush
    Undertaker' (see *The Bush Undertaker*, p. 248).
8   *The Bush Undertaker*, p. 31. Dr Roderick does not print this
    paragraph in *Short Stories and Sketches 1888–1922*.
9   Virtually every story between 1892–1895 is followed in *Short Stories
    and Sketches 1888–1922* by the asterisk which indicates that Lawson
    revised it at some time or other.
10   For a discussion of some of the most important textual difficulties, see
     Dr Roderick's notes in *The Bush Undertaker*.

The confessions of a beachcomber

1   Henry David Thoreau, *Walden and Civil Disobedience*, with an
    Afterword by Perry Miller (Signet, New York, 1960), p. 216.
2   Charles Barrett, *Koonwarra: A Naturalist's Adventures in Australia*

(Oxford University Press, Melbourne, 1939), p. 168. All future page references to *Koonwarra* are from this edition, and are incorporated in the text.

3   E. G. Banfield, *My Tropic Isle* (Unwin, London, 1911). All page references to *My Tropic Isle* are from this edition, and are incorporated in the text.

4   E. G. Banfield, *The Confessions of a Beachcomber*, with an Introduction by Alec H. Chisholm, new Australian edition (Angus & Robertson, Sydney, 1968), p. xv. All future page references to *The Confessions* are from this edition, and are incorporated in the text.

'Wherefore I think': Notes on the poetry of Kenneth Slessor

1   Kenneth Slessor, 'Writing Poetry: The Why and the How', *Southerly* IX, 3 (1948), pp. 166–71. Page references to this article are incorporated in the text.

2   R. P. Blackmur, *The Lion and the Honeycomb: Essays in Solicitude and Critique* (Methuen, London, 1956), pp. 289–309. Page references to *The Lion and the Honeycomb* are incorporated in the text.

3   Kenneth Slessor, *Poems*, 2nd ed. (Angus & Robertson, Sydney, 1957), p. 74. All future page references to *Poems* are incorporated in the text.

Wrestling with the angel: Judith Wright's poetry in the 1950s

1   Judith Wright, *Collected Poems, 1942–1970* (Angus & Robertson, Sydney, 1971), p. 17. All further quotations from Judith Wright's verse are from this edition, and page references are incorporated in the text.

Diversions and obsessions: A. D. Hope and Robert D. FitzGerald

1   A. D. Hope, *A Book of Answers* (Angus & Robertson, Sydney, 1978). Page references are incorporated in the text.

2   Robert D. FitzGerald, *Product* (Angus & Robertson, Sydney, 1977). Page references are incorporated in the text.

'A rich surplus of consciousness': A response to the poetry of Francis Webb

1   See my article 'The Very Gimbals of Unease: The Poetry of Francis Webb', *Meanjin* xxvi, 3 (Spring 1967), pp. 255–74.

2 Francis Webb, *Collected Poems* (Angus & Robertson, Sydney, 1969), p. 223. All future quotations from Webb's verse are from this edition. Page references are incorporated in the text.

3 Samuel Johnson, *Selected Poetry and Prose*, ed. Frank Brady and W. K. Wimsatt (University of California Press, Berkeley, 1977), p. 348.

4 John Donne, *Poems*, vol. I, ed. H. J. C. Grierson (Oxford University Press, Oxford, 1912), p. 44.

5 T. S. Eliot, in the essay on 'Andrew Marvell', *Selected Essays*, 2nd ed. (Faber and Faber, London, 1934), p. 293.

6 The poems are numbered 37, 38 and 72 in *The Poems of Gerard Manley Hopkins*, ed. W. H. Gardner and N. H. MacKenzie (Oxford University Press, Oxford, 1970).

7 Robert Lowell, *Life Studies* (Farrar, Straus and Giroux, New York. 1959), p. 87.

8 T. S. Eliot, *Selected Essays*, p. 137.

Eve Langley: Oscar Wilde in the Blue Mountains

1 See p. 23 of the transcript of an ABC radio documentary, 'The Shadows are Different: an Appreciation of Eve Langley' (cat JS/F55), by Meg Stewart. Page references to other quotations from the documentary are incorporated in the text, and the title is abbreviated to 'Shadows'.

2 Hal Porter, *The Extra* (Nelson, Melbourne, 1975), p. 145. Page references to other quotations from *The Extra* are incorporated in the text.

3 Eve Langley, *White Topee* (Angus & Robertson, Sydney, 1954), pp. 241–4. Page references to other quotations from *White Topee* are incorporated in the text, and the title is abbreviated to *WT*.

4 See E. Morris Miller and Frederick T. Macartney, *Australian Literature: a Bibliography to 1938, extended to 1950* (Angus & Robertson, Sydney, 1956), p. 277; H. M. Green, *A History of Australian Literature* (Angus & Robertson, Sydney, 1961), vol. II, p. 1020; Meg Stewart, as cited in note 1 above; transcript of Tape 49 — Cut 1, second side in the Hazel De Berg Collection held in the National Library. Hazel De Berg interviewed Eve Langley on 9 May 1964. Page references to other quotations from this transcript are incorporated in the text.

5 Douglas Stewart, 'A Letter to Shakespeare', in *The Flesh and the Spirit* (Angus & Robertson, Sydney, 1948), pp. 30–8.

6 Eve Langley, *The Pea-Pickers*, 2nd ed. (Angus & Robertson, Sydney, 1958), p. 161. Page references to other quotations from *The Pea-Pickers* are incorporated in the text, and the title is abbreviated to *PP*.

Hal Porter and the art of autobiography

1 Hal Porter, *The Extra* (Nelson, Melbourne, 1975), pp. 168–9.
2 Hal Porter, *The Paper Chase* (Angus & Robertson, Sydney, 1966), pp. 70–1.   Page references to all other quotations from *The Paper Chase* are incorporated in the text, and the title is abbreviated to *PC*.
3 Hal Porter, *Mr. Butterfry, and Other Tales of New Japan* (Angus & Robertson, Sydney, 1970), p. 109.
4 Hal Porter, *The Right Thing* (Rigby, Adelaide, 1971), p. 104.
5 Robert Burns, 'A Sort of Triumph Over Time: Hal Porter's Prose Narratives', in *Australian Postwar Novelists*, ed. Nancy Keesing (Jacaranda Press, Brisbane, 1975), p. 111.
6 Hal Porter, *The Watcher on the Cast-Iron Balcony* (Faber and Faber, London, 1962), pp. 147–8. Page references to all other quotations from *The Watcher on the Cast-Iron Balcony* are incorporated in the text, and the title is abbreviated to *Watcher*.

The emotional structure of The Watcher on the Cast-Iron Balcony

1 Hal Porter, *The Watcher on the Cast-Iron Balcony* (Faber & Faber, London, 1963), p. 10. All future quotations from *The Watcher* are from this edition, and page references are incorporated in the text.

Criticism and the universities

1 Henry Lawson, *Collected Verse*, ed. Colin Roderick (Angus & Robertson, Sydney, 1967), vol. I, p. 327.
2 Alfred Kazin, *Contemporaries* (Little, Brown & Co., Boston, 1962), p. 495.
3 C. S. Lewis, *A Preface to Paradise Lost* (Oxford University Press, Oxford, 1960), p. 11.
4 Graham Hough, *The Dream and the Task* (Duckworth, London, 1963), pp. 60–1.
5 Northrop Frye, *Fables of Identity* (Harcourt Brace Jovanovich, New York, 1963), pp. 8–9.
6 *Overland* 38 (March 1968), p. 40.
7 Hough, pp. 87–8.
8 *The Listener*, 29 February 1968, p. 258.
9 Kazin, p. 498.
10 Matthew Arnold, 'The Function of Criticism at the Present Time', *Essays in Criticism: First Series* (Macmillan, London, 1902), p. 6.

Criticism and the individual talent

1   A. L. Kroeber, *Configurations of Culture Growth* (University of California Press, Berkeley, 1944), p. 838.

2   Brian Kiernan, *Images of Society and Nature: Seven Essays on Australian Novels* (Oxford University Press, Melbourne, 1971). All page references are incorporated in the text.

3   John Wain, 'The Disappearing Critic', *The Listener*, 6 August 1970.

4   T. S. Eliot, 'Shakespeare and the Stoicism of Seneca', in *Selected Essays* (Faber & Faber, London, 1934), p. 137.

5   Randall Jarrell, *A Sad Heart at the Supermarket* (Eyre & Spottiswoode, London, 1965), p. 122.

6   Les A. Murray, 'An Absolutely Ordinary Rainbow', in *The Weatherboard Cathedral* (Angus & Robertson, Sydney, 1969), pp. 47–8.

7   Epigraph to *Australia Felix*. All quotations are from Henry Handel Richardson, *The Fortunes of Richard Mahony* (Heinemann, Melbourne, 1946). Page references are incorporated in the text.

8   J. G. Robertson, 'The Art of Henry Handel Richardson', in Henry Handel Richardson, *Myself When Young* (Heinemann, Melbourne, 1948), pp. 177–8.

9   A. R. Chisholm & J. J. Quinn, eds, *The Verse of Christopher Brennan* (Angus & Robertson, Sydney, 1960), p. 173.

10 Charles Harpur, 'The Tower of the Dream', in *Poems* (George Robertson, Melbourne, 1883), pp. 19–29. All page references are incorporated in the text. Elizabeth Perkins, *The Poetical Works of Charles Harpur* (Angus & Robertson, Sydney, 1984), provided a variant version of the text of 'The Tower of the Dream'.

11 See Delmore Schwartz, *In Dreams Begin Responsibilities* (New Directions, New York, 1938).

The criticism of Arthur Phillips

1   A. A. Phillips, *The Australian Tradition*, 2nd ed. (Cheshire, Melbourne, 1966), p. viii. All future page references to *The Australian Tradition* are to this edition, and are incorporated in the text.

2   The essays printed in the 1980 re-issue of the second edition reproduce those of the 1966 text. I allude later in this essay to the variations between the 1958 and 1966 editions.

3   A. A. Phillips, ed., *An Australian Muster* (Melbourne University Press, 1946), p. v.

4   A. A. Phillips was born in 1900.

5   A. A. Phillips, ed., *Five Radio Plays* (Longmans Green, Melbourne, 1949), p. 12.

6   A. Boyce Gibson and A. A. Phillips, *Thinkers at Work* (Longmans Green, Melbourne, 1946), p. 1.

5 April 1984: The two Winstons

1   James Boswell, *Life of Johnson*, ed. George Birkbeck Hill, revised and enlarged by L. F. Powell (Clarendon Press, Oxford, 1934), vol. I, p. 471.
2   George Orwell, *Nineteen Eighty-Four* (Secker and Warburg, London, 1949), p. 12. All future page references are incorporated in the text.
3   John Docker, *In A Critical Condition* (Penguin, Melbourne, 1984). All page references are incorporated in the text.
4   See 'The Confessions of a Literary Gauleiter', *Southerly* XLIII, 4 (1983), pp. 378–96.
5   George Orwell, *Homage to Catalonia*, intro. by Lionel Trilling (The Beacon Press, Boston, 1955), pp. vii–viii.
6   Susan Sontag, *Against Interpretation and Other Essays* (Noonday Press, New York, 1960), p. 32.
7   Wallace Stevens, *The Necessary Angel: Essays on Reality and the Imagination* (Vintage Books, New York, 1951), p. 61.

Index